spring into

HTML and CSS

▪▪spring into▪▪ series

Spring Into... a series of short, concise, fast-paced tutorials for professionals transitioning to new technologies.

Find us online at **www.awprofessional.com/springinto/**

Spring Into Windows XP Service Pack 2
Brian Culp
ISBN 0-13-167983-X

Spring Into PHP 5
Steven Holzner
ISBN 0-13-149862-2

Spring Into HTML and CSS
Molly E. Holzschlag
ISBN 0-13-185586-7

Spring Into Digital Photography
Joseph T. Jaynes and Rip Noel
ISBN 0-13-185353-8

Spring Into Technical Writing for Engineers and Scientists
Barry J. Rosenberg
ISBN 0-13-149863-0

Spring Into Linux®
Janet Valade
ISBN 0-13-185354-6

YOUR OPINION IS IMPORTANT TO US!

We would like to hear from you regarding the Spring Into... Series. Please visit **www.awprofessional.com/springintosurvey/** to complete our survey. Survey participants will receive a special offer for sharing their opinions.

From the Series Editor
Barry J. Rosenberg

A few years ago, I found myself in a new job in which I had to master many new skills in a very short time. I didn't have to become an instant expert, but I did have to become instantly competent.

I went to the bookstore but was shocked by how much the publishing world had changed. At a place where wit and intelligence had once been celebrated, dummies were now venerated. What happened?

Photograph courtesy of Ed Raduns

Well, I made a few phone calls, got Aunt Barbara to sew up a few costumes, and convinced Uncle Ed to let us use the barn as a stage. Oh wait… that was a different problem. Actually, I made a few phone calls and got some really talented friends to write books that clever people wouldn't be ashamed to read. We called the series "Spring Into…" because all the good names were already taken.

With Spring Into…, we feel that we've created the perfect series for busy professionals. However, there's the rub—we can't be sure unless you tell us. Maybe we're hitting the ball out of the park and straight through the uprights, bending it like Beckham, and finding nothing but net. On the other hand, maybe we've simply spun a twisted ball of clichés. Only you can tell us. Therefore, if anything—positive or negative—is on your mind about these books, please email me at

barry.rosenberg@awl.com

I promise not to add you to any email lists, spam you, or perform immoral acts with your address.

Sincerely,
Barry

▮▮▮spring into▮▮

HTML and CSS

Molly E. Holzschlag

✦Addison-Wesley

Upper Saddle River, NJ • Boston• Indianapolis • San Francisco
New York • Toronto • Montreal • London • Munich • Paris • Madrid
Cape Town • Sydney • Tokyo • Singapore • Mexico City

The publisher offers excellent discounts on this book when ordered in quantity for bulk purchases or special sales, which may include electronic versions and/or custom covers and content particular to your business, training goals, marketing focus, and branding interests. For more information, please contact:

U. S. Corporate and Government Sales
(800) 382-3419
corpsales@pearsontechgroup.com

For sales outside the U. S., please contact:

International Sales
international@pearsoned.com

Visit us on the Web: www.awprofessional.com/springinto/

Library of Congress Catalog Control Number: 2005920032

Pearson Education, Inc.
Rights and Contracts Department
501 Boylston Street, Suite 900
Boston, MA 02116
Fax (617) 671-3447

ISBN-10: 0-13-185586-7
ISBN-13: 978-0-13-185586-1

Third printing, November 2007

Contents

Preface

The Web might be the most intriguing invention of the 20th century. Certainly, it is a technology that has spread faster than a California wildfire and has, in just a decade's time, changed the ways in which most contemporary societies live, work, study—and, of course, shop.

Hard to imagine that it all began as an experiment in a particle physics laboratory. Tim Berners-Lee and his fellow physicists at CERN (European Organization for Nuclear Research) had been searching for a way to effectively share research documents across a variety of computer platforms. The Internet, with its complex, international network, was a very natural foundation upon which to house the technologies that would ultimately combine to make up the World Wide Web.

From its modest origins to the absolutely astonishing permeation into world culture, the Web, according to its father, Berners-Lee, was intended to be as much a social environment as a technical one. This idea might well have led to the fast proliferation of the Web, largely because it enables us to interact in many different ways socially via the technology, so much so that a new study of *social networking* has emerged to examine the social implications of the Web on society, and vice versa.

Who Should Read This Book?

You might, in fact, be a particle physicist, but this book is also intended for a wide range of nontechnical professionals interested in building websites and working with web documents for professional application within a given field, such as education, medicine, law, or science. To that end, I've written the book with a bit less technical jargon than I would for an audience of software developers, but you will find that this book, while very approachable, does get into some nitty-gritty concerns. The good news is you don't have to be a rocket scientist to understand it—but if you are, it'll work out for you, too!

And, while intended for nontechnical professionals, the book will most certainly also be useful for people who are working in the web design and development field, and are interested in learning contemporary approaches to working with web pages.

How Is This Book Organized?

I've organized this book into two sections. The first focuses on HTML, the language used to structure the document and its contents.

NOTE

Although HTML is still in use, it has been reformulated into a language known as Extensible Markup Language (XHTML). For general purposes, they are essentially the same, with the exception that XHTML can be extended in ways beyond the scope of the book. However, to keep up-to-date and to get you working with modern markup, XHTML is used in this book. In fact, it's an important point that I tend to use the terms *HTML* and *XHTML* interchangeably, even though they are, in fact, a bit different.

You'll learn more about HTML and XHTML in the book's first section, which contains the following chapters:

TABLE 1 Chapters in Section 1

Chapter	Title	Teaches you how to...
1	Building an HTML Page	Create a page in XHTML
2	Adding Text and Links	Format text and links
3	Adding Images, Media, and Scripts	Add dynamic content
4	Creating Tables	Build effective data tables
5	Building Forms	Create HTML forms
6	Working with Frames	Work with frames

The second section of the book focuses on Cascading Style Sheets (CSS), which is the language that integrates with HTML and XHTML to add the design features of the page: layout, colors, fonts, and anything decorative. You'll learn how to apply CSS to the pages you build by following the approaches found in the following chapters:

TABLE 2 Chapters in Section 2

Chapter	Title	Teaches you how to . . .
7	Using CSS	Integrate CSS with HTML
8	Working with Color and Images Using CSS	Add color and imagery
9	Styling Text	Work with web typography
10	Link Effects, Lists, and Navigation	Design with links and lists
11	Margins, Borders, and Padding	Gain control over space
12	Positioning, Floats, and Z-index	Position and float elements
13	CSS Layouts	Lay out pages with CSS

Along with the chapters, there are two very important appendixes. The first is "XHTML 1.0 Annotated Reference," which provides a look-up along with proper usage and tips of all the elements available in XHTML 1.0. The second is "CSS 2.1 Annotated Reference," which provides a listing, along with proper usage and tips, of all available CSS properties.

Between the chapters and the appendixes, you'll be set when it comes to the breadth of knowledge required to create great web pages using today's techniques.

What's Unusual About This Book?

This book, like the other books in the Spring Into... Series, provides the following unique approaches to the content within:

- Each topic is explained in a discrete one- or two-page unit called a "chunk."

- Each chunk builds on the previous chunks in that chapter.

- Many chunks contain sidebars and "Quantum Leaps," which provide helpful, ancillary material that is often more advanced than the main text.

The chunk style has been specifically crafted to meet the needs of busy people. I know you don't have a lot of time to spend learning complex ideas, so giving them to you in bite-size chunks is a helpful way to get you working as fast as possible, the right way, from the get-go.

Where to Get Examples from the Book

See the book's web page www.awprofessional.com/springinto/.

Acknowledgments

Writing a book feels like a lonely process, but the fact is that many people help out. Barry Rosenberg provided much needed early guidance on how to best write in the chunk style used in this series. Along the way, three reviewers provided valuable feedback: Kimberly Blessing and Eris Free pointed out ways I could improve the text, and Daniel Smith lent his fine eye and found mistakes and points of clarification, and provided very supportive tips along the way. A special thanks to Mark Taub, who offered the fine opportunity as well as shepherded it through. Finally, to David Fugate, literary agent extraordinaire, who is always there with wit, wisdom, and great movie advice, to boot.

About the Author

Coined "one of the greatest digerati" and deemed one of the "Top 25 Most Influential Women on the Web," there is little doubt that in the world of web design and development, **Molly E. Holzschlag** is a vibrant and influential thinker, teacher, and author. With more than 30 web development book titles to her credit, Molly is a Steering Committee member for the Web Standards Project (WaSP and an advisory board member to the World Organization of Webmasters. She also has taught Webmaster courses for the University of Arizona, University of Phoenix, New School University, and Pima Community College. Many recognize Molly from her books, feature articles, and popular website, molly.com.

About the Series Editor

Barry Rosenberg wrote the cult classic, *KornShell Programming Tutorial* (Addison-Wesley, 1991), which pioneered many of the chunk-oriented techniques found in the Spring Into... Series. He is the author of more than sixty corporate technical manuals, primarily on programming. An experienced instructor, Barry has taught everything from high-school physics to weeklong corporate seminars on data structures.

Most recently, Barry spent four semesters at MIT where he taught advanced technical writing. Barry is also a professional juggler who has performed more than 1,200 shows, including a three-week run in Japan. Juggling serves as the backdrop for his novel, *Cascade* (not yet published). Barry currently works as the documentation manager at 170 Systems.

CHAPTER 1

Building an HTML Page

Web documents are meant to be constructed logically. You must have certain elements in place for your document to conform and validate. Conformance means that the document actually follows the language and language version in which it is being written. Validation is the technical process by which we test conformance, allowing us to find errors and fix mistakes.

The first thing you can do to make absolutely certain that your pages are given the best fighting chance at conformance is to begin with all the required and structural elements that are needed *before* you begin to add text and other content.

Ironically, it's only been in hindsight that the majority of people working on websites have improved upon the way they use markup. The Web was in such a state of evolutionary, rapid growth that new elements and features were being added to browsers—and HTML—all the time. Many of these features made it into the actual specifications, but many did not. What's more, elements of HTML pages that should have been included from the beginning have often been left out, even by professionals.

How is this possible, you might wonder? Well, the primary piece of software used to interpret HTML is the desktop web browser. These browsers have a long history of forgiving errors. Of course, they also have a long history of introducing errors! Browsers have been both the blessing and the curse of the Web because they have allowed for innovation but often spent more time adding fun features rather than basic support for the languages they are meant to support. As a result, the Web is a mishmash of HTML use—most of it not conforming or valid—and, in light of this chapter's discussion, many times authored without the basic structural components required by the language.

A movement is afoot to bring better standards to browsers, to the tools that people use to develop websites, and to those of us interested in creating pages that not only work, but work well, regardless of whether our goals are personal or professional.

In this chapter, you learn to create a template that will serve as the foundation for everything you do in this book. This template will contain all the necessary and helpful technical and structural bits that form the basis of a document that will conform and validate, too.

Declaring and Identifying the Document

The first thing you'll want to do in your page is add a bit of code that declares which type of document you're using and identifies the language version. This is done with Standardized General Markup Language (SGML), which is the parent language to HTML and appears in this important declaration, known as the *DOCTYPE declaration*. This declaration is a unique piece of code, and a suitable declaration must be used in every document you create.

Example 1-1 shows the DOCTYPE declaration we'll be using in all examples in this book:

EXAMPLE 1-1 The DOCTYPE declaration for XHTML 1.0 Transitional

```
<!DOCTYPE html PUBLIC "-//W3C//DTD XHTML 1.0 Transitional//EN"
"http://www.w3.org/TR/xhtml1/DTD/xhtml1-transitional.dtd">
```

Look a little weird? Not to worry. I'll go through it with you so you have a firm understanding of what each bit of this declaration means. First, there's the opening <!, which many readers who have looked at HTML before might wonder about. The angle bracket is a familiar component in HTML, but the exclamation mark appears in only one other situation with HTML: in comments, which you'll also learn about in this chapter. This symbol isn't used too often because it's SGML syntax being used in the context of HTML. Here, it simply means that a declaration is about to begin. This is then followed by the term DOCTYPE, which states that this code is declaring the *document type*.

The next bit is html, which defines this document type as being written in HTML. Note that it's in lower case here. This is significant because we're using XHTML—and because XHTML is case sensitive, this particular part of the declaration must be in lower case. If it's not, your document will not validate. The word PUBLIC is an important piece of information. This means that the particular document type being referenced is a public document. Many companies create unique versions of XHTML, with customized elements and attributes. For our purposes, the public version of HTML that we're going to use is absolutely sufficient.

The ensuing syntax "-//W3C//DTD XHTML 1.0 Transitional//EN" defines the host of the document's language type and version (The World Wide Web Consortium, W3C), and states that the document is being written according to the XHTML 1.0 Transitional Document Type Definition (DTD). A DTD is simply a long laundry list of allowed elements and attributes for that language and language version. Finally, there's a complete URL that goes to the DTD, "http://www.w3.org/TR/xhtml1/DTD/xhtml1-transitional.dtd". If you were to load this into your browser, you'd see the actual DTD, for XHTML 1.0 Transitional (see Figure 1-1).

```
<!-- There are also 16 widely known color names with their sRGB values:

     Black   = #000000    Green  = #008000
     Silver  = #C0C0C0    Lime   = #00FF00
     Gray    = #808080    Olive  = #808000
     White   = #FFFFFF    Yellow = #FFFF00
     Maroon  = #800000    Navy   = #000080
     Red     = #FF0000    Blue   = #0000FF
     Purple  = #800080    Teal   = #008080
     Fuchsia= #FF00FF     Aqua   = #00FFFF
-->
```

FIGURE 1-1 A portion of the XHTML Transitional DTD.

With this declaration at the top of your document, you will be able to author the document and then run it through a validator to check for conformance. The validator uses the information in the declaration and compares your document to the DTD you've declared. If you've followed the rules allowed in the DTD you've declared here, you should have no errors whatsoever, which is, of course, our goal.

QUANTUM LEAP

Due to discrepancies in the way that many browsers were handling various aspects of HTML and CSS, a means of gaining better performance for those documents written to specification became evident. Tantek Celik, then a developer for Microsoft, created a switching mechanism in IE that corrected numerous problems. This switch uses properly formed DOCTYPE declarations to switch the browser from "quirks" mode (the forgiving mode I described in this chapter's introduction) to "compliance" mode, which allows sites written in compliant markup and CSS to perform much more efficiently. One important point: Never place anything above a DOCTYPE declaration, or you might end up with browser display issues.

To learn more about DOCTYPE switching, see http://gutfeldt.ch/matthias/articles/doctypeswitch.html. There's also a great chart there showing numerous declarations and which ones actually flip the switch. XHTML 1.0 Transitional with a proper DOCTYPE as shown in this section was chosen also because it performs this function.

Although DOCTYPE declarations are never displayed, their necessity is inarguable. Using these properly, you can't go wrong: You'll have valid pages that are also interpreted by the browser in as optimal of a situation as possible.

Adding the *html* Element

After the DOCTYPE declaration, you'll want to begin building your document from its root element. I use the term *root* purposely because all documents create a document tree, something that we'll be exploring at length. Understanding the tree created by HTML documents plays an important role in being able to effectively style those documents using CSS.

The `html` element is considered the root element of any HTML document. Remember, the declaration isn't an HTML element—it's SGML. So the first element to appear takes on the important root status.

Example 1-2 shows the `html` element, with its opening tag and closing tag.

EXAMPLE 1-2   The root HTML element

```
<html>

</html>
```

Pretty basic, right? Well, in XHTML, we have to add one other important piece to the opening tag, and that's the XML namespace for XHTML. This is just another way of identifying the language being used within the document. I won't go into the ideological reasons we do this, but suffice it to say that it must be there to validate (see Example 1-3).

EXAMPLE 1-3   The root HTML element with the XML namespace attribute and value

```
<html xmlns="http://www.w3.org/1999/xhtml" xml:lang="en" lang="en">

</html>
```

You can see the `xmlns` attribute, which stands for "XML namespace" and the value is a URL, which, if you follow it, leads nowhere exciting, I promise! You'll just get a page saying you've reached the XML namespace for XHTML. Again, this is just another identifier.

NOTE
You'll notice a few other bits of syntax, including the `xml:lang` attribute, which defines the language of the document using XML syntax (remember, XHTML is a combo of HTML and XML), in this case `en` for English, and the `lang` attribute from HTML, declaring the same information. These are optional attributes, but we'll use them both, for full compatibility.

The *head* and *title* Elements

Now you've got the very basic beginnings of a document, with the DOCTYPE declaration in place and the root element at the ready. You'll now begin adding other important pieces of the document, beginning with the head element. This element is where all things necessary for the document's display and performance are placed—but are not literally seen within the browser window. To create the head section, you simply add the head tags within the upper portion of your template, right below the opening <html> tag (see Example 1-4).

EXAMPLE 1-4 Building the template: Adding a head section

```
<!DOCTYPE html PUBLIC "-//W3C//DTD XHTML 1.0 Transitional//EN"
"http://www.w3.org/TR/xhtml1/DTD/xhtml1-transitional.dtd">

<html xmlns="http://www.w3.org/1999/xhtml" xml:lang="en" lang="en">
<head>

</head>

</html>
```

Notice that the head element requires no attributes but simply has the opening and closing tags. This identifies the head region. Table 1-1 shows some of the various elements that you can place within the head of your document.

TABLE 1-1 Elements in the Head Portion of the Document

Element	What It Does
title	This element enables you to title your document. This title will then appear in the title bar of your browser. The title element is required.
meta	The meta element is used for numerous concerns, including keywords and descriptions, character encoding, and document authorship. The meta element is not required, and your use of it will vary according to your specific needs.
script	This element enables you to insert scripts directly into your document or, as is the preference, link from the page to the script you'd like to use. It is used as needed.
style	The style element enables you to place style information into the individual page. This is known as *embedded* style, which you'll read more about in Chapter 7, "Using CSS." It is used as needed.
link	The link element is most commonly used to link to an external style sheet, although it can be used for other purposes, such as linking to an alternative page for accessibility, or to link to a favicon, those popular icons you see in the address bar on certain websites.

The *title* Element in Detail

The `title` element is the only *required* element within the head element. This element displays any text within it in the browser bar (see Figure 1-2) along with the browser's name at the end of the text.

FIGURE 1-2   The title element text will appear in the browser's title bar.

Aside from the fact that you have to have the `title` element in place, writing good titles is a first-line technique that accomplishes three things:

- Provides a title for the page,
- Offers users *orientation*—that is, it helps them know where they are on the Web and within the site itself
- Provides additional information about the site page

Writing effective titles means addressing these three concerns. A good title example appears in Example 1-5.

EXAMPLE 1-5   Title example with site name and location for user orientation

```
<title>molly.com - books - HTML &amp; CSS</title>
```

Note that the page is titled using the site name, the site section, and the subsection, providing useful information for the visitor.

An ineffective example can be seen in Example 1-6.

EXAMPLE 1-6   Title example with site name and location for user orientation

```
<title>Read my books!</title>
```

Here, there's no information that helps us. So while the technical requirement of having a title is fulfilled, the practical needs are not.

NOTE

Although you cannot use HTML inside a title, you can use character entities, as you can see in Example 1-5, where I used the entity & to create the & symbol. For more information on available character entities, see Appendix A, "XHTML Reference."

The *meta* Element

Although it is not required in a document, the meta element performs so many different functions that it's a good idea to become familiar with it right away.

Document Encoding

Document encoding means setting the character set for your page, which is particularly important when writing documents in other languages. For many years, those of us writing in Latin characters (including English) used the ISO 8859-1 character set. The ISO sets and subsets cover a wide range of languages. But nowadays, we have UTF-8, a more universal format following a different standard than ISO values. UTF-8 can be helpful in a variety of browsers, but there are some limitations. If you are publishing in another language, such as Russian or Japanese, you'll want to have your document encoding set up under ISO rather than Unicode character sets.

NOTE

Ideally, character encoding is set on the server and not in a meta element. However, you can set it using a meta element. See
http://www.webstandards.org/learn/askw3c/dec2002.html.

Example 1-7 shows a meta element that defines the UTF-8 format, suitable for documents in English as well as other languages, depending upon your browser support.

EXAMPLE 1-7   Using meta to declare document encoding with Unicode

```
<meta http-equiv="Content-Type" content="text/html; charset=UTF-8" />
```

Example 1-8 shows a meta element for a document written in Russian, using the ISO method.

EXAMPLE 1-8   Using meta to declare document encoding for Cyrillic, using ISO

```
<meta http-equiv="Content-Type" content="text/html; charset= iso-8859-5" />
```

Keywords, Description, and Authorship

The meta element can be used to describe keywords, describe the site, and define the author, too. This is extremely helpful for public search engines as well as for any search engine you might be running on your own site.

Keywords are single words and word combinations that would be used during a search. This assists people looking for specific topics to find the information you're providing (see Example 1-9).

EXAMPLE 1-9   Using meta for keywords and keyword combinations

```
<meta name="keywords" content="molly, molly.com, html, xhtml, css, design, web
design, development, web development, perl, color, web color, blog, web log,
weblog, books, computer books, articles, tutorials, learn, author, instructor,
instruction, instructing, training, education, consult, consultation, consultant,
famous people page, famous people list, standards, web standards, web standards
project, wsp, wasp, digital web, digital web magazine, web techniques, web
techniques magazine, web review, webreview, webreview.com, wow, world organization
of webmasters, conference, conferences, user interface, usability, accessibility,
internationalization, web culture" />
```

You'll notice that although I use the word *web* a great deal, it's in combination with other keywords. Most search engines will lock you out if you use multiple single keywords. This used to be a way of getting higher ranking, but no longer. Use keywords that make sense, or if you want to have multiple instances of a word, use it in a realistic combination.

Descriptions are typically 25 words or less and describe the purpose of your document (see Example 1-10).

EXAMPLE 1-10   The meta element used for site or page description

```
<meta name="description" content="I'm Molly E. Holzschlag, and this Web site
shares my Web development work and personal thoughts." />
```

Short and to the point! Another use is to define the author of the document, as shown in Example 1-11.

EXAMPLE 1-11   Using meta to describe page authorship

```
<meta name="Author" content="Molly E. Holzschlag" />
```

Of course, this information is never displayed on your web page itself. Instead, as with all elements and attributes within the head portion of a document, this information is used by the browser and other resources such as search engines.

NOTE

Other uses for the meta element are to refresh documents automatically and to restrict search engines from logging specific pages. Learn more at http://www.learnthat.com/courses/computer/metatags/meta.html.

The *body* Element

The body element is where all the action takes place. It's the element where you'll be placing the content of your page and marking it up using XHTML to structure it accordingly. The element goes within the html element, directly below the head——makes sense, doesn't it? (See Example 1-12.)

EXAMPLE 1-12   Placing the body element

```
<html>
<head>
<title>Appropriate Title Text Here</title>
</head>
<body>
</body>
</html>
```

When viewed in a browser, the information within the body element is what is displayed in the browser window, also referred to as the *viewport*. This is the content area only—no browser chrome (which refers to the browser's interface components, such as scrollbars and status bars). Figure 1-3 shows Google in a web browser. Only the displayed content is within the viewport.

FIGURE 1-3   Viewing body text within the browser viewport.

HTML Comments

Another important piece of markup that you'll want to get started using right away is HTML comments. Comments enable you to hide content or markup for temporary purposes or backward compatibility, to identify sections within your document, and to provide directives for other folks who might be working on the page.

The syntax for an HTML comment looks like this:

```
<!-- -->
```

What you are hiding, identifying, or providing in terms of guidance goes between the opening and closing portions of a comment. Example 1-13 hides the text content within the body using comments.

EXAMPLE 1-13 Hiding text content and markup

```
<body>
<!--
<p>The content of this paragraph will not appear within the body so long as it's
within a comment.</p>
-->
<p>The content of this paragraph will be displayed, because it's outside of the
comment field.</p>
</body>
```

You can denote sections within your document, as shown in Example 1-14.

EXAMPLE 1-14 Hiding text content and markup

```
<body>

<!-- begin primary content -->

<!--begin footer information-->

</body>
```

Finally, comments are a useful way to provide directives (see Example 1-15).

EXAMPLE 1-15 Providing guidance inside a comment

```
<body>
<!-- Angie: please be sure to use lists instead of tables in this section  -->
</body>
```

Reviewing the Template

Time to wrap up our exploration of a template by actually putting all the components together (see Example 1-16).

EXAMPLE 1-16   Viewing the structure of an XHTML document

```
<!DOCTYPE html PUBLIC "-//W3C//DTD XHTML 1.0 Transitional//EN"
"http://www.w3.org/TR/xhtml1/DTD/xhtml1-transitional.dtd">

<head>

<title>your site : location within site : topic title</title>

<meta http-equiv="Content-Type" content="text/html; charset=UTF-8" />
<meta name="keywords" content="your, keywords, here" />
<meta name="description" content="your description here" />
<meta name="author" content="your name here" />

</head>

<body>

<!-- main content section  -->

</body>
</html>
```

Copy this markup, save it to a work folder on your computer, and name it index.html. This will be the file you'll open and add content and additional markup to as we progress.

Text Is Next!

Of course, if you were to open the document you just created in a web browser, the viewport section—where content normally is displayed—would be completely blank! This is because the only thing in the body is a comment, which hides the text within it. The one thing you will notice is the title of your site, which appears in the title bar at the top of your browser.

Beginning with structure is a great way to learn how to create great pages right away. Although it might seem frustrating to do all this complicated stuff and end up with no visible results, I promise you that the long-term rewards are worth it. You'll end up with far more control and understanding of everything to do with markup and CSS, I assure you.

So after you've saved your document, go ahead and validate it. Browse to http://validate.w3.org/, find the file upload section, and upload your file. Run it through the validator. Find any errors? Fix them and try again. No errors? Great job.

And I promise you that in the next chapter, "Adding Text and Links," you'll end up with something to actually view within your browser!

CHAPTER 2

Adding Text and Links

I f content is king, then text is what helped him get to his royal throne! Without well-formatted, organized text and intelligent linking, any individual trying to create kingly content will be at quite a disadvantage.

If you step back in history a bit, you'll find that the Web was, at first, all about text and links. That it's become a vibrant, colorful, visual environment for the majority of its users was an accident, really. The original intention of the Web's inventor, Tim Berners-Lee, was to create a multiplatform means for his fellow scientists to share information, publish their data, and be able to link a reference within an essay directly to that related reference. The man was a physicist, not a designer, and he was working in an environment that didn't even have a graphical user interface. I'm talking the old-fashioned Internet, seen as green or amber text on a black background.

Given its humble origins, the Web has come a long way. It's a highly visual environment now, and before CSS became widely available for use, people creating websites relied on elements meant for text to create visual results, such as adding extra line breaks to get additional whitespace on the page.

Now that you can use CSS to effectively manage such visual concerns, the focus has shifted back to using text elements as they should be used: to format text. So despite the emergence of a highly visual, highly interactive Web, text and linking remain the primary meat and potatoes of any website worth its salt. Anyone working with text is encouraged to use text and links in a meaningful way.

In this chapter, you'll learn how to work with text and links efficiently and appropriately. From the logic of headers and lists to a variety of linking options, you'll find out what it means to create great text in noble fashion, making your content as royal as can be.

Using Headers Properly

Headers in HTML and XHTML are tags used to define the headings within your page. There are six levels of headings, from <h1> . . . </h1> to <h6> . . .</h6>. The <h1> . . . </h1> level header is considered the most significant header, such as a page title, with an <h2> . . .</h2> level header performing as a subhead and so on. Headers at the fifth and sixth levels are rarely used, although you will find them occasionally in very complex documents. Example 2-1 shows a list of headers as they might appear in a document, although there would be text between each header.

EXAMPLE 2-1   Headers with logical content contained with them

```
<h1>Welcome to Molly's Home Page!</h1>
<h2>Books</h2>
<h3>As Author</h3>
<h4>Book Title</h4>
```

Typically, you'll want more than one subheading per section—it helps your content to be more understandable to readers. As you can see from Figure 2-1, each level header I've used has been visually formatted to be larger at the <h1> level and become progressively smaller.

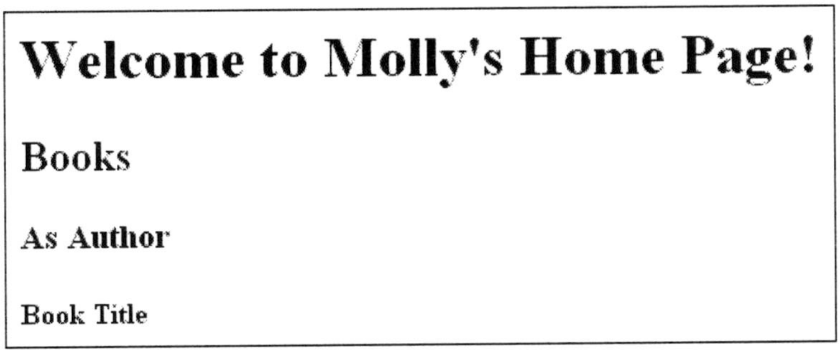

Welcome to Molly's Home Page!

Books

As Author

Book Title

FIGURE 2-1   Headers as rendered in a web browser.

Headers Are Structural, Not Visual

Display is considered discretionary to the browser manufacturer. You will use CSS to style your headers later. Headers should be used in a hierarchical fashion because the tags are describing the text being formatted.

Adding Paragraphs

Paragraphs are managed using the paragraph element, represented by an opening and closing tag <p>. . .</p>, with text content in between (see Example 2-2).

EXAMPLE 2-2   Marking up paragraphs with an opening and closing tag

```
<p>Mentally, too, they were almost moribund. They stared vacantly, straight out to
sea. They stared with the unwinking fixedness of those whose gaze is caught in
hypnotic trance.</p>

<p>It was Frank Merrill who broke the silence finally. Merrill still looked like a
man of marble and his voice still kept its unnatural tone, level, monotonous,
metallic.</p>
```

Figure 2-2 shows how the paragraphs will appear within a web browser. You'll note that all the necessary carriage returns are handled when the browser interprets the paragraph tags.

> It was the morning after the shipwreck. The five men still lay where they had slept. A long time had passed since anybody had spoken. A long time had passed since anybody had moved.
>
> Indeed, it, looked almost as if they would never speak or move again. So bruised and bloodless of skin were they, so bleak and sharp of feature, so stark and hollow of eye, so rigid and moveless of limb that they might have been corpses.

FIGURE 2-2   Paragraph formatting in the web browser.

NOTE
You will see instances when there's no closing tag in paragraphs. This is legal in HTML, but even when using HTML instead of XHTML, it's good practice to close your paragraph tags. The display is the same no matter which approach you use.

Text lines in paragraphs will break only in accordance with the size of the browser window and will flow to fill any available space until the end of the paragraph. At that point, there is a full break plus a line before the ensuing content.

Working with Page Breaks

Page breaks force a break in a line found within a paragraph. They are especially useful when forced line breaks are important to the flow of the text, such as in a poem (see Example 2-3).

EXAMPLE 2-3 Working with page breaks

```
<p>What earthly tongue, and, oh! what human pen<br />
Can tell that scene of suffering, too severe.<br />
'Tis ever present to my sight, oh! When<br />
Will the sound cease its torture on mine ear?</p>
```

You'll note that I've first placed these lines of markup in a paragraph because you'll want them to have some kind of structure. The paragraph is a logical choice because a poem is really a series of paragraphs, broken by line. Figure 2-3 shows the way the browser displays breaks.

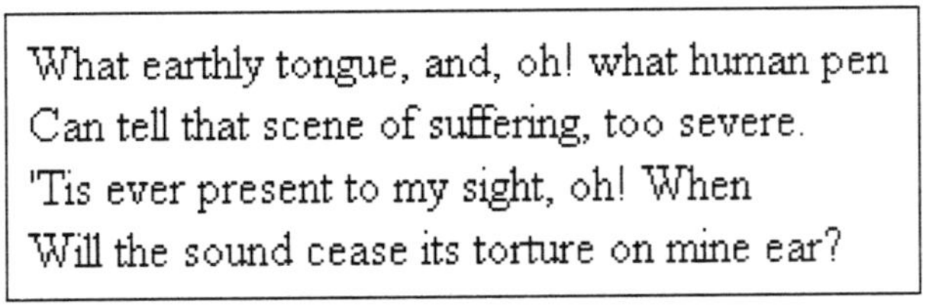

What earthly tongue, and, oh! what human pen
Can tell that scene of suffering, too severe.
'Tis ever present to my sight, oh! When
Will the sound cease its torture on mine ear?

FIGURE 2-3 A paragraph with forced line breaks.

NOTE

You will also see breaks that look like this: <br>. This is how breaks are written in HTML.

Avoid Paragraphs and Breaks for Use in Display

As mentioned earlier, many people creating web pages rely on tags they shouldn't to achieve display. For example, some people stack breaks on top of one another to get whitespace into the document.

This is problematic because it causes the document to have markup in it that is not being used meaningfully. Because we now can use CSS confidently for these types of display concerns, use paragraphs and breaks for their intended use only: the formatting of paragraphs and line breaks.

Ordered Lists

An ordered list is a list of items that must be followed in a specific order, such as in a recipe or directions to someone's home. Ordered lists are also called numbered lists.

Two elements are required to create an ordered list. The first is the <ol>. . . </ol> (ordered list) element, and the second is the <li> . . . </li> (list item) element (see Example 2-4).

EXAMPLE 2-4   Creating an ordered list

```
<ol>
<li>Take I-10 to the Speedway Exit</li>
<li>After you've exited, make a left onto Speedway Boulevard</li>
<li>Follow Speedway for several miles until you reach Park Avenue. </li>
</ol>
```

The ordered list element alerts the browser that any list items contained within the list will be numbered sequentially by the browser (see Figure 2-4).

1. Take I-10 to the Speedway Exit
2. After you've exited, make a left onto Speedway Boulevard
3. Follow Speedway for several miles until you reach Park Avenue.

FIGURE 2-4   An ordered list as interpreted by the browser.

The browser has automatically generated a numeric value for each list item. You can style these with a range of numeric values, such as Roman numerals, by using CSS to modify the behavior of the browser.

NOTE

As with the paragraph element, list item elements *do not have to be closed* in HTML (although it's good practice to close them).

Unordered Lists

An unordered list is a list in which items do not have to take place sequentially. You'll be most familiar with the term *bulleted list*. Bulleted lists can be used to display such items as product lists, featured items, and short but concisely organized content.

An unordered list works exactly the same way that an ordered list does, but it simply uses the <ul>. . .</ul> (unordered list) element instead of the ordered list element (see Example 2-5). This tag allows the browser to display the list items with bullets rather than numbers.

EXAMPLE 2-5   An unordered list

```
<p>Site sections include:</p>

<ul>
<li>Books</li>
<li>CDs and DVDs</li>
<li>Electronics</li>
<li>Photographic Equipment</li>
<li>Software</li>
</ul>
```

I've used the closing list item </li> tag here, which is fine in HTML (where it's not required, but you can use it) and is necessary in XHTML.

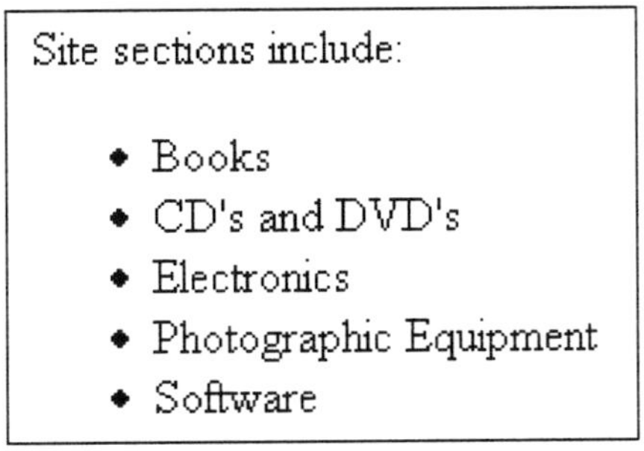

Site sections include:

- Books
- CD's and DVD's
- Electronics
- Photographic Equipment
- Software

FIGURE 2-5   An unordered list.

The browser has interpreted the <ul>. . .</ul> element properly by displaying bullets for each list item rather than a numeric value. There are options in CSS to change the style of the bullets, such as having square rather than round bullets.

Nesting Lists

Sometimes it's very helpful to have nested lists when using both unordered and ordered lists. A nested list is a list within a list. To create a correctly nested list in XHTML, the trick is to be sure the nest is contained completely within an open and closing list item element (see Example 2-6).

EXAMPLE 2-6   Nesting an Ordered List Within Another Ordered List

```
<ol>
<li>Beat eggs, flour, butter and sugar until creamy</li>
<li>Pour into round baking pan</li>
<li>Slowly add and swirl the following ingredients in order:
     <ol>
     <li>Add the chocolate sauce, </li>
     <li>Now, add the cinnamon crunchies, </li>
     <li>Add 1 tsp nutmeg</li>
     </ol>
</li>
<li>Place in oven and bake for 40 minutes</li>
</ol>
```

Figure 2-6 displays the results.

1. Beat eggs, flour, butter and sugar until creamy
2. Pour into round baking pan
3. Slowly add and swirl the following ingredients in order:
    1. Add the chocolate sauce,
    2. Now, add the cinnamon crunchies,
    3. Add 1 tsp nutmeg
4. Place in oven and bake for 40 minutes

FIGURE 2-6   Nesting ordered lists.

You can use a variety of list types in combination when nesting, as follows:

- Ordered lists within ordered lists
- Ordered lists within numbered lists
- Numbered lists within numbered lists
- Numbered lists within ordered lists

Say you have an ordered list describing your recipe, but the added ingredients are optional rather than sequential (see Example 2-7).

EXAMPLE 2-7   Combining nested list types

```
<ol>
<li>Beat eggs, flour, butter and sugar until creamy</li>
<li>Pour into round baking pan</li>
<li>Slowly add and swirl any one or combination of the following ingredients:
    <ul>
    <li>chocolate sauce</li>
    <li>cinnamon crunchies,</li>
    <li>1 tsp nutmeg</li>
    </ul>
</li>
<li>Place in oven and bake for 40 minutes</li>
</ol>
```

1. Beat eggs, flour, butter and sugar until creamy
2. Pour into round baking pan
3. Slowly add and swirl any one or combination of the following ingredients:
    ◇ chocolate sauce
    ◇ cinnamon crunchies,
    ◇ 1 tsp nutmeg
4. Place in oven and bake for 40 minutes

FIGURE 2-7   Mixed ordered and unordered lists as displayed within a browser.

You'll notice right away that any nested unordered list has an open rather than solid bullet. This is typical default browser behavior. Using CSS, you can modify the numbered and bullet styles for your nested lists.

Beware: Overuse of Nests

Nesting lists can be a great way to get information across to readers quickly and easily, but they can also be overused. If you have a list more than three nests deep and it's not a complex outline, you might want to rethink the approach you're taking in organizing your information.

Definition Lists

A definition list is as ancient of an HTML construct as you can find. However, these are sorely underused, which is a shame because they provide a great way to define terms and concepts.

Definition lists consist of three elements: the definition list element, `<dl>. . . </dl>`; the definition term element, `<dt>. . .</dt>`, and the definition description element, `<dd>. . .</dd>`.

You can have multiple instances of terms within a definition list (see Example 2-8).

EXAMPLE 2-8   Multiple definitions within a list

```
<dl>
    <dt>Furkid (n)</dt>
    <dd>A pet treated as though it were one's child.</dd>

    <dt>Nearshoring (v)</dt>
    <dd>Restructuring a company's workforce by moving jobs to a nearby
        foreign country.</dd>

    <dt>Neurodiversity (n)</dt>
    <dd>The variety of non-debilitating neurological behaviors and
        abilities exhibited by the human race.</dd>
</dl>
```

The browser displays the term, and the definition itself is indented (see Figure 2-8).

Furkid (n)
    A pet treated as though it were one's child.
Nearshoring (v)
    Restructuring a company's workforce by moving jobs to a nearby
    foreign country.
Neurodiversity (n)
    The variety of non-debilitating neurological behaviors and abilities
    exhibited by the human race.

FIGURE 2-8   Definition list displayed in a browser.

You'll be able to use CSS to add styles such as fonts and color if you want to add a little flair to your list.

The Good Old Link

Without the link, the Web would simply not exist. It's the heart and soul of the Web and, as such, should be treated with kindness!

Linking is easy to accomplish, but there are a few important issues to discuss when it comes to linking. Before you get to the code, I want to offer a little insight into two primary types of linking: absolute and relative.

Absolute linking is using the exact address to the file you'd like the link to point to. This means including the domain, any subdirectories, and the filename (see Example 2-9).

EXAMPLE 2-9   An absolute address example

```
http://www.molly.com/books/springboard.html
```

Relative linking means linking to files associated on the same server—files that are in the neighborhood, so to speak. You can link a document to another document in the same directory simply by using its filename: `springboard.html`.

Or, if it's in a subdirectory, you use the subdirectory: `books/springboard.html`.

You can move up from a directory into another: `../books/springboard.html`.

And on some servers, you can use a global identifier to signify "wherever this document is found on this server": `/includes/springboard.html`.

> **Beware: Links in Blogs and CM**
>
> Although most people advocate always using relative linking when working with documents on the same server, this isn't always the best option.
>
> Blogging tools and content-management systems (CMS) generate archives. That means relative references might become unusable in the archive file, which is found somewhere else than the original file.
>
> Because of this, I suggest using absolute linking in those cases.

In the link samples coming up, you'll see me use a range of absolute and relative linking.

Standard links are generated using the anchor element <a>. . .</a>. The hypertext reference attribute (href) is used to denote the link address, and text content within the opening and closing tags will appear as linked text (see Example 2-10).

EXAMPLE 2-10   Linking to an absolute address

```
<a href="http://www.molly.com/books/aw.html">Read about HTML and CSS</a>
```

Figure 2-9 displays the results.

> Read about HTML and CSS

FIGURE 2-9   The incredible hyperlink.

An important concern involves links and accessibility. To make links more accessible to those with disabilities, you can add attributes that provide additional cues to those individuals. The title attribute is very helpful to use. Here, you'll add the attribute and a more detailed description of the link (see Example 2-11).

EXAMPLE 2-11   Adding the title attribute and value

```
<a href="http://www.molly.com/books/springboard.html" title="read about the
upcoming book from Addison-Wesley covering HTML and CSS">Read about HTML and
CSS</a>
```

As the mouse passes over the link, a ToolTip appears along with the additional details (see Figure 2-10).

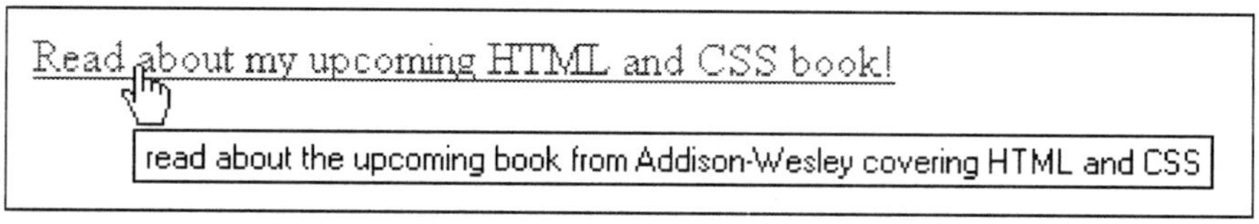

> Read about my upcoming HTML and CSS book!
>
> read about the upcoming book from Addison-Wesley covering HTML and CSS

FIGURE 2-10   Using a title and description makes your links more accessible.

Another important attribute for link accessibility is tabindex, which enables you to denote links in a custom, specific sequence for those individuals who are tabbing instead of clicking through the page.

So if you wanted a link to be the second most important link on the page, you would give the link a tabindex value <a href="springboard.html" tabindex="2">. . .</a>.

Email Links

An email link is just like a standard link, except that, instead of sending you to another page, the link opens the associated email application so you can email the individual directly. Email links are especially useful for contact emails for individuals, staff members on a company site, and customer service and support feedback.

Email links use the `mailto:` attribute along with the `href` attribute and the recipient's email address to accomplish this function (see Example 2-12).

EXAMPLE 2-12 Using the mailto: attribute to create an email link

```
<a href="mailto:molly@molly.com">email molly</a>
```

Figure 2-11 shows the results.

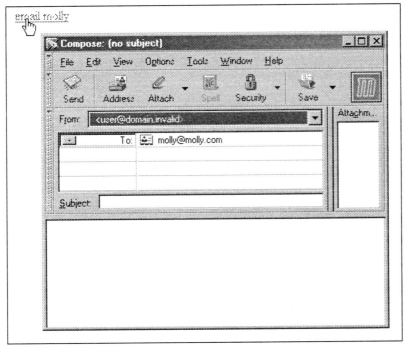

FIGURE 2-11 Clicking on a `mailto:` link opens your email software and inserts the email address into the To field.

If you'd like to make your link a little more user-friendly, you can also add a subject line by following the email address with a question mark (?) and the subject attribute and value (see Example 2-13).

EXAMPLE 2-13   Adding a subject to the email

```
<a href="mailto:molly@molly.com?subject=feedback">email molly</a>
```

Figure 2-12 displays the results.

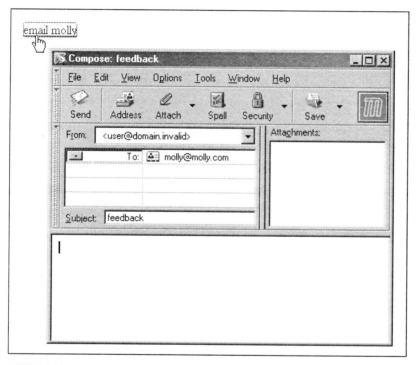

FIGURE 2-12   `Mailto:` link with subject line added.

You'll want to consider accessibility features for your links as well, especially the `title` attribute and a description, and `tabindex` if the sequential order of links on a given page is particularly important to your site visitors (see Example 2-14).

EXAMPLE 2-14   Adding accessibility features to `mailto:` links

```
<a href="mailto:molly@molly.com?subject=feedback" title="email molly regarding
book feedback" tabindex="3">email molly</a>
```

The title text now appears in a ToolTip as the mouse passes over the link. The `tabindex` is set to 3, so the site visitor can press the Tab key three times to reach the link, a very helpful offering to those individuals with mobility impairments.

Intrapage Linking

Intrapage linking enables you to have a link in a document that will automatically go to another location within the same document. This is achieved by creating a link to the location using an octothorpe (#) followed by a relevant name, and then defining the location using an anchor element and the name attribute with that name.

You can use as many such links in a document as is reasonable to achieve your goals. This technique is most helpful for navigating very long documents (see Example 2-15).

EXAMPLE 2-15   Setting up intrapage links

```
<p><a href="#news">Go to the News</a></p>
<h1>Welcome</h1>
<p>This paragraph welcomes you.</p>
<h2>About</h2>
<p>This paragraph talks about us.</p>
<h2><a name="news">News</a></h2>
<p>This is the section your link will go to.</p>
```

Figures 2-13 and 2-14 demonstrate how this works.

Go to the News

Welcome

This paragraph welcomes you.

FIGURE 2-13   Clicking the intrapage link.

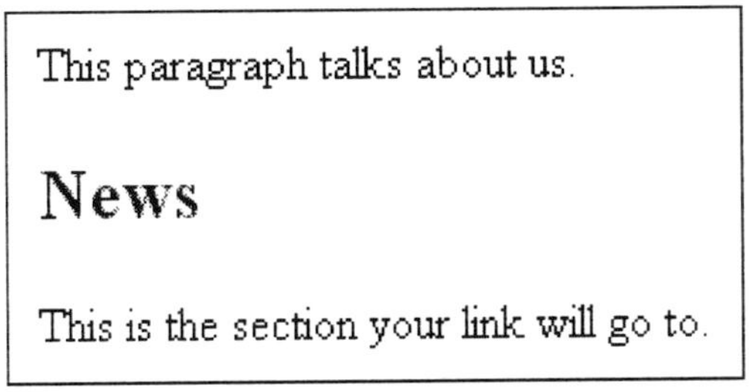

This paragraph talks about us.

News

This is the section your link will go to.

FIGURE 2-14   The browser moves the document to the named location.

Using the same technique as with intrapage linking, you can link from one document to a specific place in another document. This technique is useful when you're referencing a specific notation within text that might be on another page. To achieve this, you simply use an absolute URL plus the octothorpe followed by the named location in the first document (see Example 2-16).

EXAMPLE 2-16   Using links to jump to a specific place in another document

```
<p><a href="http://www.molly.com/headers.html#h2">Follow this link to read about
h2 level headers</a></p>
```

You name the section in the document to which you are referring appropriately (see Example 2-17).

EXAMPLE 2-17   The desired location

```
<h1><a name="h2">All about h2 level headers</a></h1>
```

The first document then contains a link to the specific location within the other document.

Beware Name and ID

In XHTML 1.1, the name attribute has been completely replaced with the id attribute. As a result, if you're using XHTML 1.1, you'll need to replace all instances of name with id in the anchor element.

Some browsers do not recognize this, so use XHTML 1.0 or HTML documents for any pages of this nature to avoid problems.

Adding Content to the Template

Example 2-18 takes the template created in Chapter 1, "Building an HTML Page," and has added some of the features introduced in this chapter so you can get context for them in a working document.

EXAMPLE 2-18 Adding content to the template

```
<!DOCTYPE html PUBLIC "-//W3C//DTD XHTML 1.0 Transitional//EN"
"http://www.w3.org/TR/xhtml1/DTD/xhtml1-transitional.dtd">

<head>

<title>your site : location within site : topic title</title>

<meta http-equiv="Content-Type" content="text/html; charset=UTF-8" />
<meta name="keywords" content="your, keywords, here" />
<meta name="description" content="your description here" />
<meta name="author" content="your name here" />

</head>

<body>

<h1>Welcome!</h1>

<p>Here are a few things I enjoy.</p>

<h2>A poem . . .</h2>

<p>What earthly tongue, and, oh! what human pen<br />
Can tell that scene of suffering, too severe.<br />
'Tis ever present to my sight, oh! When<br />
Will the sound cease its torture on mine ear?</p>

<h2>A recipe</h2>

<p>I like this recipe so much, I tell all my friends about it!</p>

<h3>Swirled coffee cake</h3>

<ol>
<li>Beat eggs, flour, butter and sugar until creamy</li>
<li>Pour into round baking pan</li>
<li>Slowly add and swirl any one or combination of the following ingredients:
     <ul>
     <li>chocolate sauce</li>
     <li>cinnamon crunchies,</li>
     <li>1 tsp nutmeg</li>
```

```
        </ul>
    </li>
    <li>Place in oven and bake for 40 minutes</li>
</ol>

<h2>Unusual terms</h2>

<dl>
    <dt>Furkid (n)</dt>
    <dd>A pet treated as though it were one's child.</dd>

    <dt>Nearshoring (v)</dt>
    <dd>Restructuring a company's workforce by moving jobs to a nearby
        foreign country.</dd>

    <dt>Neurodiversity (n)</dt>
    <dd>The variety of non-debilitating neurological behaviors and
        abilities exhibited by the human race.</dd>
</dl>

<h2>When friends get in touch . . .</h2>

<p><a href="mailto:molly@molly.com?subject=feedback">email molly</a></p>

</body>
</html>
```

Load this on up in your web browser and take a look!

QUANTUM JUMP: THE IMPORTANCE OF STRUCTURE

In this chapter, you've gotten a great start learning about two of the most important aspects of a web page: text and links. But along the way, you also learned a bit about the importance of semantics, or meaning, of elements and their tags.

This understanding is so important because when you misuse elements to achieve visual results rather than to convey meaning, you limit the document a great deal. The meaning of these elements is a part of logical document structure, and a logical document structure, in turn, generates what's known as a *document tree*.

A document tree is simply the hierarchical logic of your document's structure, based on the semantics of the tags you're using to mark up your content. This tree isn't particularly relevant on its own, but the moment you begin applying CSS, JavaScript, or server-side scripts for dynamic content generation, the document tree becomes incredibly important.

A clean document generates a logical document tree, making the CSS and scripting all the more easy because you can rely on advanced concepts in both that rely on such issues as inheritance. Without a clear document tree, you will be at a disadvantage when trying to debug documents.

Wrapping It Up

Being able to properly format text and manage content goes a long way toward helping you create a web page that makes sense not only to you and other people who might update your documents, but to those good folks who visit your site as well.

Advantages to well-formatted content include these:

- Site visitors will have a clear understanding of your site's intent.

- You can help guide your visitors through the site in a way that that makes sense.

- You will keep your content well organized.

- Your links will be carefully thought out and, therefore, will be more useful to your audience.

- You can persuade your visitors through your text content and links to visit other areas of your site, especially those areas where you most want them.

Essentially, the way you manage text and linking will ensure not only that your content is king, but that your site visitors feel like royalty while visiting, too.

Text Isn't Everything

Of course, text isn't the only way in which we can persuade, entertain, and inform our guests. Adding images, media, and interactive options can go a very long way to making the experience of your web site a rich one.

So, next up, I'll be showing you how to add images, media, and scripts to your documents. If it seems a little early in the game to be jumping into what might feel like a more complex topic, worry not! The idea is to get you putting your knowledge to work right away, in satisfying and fun ways that will keep you interested in learning more, too.

CHAPTER 3

Adding Images, Media, and Scripts

Images, media, and scripting help a site become "dynamic and rich." This is called *dynamic* because many of these features offer the opportunity for the site visitor to interact in an active way with the site. It's *rich* because the site becomes richer visually and in terms of content. *Images* in this chapter refers specifically to images you'll be adding to your page as part of the design itself or as a means of enhancing the content, such as with photos. Images must be processed in a specific way for the Web, using a good image editor; you can quickly learn the details.

NOTE

Web graphics can be created by a wide range of programs, but typically you're going to want to have a decent image editor, such as Photoshop (if your wallet is a little smaller, you can try Jasc's Paint Shop Pro). There are numerous other web graphic programs; you can find them by searching for "web graphics software" at your favorite search engine.

Two primary types of web graphic formats exist: GIF and JPEG. The GIF file format is best for images with few, flat colors and line drawings; JPEGs are best for images with many colors and color gradients, such as photos. A third type of web graphic format is PNG, but the lack of support for PNG in some browsers makes it a less stable choice.

Multimedia on the Web can refer to a number of things, including animated GIFs, Flash animations, audio, video, and Java applets. *Scripts* in this chapter refers to JavaScript and DHTML effects that you can add to your documents, creating a richer user experience.

NOTE

Although images, media, and scripting can bring more options to your site, they also can add unnecessary clutter and download time. I like to think of most content of this nature to be decorative. Just as you wouldn't want to overdecorate a house, think about how less can be more when it comes to your page.

The *img* Element

When working with images, the element you'll be using is `img`. This is an empty element—in other words, it does not contain any text content. As a result, it doesn't require a closing tag. It's written in XHTML as follows:

```
<img />
```

Placed all by itself within the body of your document, this will do nothing at all. So along with the `img` element itself, you'll need to point to the location of the image. This is done using the `src` attribute, which stands for "source."

In the value of the source attribute, you'll add the location and the name of the actual web graphic file, along with its extension. Example 3-1 shows a complete document with the image source included.

EXAMPLE 3-1   Adding the image into the document body

```
<!DOCTYPE html PUBLIC "-//W3C//DTD XHTML 1.0 Transitional//EN"
    "http://www.w3.org/TR/xhtml1/DTD/xhtml1-transitional.dtd">

<html xmlns="http://www.w3.org/1999/xhtml" xml:lang="en">

<head>

<title>Chapter 3</title>

</head>

<body>

<img src="images/photo.jpg" />

</body>
</html>
```

NOTE
You'll notice that I've used a subdirectory called images in which to store my web graphics. It's conventional to place images in a subdirectory beneath the documents that use them or, if you have a fairly small site, in one image location off the root directory.

This causes the image to appear in your browser window (see Figure 3-1).

FIGURE 3-1 The image appears within the browser window.

Without any content in the document, the image automatically is placed in the upper-left corner. You'll ultimately be doing a lot more with this image to make it more useful:

- Assist browsers with better rendering

- Provide helpful information to those who might not be able to view the image

- Link the image

NOTE

You'll explore how to do these things using XHTML first, but in Chapter 8, "Working with Color and Images Using CSS," you'll learn more advanced methods to control an image's presentation using CSS.

Adding *width* and *height* Values

The next thing you'll want to do for your image is add `width` and `height` values. This actually assists browsers in rendering images more efficiently, so it's always a good idea to add this information.

You can find the image's width and height in a couple ways. The first way is that you can look for it in your imaging editor (see Figure 3-2).

Another way to find width and height is to open the image itself in your browser.

Figure 3-3 depicts the image itself (not the HTML file), and you can see in the title bar that the width and height are displayed.

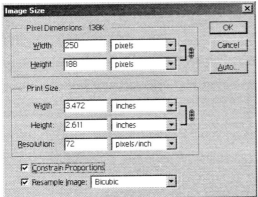

FIGURE 3-2   Look for the width and height in pixels for your image—here, Photoshop displays the width and height at the top of the Image Size dialog box.

FIGURE 3-3   I opened the image in my browser, and the image width and height appear within the browser's title bar.

NOTE
Not all browsers have this feature, but most common ones do.

When you've got the image dimensions—in this case, 250 pixels wide by 188 pixels high—you can place it into your image markup:

```
<img src="photo.jpg" width="250" height="188" />
```

NOTE
You should always include the correct width and height. If the `width` and `height` values are larger than the actual image, the browser will stretch the image to make it fit. If you note smaller values, the browser will squeeze the image into the smaller size, scrunching it up.

Providing Alternative Text

Some people surf the Web without images turned on. Sounds strange in today's world of high bandwidth, but some people still don't have high-speed access, so images can slow down their access to your page's content, and they will disable the images. Another important concern is that many people visiting the Web are visually impaired or blind. In all these cases, it's helpful to provide some clues to your visitor as to what the image represents.

This is done using *alternative text*, which uses the alt attribute and a description, as shown in Example 3-2.

EXAMPLE 3-2   Adding an alt text description

```
<img src="photo.jpg" width="250" height="188" alt="photograph of a delicious
Vietnamese noodle dish from restaurant Pho 88" />
```

Alternative text descriptions appear in two ways on the site. First, they appear in the location of the image before the image load and when images are disabled (see Figure 3-4).

FIGURE 3-4   Alternative text in a browser where images are disabled.

The second way alternative text appears is upon mouseover of an image. This assists everyone because it provides more contextual clues on the image's purpose (see Figure 3-5).

FIGURE 3-5   Alternative text in a ToolTip as the mouse passes over the image.

Linking the Image

Many times you will want to link an image to either another HTML document or a detailed version of the image. In either case, linking an image works the same way as linking text. You surround the image code with the anchor element and the reference to where the image is linking, just as if it were the text content (see Example 3-3).

EXAMPLE 3-3   Linking the image

```
<a href="detail.html">
<img src="images/photo.jpg" width="250" height="188" alt="photograph of a
delicious Vietnamese noodle dish from restaurant Pho 88" />
</a>
```

The image is now linked, and when clicked on, it will take the visitor to the detail.html page. You can even add a title attribute to the link if you want further details about the link to be available to your visitors. By default, browsers place a border around the image to highlight the fact that it is a linked image, and the hand cursor appears upon mouseover, too (see Figure 3-6).

FIGURE 3-6   A linked image.

If the image link is followed, the browser will use the default visited link color around the image. Of course, many people find the link border unsightly. If you'd like to get rid of your border immediately, you can do so by turning it off directly in the HTML, as shown in Example 3-4.

EXAMPLE 3-4   Using the `border` attribute

```
<a href="detail.html">
<img src="images/photo.jpg" width="250" height="188" alt="photograph of a
delicious Vietnamese noodle dish from restaurant Pho 88" border="0" />
</a>
```

The image, while still linked, now displays no border (see Figure 3-7).

FIGURE 3-7   The image, while still linked, has no visible border.

Beware: Borders Are Presentational

The `border` attribute is considered presentational because it can be used decoratively. By providing a value greater than 0, the border size changes, whether the image is linked or not. Ideally, you will use CSS instead of the `border` attribute to modify your borders. CSS will also be used to position or float the image within its content. You'll learn more about this in Chapter 11, "Margins, Borders, and Padding," and Chapter 12, "Positioning, Floats, and Z-index."

Linking to an Audio or Video File

If you'd like to provide links to media on your site, you can do so just as easily as linking an image. Many file types exist for audio and video, the most popular these days being the MP3, QuickTime, Real, and Windows Media files.

You first place your media file into a subdirectory. As with images, this is a convention that helps you keep all your various files organized. In this case, I've named the subdirectory media (how's that for brilliant?) and placed two files in it, one an MP3 audio file and the other an .avi video file. Example 3-5 shows my document and how I've linked to my media files.

EXAMPLE 3-5 Linking to audio and video

```
<!DOCTYPE html PUBLIC "-//W3C//DTD XHTML 1.0 Transitional//EN"
      "http://www.w3.org/TR/xhtml1/DTD/xhtml1-transitional.dtd">

<html xmlns="http://www.w3.org/1999/xhtml" xml:lang="en">
<head>
<title>Chapter 3</title>
</head>

<body>

<a href="media/audio-sample.mp3">Link to Audio Sample</a><br />
<a href="media/video-sample.avi">Link to Video Sample</a>

</body>
</html>
```

I've added text within the links and placed a break between the two links so they appear on top of one another rather than side by side, for the sake of clarity. This results in the links as shown in Figure 3-8.

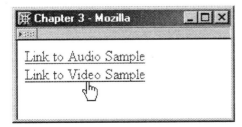

FIGURE 3-8 Links to audio and video samples.

So far, pretty easy, right? Well, there are a few more things to do with links to give visitors an easier time managing the audio and video.

Beware Browser Behavior Differs

Different browsers and different browser configurations influence the way that linked audio and video is displayed. As the link is selected, some browsers automatically download the file into an external media player and play the audio or video clip. Other browsers provide a pop-up option asking whether you'd like to open the file with the appropriate application, or download it and save it to your hard drive. Because of these differences in behavior, it's helpful to let your visitors know as much about the link they're about to click on as possible.

Because most audio and video clips are quite large, it's helpful to provide the file sizes on the page so visitors are prepared. You can do this by simply typing the details into the link or directly after it.

> **NOTE**
>
> Some folks even go so far as to provide a range of file sizes for their low-, medium-, and high-bandwidth visitors.

Another way to assist is to place a description of the file into the `title` attribute of the link (see Figure 3-9).

This helps provide more detail to all and also alerts those folks who can't see or hear to understand what the link is for (see Example 3-6).

EXAMPLE 3-6   Adding details for your visitors

```
<a href="media/audio-sample.mp3" title="audio of molly singing">Link to Audio
Sample</a>. Size: 1,300KB<br />
<a href="media/video-sample.avi" title="video of sarah's dance class">Link to
Video Sample</a>. Size: 29,000KB
```

FIGURE 3-9   Providing helpful details for audio and video links.

Embedding Files Using the *object* Element

Another means of providing audio, video, and other multimedia such as Flash animations and Java applets is to embed them directly into the page. This means that the software plug-in automatically loads with the page.

All external files are considered *objects*. This includes images as well as multimedia files. In contemporary HTML and XHTML specifications, the proper way to include all multimedia is to use the object element to embed a file directly:

```
<object data="media/video-sample.avi" type="video/avi" />
```

This results in the player application appearing on the page. The video can then be played (see Figure 3-10).

FIGURE 3-10   The embedded player loaded into Internet Explorer.

NOTE
Of course, you can do a lot more in terms of providing advanced settings. To learn more about the many available settings for multimedia, see the excellent tutorial at http://www.w3schools.com/media/default.asp.

In instances with Flash files, you use the `object` element to achieve inline results, as you can see in Example 3-7.

EXAMPLE 3-7   Embedding a Flash movie file (SWF) into a page using `<object>`

```
<object classid="clsid:d27cdb6e-ae6d-11cf-96b8-444553540000" width="100"
height="100" codebase="http://active.macromedia.com/flash6/cabs/
swflash.cab#version=6,0,0,0">
<param name="movie" value="media/ava.swf" />
<param name="play" value="true" />
<param name="loop" value="true" />
<param name="quality" value="high" />
</object>
```

In most standards-compliant browsers that also have Flash enabled, the file should play directly upon loading, as shown in Figure 3-11.

FIGURE 3-11   The Flash animation of the AVA logo plays inline in Internet Explorer.

NOTE

As you can see, quite a bit of information has to go along with objects, including `codebase` information and use of the `parameter` element to define not only the location of the file, but also aspects about how it's to be played. These options are all generated by Macromedia Flash when you create the Flash file. For more information on Flash, see http://www.macromedia.com/software/flash/.

You can use the `object` element for audio and Java applets, too. Simply add the correct codebase information and desired parameters, and you'll be good to go.

But Your Honor, I Object!

Okay, the entire last section was filled with lies. Not that I'm trying to steer you wrong—I'm trying to do quite the opposite. All external media should be addressed using the `object` element if you want to be using markup that exists in the valid world of HTML and XHTML.

However, there's a big stumbling block with using the `object` element, and that is that support for it is inconsistent across browsers and platforms. This is very disturbing from a purist's point of view because there's no other alternative *within the specifications.*

QUANTUM LEAP: OBJECT HANDLING IN XHTML 2.0

In XHTML 2.0, the `object` element becomes ubiquitous. In other words, any other elements for external objects, including the `img` element, are made obsolete. Obviously, it's preliminary to use XHTML 2.0 because your results will be limited to those very few browsers that support `object` for `img`. But it gives you a good idea of the direction XHTML is taking.

Here's what it boils down to, in simple terms: If you want your multimedia to be as consistent as possible across browsers, you have to turn to a proprietary element, the `embed` element. This element has never existed in any of the formal specs, but most all browsers support it; although your pages with the `embed` element will cause validation errors, they're going to work.

Conventional wisdom mixes both `object` and `embed`. So if you were to use this approach with the same Flash file just described, you'd end up with the markup shown in Example 3-8.

EXAMPLE 3-8   Embedding a Flash movie file (SWF) into a page using <object> and <embed>

```
<object classid="clsid:d27cdb6e-ae6d-11cf-96b8-444553540000" width="100"
height="100" codebase="http://active.macromedia.com/flash6/cabs/
swflash.cab#version=6,0,0,0">
<param name="movie" value="media/ava.swf" />
<param name="play" value="true" />
<param name="loop" value="true" />
<param name="quality" value="high" />
<embed src="media/ava.swf" width="100" height="100" play="true"
loop="true" quality="high"></embed>
</object>
```

The Flash movie will now play inline in almost every browser.

Adding Scripts

Another means of bringing interactivity and interest to your pages is adding scripts to them. Typically, this refers to JavaScript or what is known as *Dynamic HTML* or DHTML, which is a combination of technologies, including HTML, CSS, JavaScript, and the Document Object Model. Combining these technologies gives you rich features such as drop-down menus and interactive games.

QUANTUM LEAP: THE DOCUMENT OBJECT MODEL
The Document Object Model, also referred to as the DOM, is the interface within browsers that enables you to attach scripting to specific elements. Part of the reason DHTML has been controversial and problematic is that browsers have implemented nonstandard DOMs, which have resulted in poor consistency. When you are looking for DHTML scripts, be sure that you're using those scripts that offer the most cross-browser support. The DOM is standardized, and all contemporary, standards-based browsers are working to implement DOM standards efficiently.

You can add scripts to your document in two primary ways. One is to place the script into the head portion of your document. This is referred to as an *embedded* script. The other way is to place your script external to the document, which is referred to as a *linked* script.

Embedding a Script

To embed a JavaScript in the head portion of your document, you use the `script` element to contain the script (see Example 3-9).

EXAMPLE 3-9   Embedding a script into the head of a document

```
<head>
        <script type="text/javascript">
        function newWindow() {foodWindow = window.open("images/photo.jpg",
        "foodWin", "width=250,height=188")}
        </script>
</head>
```

The purpose of this script is to set up the document to open the image `photo.jpg` in a new window when a specific link is clicked. You also need a bit of script in the actual link found in the body of the document, as follows:

```
<a href="javascript:newWindow()">Delicious Vietnamese Lunch</a>
```

Figure 3-12 demonstrates how clicking on the link makes the pop-up window appear with the image intact.

FIGURE 3-12 The results of the embedded script.

Linking to a Script

In terms of best practices, the more you can get out of your document and into external files in terms of scripting and style, the better. You can have many pages pointing to one script, and if you require changes to the script, you can make them to the one script file instead of to many documents with embedded scripts.

To link to the script, first place the script code (without any HTML) into a separate file, and name the file with a `.js` extension, as in `popup.js`. You can place that file into a subdirectory named scripts (just as you did with images and media), and then use the `script` element to link it to the document (see Example 3-10).

EXAMPLE 3-10 Linking to the script

```
<head>
<script src="scripts/popup.js" type="text/javascript"></script>
</head>
```

Leave the link code as is within the body of the document, and the results will be exactly the same as demonstrated in Figure 3-12.

Scripting and Browser Concerns

In some instances, people are using old browsers with no JavaScript support or poor support for the script element itself, or have JavaScript disabled. Working around these issues requires some additional markup.

NOTE

Most contemporary web designers do not use the workarounds here unless they absolutely know that they have to support older browsers. However, you might want to use them. At the very least, it's important that you see these techniques in action so you'll recognize them when viewing HTML from other sources.

Hiding Scripts from Older Browsers

If you're using embedded JavaScript, some older browsers attempt to display whatever is contained within the script element as body text.

To avoid this, many people got into the habit of "commenting out" their scripts—in other words, using comment syntax to prevent the script from being displayed (see Example 3-11).

EXAMPLE 3-11   Hiding a script with comments

```
<head>
        <script type="text/javascript">
        <!-- this hides the script from older browsers
        function newWindow() {foodWindow = window.open("images/photo.jpg",
        "foodWin", "width=250,height=188")}
        // End hiding script from old browsers -->
        </script>
</head>
```

Note the //. This is JavaScript syntax that enables you to write in a comment after that point that won't be displayed, either. The commenting used here will *not* prevent the script from operating normally in any browser that supports it.

Using the *noscript* Element

If you'd like to add some text so supporting browsers will display a message regarding script support, you can do so using the noscript element (see Example 3-12).

EXAMPLE 3-12 Using the noscript element

```
<head>
        <script type="text/javascript">
        <!-- this hides the script from older browsers
        function newWindow() {foodWindow = window.open("images/photo.jpg",
        "foodWin", "width=250,height=188")}
        // End hiding script from old browsers -->
        </script>

        <noscript>Attention: Your browser does not support JavaScript or you
        have disabled JavaScript.
        </noscript>
</head>
```

Browsers that support scripting and do not have scripting disabled will *not* see the contents of the noscript element.

However, those browsers without JavaScript or, as in the case with Figure 3-13, browsers with JavaScript purposely turned off will display the text within the noscript element.

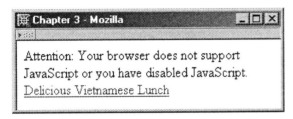

FIGURE 3-13 The noscript text within a browser with disabled JavaScript.

As you can see, the link is still intact, but the pop-up script will not work if JavaScript is disabled or unavailable.

Finding Scripts Online

One of the great things about JavaScript and DHTML is that so many free scripts are available. Of course, the downside of having so many free scripts available means that many of those scripts might be substandard or that newer, better scripts have come along since. Because of that, use discretion and read the fine print. A few sites that I like include http://javascriptkit.com/, http://simplythebest.net/ scripts/DHTML_scripts/, http://www.javascripts.com/, and http://www.dynamic-drive.com/.

Imagine That!

From structure to well-formatted text, to great imagery and interactive features, you've sure come a long way in three short chapters.

Of course, if you're getting frustrated because all of this seems very much like building a house while you're imagining how it's going to be decorated, that's understandable. It's important to keep in mind that building great web pages in today's world means taking the extra time to organize your materials, have clear goals, and take pride in the crafting of your documents.

As with a home, the better the foundation, the more well-built and finely crafted the structure, the easier it will be to make aesthetic modifications. This is really what we're after by taking the time to build our pages correctly. Just something as simple as placing all your images in an image directory, scripts in a script directory, and additional media in corresponding directories means having an internal site structure that will grow with you instead of causing collapse as your site grows and changes to meet your needs.

Imagine if you hadn't taken the time early on to build the structure well. Take the advice of professional web developers who have learned the hard way: Not building the infrastructure well can lead to all kinds of expensive, time-consuming, and downright frustrating problems along the way.

Now that you're a bit more organized in terms of your document, text, and image and media management, it's time to get fancier. In the next chapter, you'll be learning how to build effective tables. Once the holy grail of how websites were laid out visually, tables are being revisited for their structural integrity.

What we're learning is that CSS is a lot more efficient and flexible for the presentational aspects of our site, but tables can be extremely useful for displaying a range of information in effective ways. Depending upon your needs, you might find tables an excellent way of managing data, further assisting your site visitors to easily get to and understand the information you're sharing with them.

CHAPTER 4

Creating Tables

Tables are a very helpful way of presenting data on a website. Tables have an interesting history on the Web, though—one that bears a little discussion before you dig in and begin creating them.

As many readers might be aware, the Web was created by a physicist. Tim Berners-Lee had a vision that the technology could be used as a highly efficient means of distributing and sharing research documents. So tables are an extension of that original idea: They were added to the growing language of HTML as a means to share data with other researchers and scientists.

At the time, CSS hadn't emerged, so there was no technology available to specifically address the way pages were laid out. Because tables create a grid, it quickly became convention to use tables as a means of displaying content rather than data—a de facto layout tool because nothing better existed.

To this day, tables remain the primary means of laying out web documents visually. But this approach is fraught with problems. Table-based layouts take longer to load and are often extremely detailed, making them difficult to manage effectively. Tables for layout do not follow the structural premise so important for search engine rankings, so using them can inhibit the capability to improve ranking. Finally, and perhaps most importantly, table layouts create numerous barriers to accessibility.

The use of tables for layout is the biggest hack in HTML history because it forces elements and attributes created for one specific thing: the display of tabular data, to be used for something entirely different. There is no doubt that table layouts changed the face of the Web, but now that we have CSS, there's no reason to use tables for most layouts anymore. Instead, tables are once again being looked upon in their true light: as a means of displaying data.

An approach known as *transitional design* incorporates the use of lightly crafted tables along with CSS to achieve layouts that are compatible in older browsers. This technique is an excellent approach if you have concerns about supporting browsers other than contemporary ones. However, the ideal is to avoid tables altogether, except for the purpose for which they were intended.

The *table* Element

To begin creating tables, you start with the `table` element. This element alerts the browser that a table is about to be drawn. The `table` element is considered not empty because it contains text content. So it's written with an open and closing tag, as follows:

```
<table>
</table>
```

As is, nothing displays in the browser—you still have to add other elements to make that happen. But the `table` element uses a few attributes that you'll want to explore.

Table Width

If you'd like to set your table width, you can do so in the opening `table` tag. There are two width values to choose from, pixel and percentage. A pixel value is considered a *fixed* value, in that the table will be fixed to that width (see Example 4-1).

EXAMPLE 4-1   A table with a pixel, or *fixed*, width

```
<table width="250">

</table>
```

A fixed table with a width of 250 pixels will take up exactly 250 pixels width of the available browser window (see Figure 4-1).

FIGURE 4-1   No matter how wide the browser window becomes, a fixed-width table remains fixed—in this case, to 250 pixels.

A percentage value is considered a *fluid* value (also referred to as *dynamic* or *liquid*) because the table will expand to the noted percentage of space available (see Example 4-2).

EXAMPLE 4-2   A table with a percentage, or *fluid* width

```
<table width="90%">

</table>
```

In this case, the table will take up 90% of the available browser window width (see Figure 4-2).

FIGURE 4-2   A percentage-based table width will cause the table to fill the browser window to that percentage—in this case, 90%.

NOTE
Width changes vary because of resolution differences between computer displays and also because people tend to resize their browsers on the desktop. A fluid table will always reflow to fit the available space.

Table Borders and Spacing

You can add a border to your table using HTML, as follows:

```
<table width="250" border="1">
```

Doing this places a 1-pixel border around your table and any of its rows and cells.

To add spacing between cells, you use the cellspacing attribute. To add spacing between the content in a cell and the cell itself, you can use the cellpadding attribute:

```
<table width="90%" border="1" cellspacing="5" cellpadding="5">
```

As with all presentational attributes, width, border, cellspacing, and cellpadding are all going to be ultimately managed with CSS, which provides many more options in terms of how such presentation is applied. However, it's important to be familiar with these attributes and to use them in this chapter as you create your data table. You'll modify these features later with CSS.

NOTE
To learn more about how to make your data tables look fantastic, see Chapter 8, "Working with Color and Images Using CSS."

Adding a Table Row

Another critical building block of an HTML table is the table row, represented by the `tr` element (see Example 4-3).

EXAMPLE 4-3   A table with a table row

```
<table width="90%" border="1" cellspacing="5" cellpadding="5">
<tr>

</tr>
</table>
```

Every table requires at least one row. Rows are the horizontal aspects of the table. Although this markup alone will not display in and of itself, I've added the necessary components so you can visualize the row clearly (see Figure 4-3).

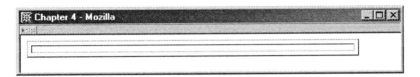

FIGURE 4-3   A table with one row—the spacing between the row's outline and the table's outline is created by the `cellspacing` and `cellpadding` attributes.

You can add as many rows as your table requires.

For the next example, I've added two rows to provide you with an example of three rows within the table. I then added some more markup necessary to help visualize the three rows (see Figure 4-4).

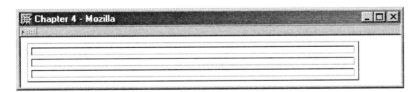

FIGURE 4-4   A table with three rows.

Adding Table Cells

Table cells provide the vertical columns of your table. They are represented by the table data tags:

```
<td>
</td>
```

Along with the `table` and `tr` elements, the table data element comprises the three essential building blocks of any table (see Example 4-4).

EXAMPLE 4-4   A table with a single table row and three columns

```
<table width="90%" border="1" cellspacing="5" cellpadding="5">
<tr>
<td></td>
<td></td>
<td></td>
</tr>
</table>
```

Because you have all the necessary building blocks, this table displays in a web browser without any additional help (see Figure 4-5).

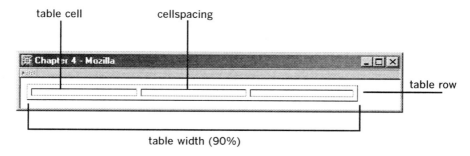

FIGURE 4-5   Anatomy of a simple table: three cells, one row, width of 90%, cellspacing of 5.

Of course, you can add as many table cells as you need for columns. Even better, you can enhance your table cells with table headers, to distinguish the column headers from the column data.

Adding Table Headers

A table header denotes the header of a column or row within a table.

```
<th>
</th>
```

To have your headers describe the column beneath them, place all the headers in a row, and place the columns that will appear underneath in subsequent rows (see Example 4-5).

EXAMPLE 4-5   Table headers for table cells

```
<table width="90%" border="1" cellspacing="5" cellpadding="5">
<tr>
<th>Location</th>
<th>Weather</th>
<th>Time Zone</th>
</tr>
<tr>
<td>Tucson, Arizona</td>
<td>Warm to Hot</td>
<td>No Daylight Savings</td>
</tr>
</table>
```

By default, the browser renders table headers in bold type. As you can see in Figure 4-6, the header text is centered. You can, of course, modify the header weight, color, and other styles using CSS.

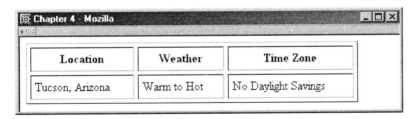

FIGURE 4-6   Adding table headers to the table.

You can also use table headers to describe the row headers (see Example 4-6). The table header then appears within the row (see Figure 4-7).

EXAMPLE 4-6   Table headers for table cells

```
<table width="90%" border="1" cellspacing="5" cellpadding="5">
<tr>
<th>Location</th>
<td>Tucson, Arizona</td>
</tr>
<tr>
<th>Weather</th>
<td>Warm to Hot</td>
</tr>
<tr>
<th>Time Zone</th>
<td>No Daylight Savings</td>
</tr>
</table>
```

FIGURE 4-7   Using table headers to head up the rows within the table.

Many data tables require headers for columns and rows, so you can combine the technique as needed (see Figure 4-8).

FIGURE 4-8   Table headers heading up rows and columns within the table.

Adding a Caption

You can caption your table using the caption element.

```
<caption>. . . </caption>
```

Place your caption content between the opening and closing tag of the caption element. The caption goes directly beneath the opening table tag and is displayed by most browsers centered above the table (see Example 4-7).

EXAMPLE 4-7   Adding a caption to the table

```
<table width="90%" border="1" cellspacing="5" cellpadding="5">
<caption>Comparing weather and time zones</caption>
<tr>
<th>Location</th>
<th>Tucson, Arizona</th>
<th>Las Vegas, Nevada</th>
</tr>
<tr>
<th>Weather</th>
<td>Warm to Hot</td>
<td>Warm to Hot</td>
</tr>
<tr>
<th>Time Zone</th>
<td>No Daylight Savings</td>
<td>Mountain Standard Time</td>
</tr>
</table>
```

Figure 4-9 shows the results.

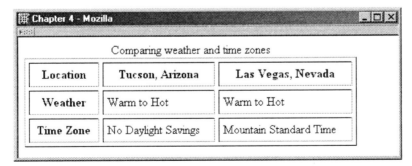

FIGURE 4-9   Adding a caption.

Table Summaries

You can summarize the content of your table using the `summary` attribute within the `table` element:

```
<table summary="text description">
```

If you're thinking "Hey, I bet this has something to do with accessibility," you're spot-on. Providing summaries does, in fact, assist people with disabilities who require more contextual information about the table.

Summaries won't appear onscreen, unlike alternative text or the `title` attribute used in links, which include the information as a ToolTip as the mouse passes over the table. In the case of summaries, they are read only by the assistive device, such as a screen reader for a blind user.

Example 4-8 shows the table so far, with a summary added.

EXAMPLE 4-8   Adding a table summary

```
<table width="90%" border="1" cellspacing="5" cellpadding="5" summary="This table
displays locations and their associated weather and time zone information">
<caption>Comparing weather and time zones</caption>
<tr>
<th>Location</th>
<th>Tucson, Arizona</th>
<th>Las Vegas, Nevada</th>
</tr>
<tr>
<th>Weather</th>
<td>Warm to Hot</td>
<td>Warm to Hot</td>
</tr>
<tr>
<th>Time Zone</th>
<td>No Daylight Savings</td>
<td>Mountain Standard Time</td>
</tr>
</table>
```

QUANTUM LEAP

Using captions and summaries goes a long way to helping make data tables more accessible for those with disabilities—and more understandable for everyone. To dig deeper into accessibility techniques for tables, see *Creating Accessible Tables* found at WebAIM (http://www.webaim.org/techniques/tables/), which is an excellent source for accessibility information in general.

Spanning Rows

As you're setting up your data table, you might find that you need to have a single column span a number of rows within the table. To do this, you'll use the rowspan attribute with the value of rows you want to span to the table header or table cell in question (see Example 4-9).

EXAMPLE 4-9   Using rowspan to span two rows

```
<table width="90%" border="1" cellspacing="5" cellpadding="5" summary="This table
demonstrates rowspan">
<caption>Demonstrating rowspan</caption>
<tr>
<th rowspan="2">Header (spans 2 rows)</th>
<td>data</td>
<td>data</td>
</tr>
<tr>
<td>data</td>
<td>data</td>
</tr>
<tr>
<th>Header (no span)</th>
<td>data</td>
<td>data</td>
</tr>
</table>
```

Figure 4-10 shows the spanned header rows.

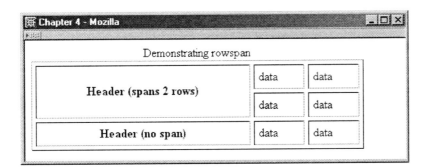

FIGURE 4-10   Spanning rows within table headers.

You can also span rows within table cells. If you wanted to make the second column span all three rows, you could do so by using the rowspan attribute in the appropriate table data cell (see Example 4-10).

EXAMPLE 4-10   Spanning three rows in a table cell

```
<table width="90%" border="1" cellspacing="5" cellpadding="5" summary="This table
demonstrates rowspan">
<caption>Demonstrating rowspan</caption>
<tr>
<th rowspan="2">Header (spans 2 rows)</th>
<td rowspan="3">data (spans 3 rows)</td>
<td>data</td>
</tr>
<tr>
<td>data</td>
</tr>
<tr>
<th>Header (no span)</th>
<td>data</td>
</tr>
</table>
```

You'll notice that I've removed any unnecessary table cells (see Figure 4-11).

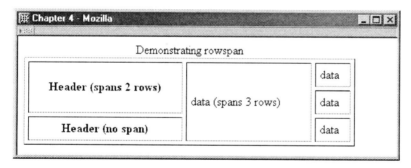

FIGURE 4-11   Adding rowspan to a table cell.

Beware Overlapping Cells

If you don't remove the cells that are overlapped by a span, you'll end up with a big mess! So you've got to do just a bit of simple math and subtract the appropriate number of cells in relation to your table and row spanning. You know you've done your work properly when there's no additional whitespace or seemingly empty spaces within the table. If you do see any odd spaces, go back and rethink the table's structure—you'll quickly find your overlap and correct the overlap problems.

Spanning Columns

Just as you can span rows, you can span columns. You use the `colspan` attribute in table header or table cells (see Example 4-11).

EXAMPLE 4-11   Spanning columns within a table header

```
<table width="90%" border="1" cellspacing="5" cellpadding="5" summary="This table
demonstrates colspan">
<caption>Demonstrating colspan</caption>
<tr>
<th colspan=2>Header (spans 2 columns)</th>
<th>Header (no span)</th>
</tr>
<tr>
<td>data</td>
<td>data</td>
<td>data</td>
</tr>
<tr>
<td>data</td>
<td>data</td>
<td>data</td>
</tr>
</table>
```

Figure 4-12 shows the results.

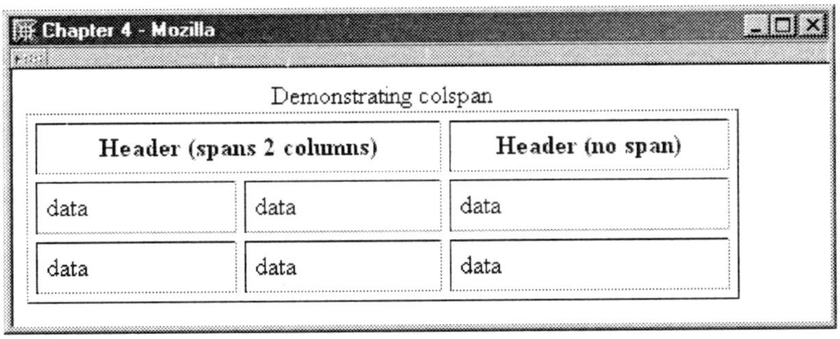

FIGURE 4-12   Spanning two columns with a table header.

Similarly, you can span table cells. In Example 4-12, the bottom table cell spans the entire row. Keep your hat on—I know, the distinction between `rowspan` and `colspan` can get a little tricky. Just keep in mind that row spanning means spanning vertically, whereas column spanning means spanning along the horizon.

EXAMPLE 4-12   Spanning three columns

```
<table width="90%" border="1" cellspacing="5" cellpadding="5" summary="This table
demonstrates colspan">
<caption>Demonstrating colspan</caption>
<tr>
<th colspan=2">Header (spans 2 columns)</th>
<th>Header (no span)</th>
</tr>
<tr>
<td>data</td>
<td>data</td>
<td>data</td>
</tr>
<tr>
<td colspan="3">data (spans 3 columns)</td>
</tr>
</table>
```

You can see the results in Figure 4-13.

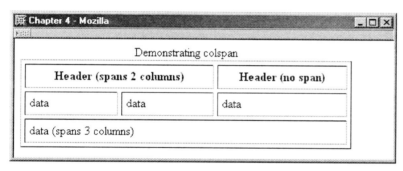

FIGURE 4-13   Spanning columns within a table cell.

QUANTUM LEAP

As you get more skilled in structuring tables, it becomes easy to see why tables for layout was such an obvious solution to creating a grid system upon which to design sites in the early days of the Web. You can see how adding graphics and text to table cells and removing any borders could create an effective design. Web designers who learned this technique first have had significant difficulty making the switch to pure CSS layouts, which work in a different way. The leap for you is to understand that although tables used for layout revolutionized web design, their problems as described in the intro to this chapter outweigh the contemporary options we have with CSS to create amazing layouts that are highly accessible and usable.

Combining *colspan* and *rowspan*

Of course, you can mix colspan and rowspan to get a range of various tables. Example 4-13 demonstrates a mix of column and row spanning.

EXAMPLE 4-13 Combining colspan and rowspan

```
<table width="90%" border="1" cellspacing="5" cellpadding="5" summary="This table
combines colspan and rowspan">
<caption>Combining colspan and rowspan</caption>
<tr>
<th colspan=2" rowspan="2">Header (spans 2 columns and 2 rows)</th>
<td>data</td>
</tr>
<tr>
<td>data</td>
</tr>
<tr>
<td>data</td>
<td>data</td>
<td>data</td>
</tr>
</table>
```

Figure 4-14 shows the results.

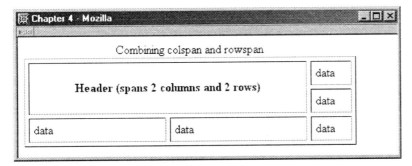

FIGURE 4-14 Combining colspan and rowspan.

NOTE

You can mix and match colspan and rowspan into as wide a range of mixes as imaginable. Two caveats remain: Be sure to get rid of any cells or headers that will be overlapped by your spanning, and know that the more complex your table becomes, the less accessible it will be for the majority of screen reader software used by blind and visually impaired users.

Grouping Table Columns: The *col* Element

If you are very concerned about accessibility, or if your data tables are long, it becomes helpful to group columns to keep them organized and logical. Two elements can assist you with grouping columns for better management and accessibility.

The first of these elements is the col element. The col element is a way to group columns to specify attributes or apply style.

The col element must appear after the caption element, if one exists, and it supports a number of attributes. Of particular importance is the span attribute, which defines how many columns the col element will span.

Example 4-14 demonstrates the use of the col element with a span attribute of 2. You'll notice I've also added the width attribute, defining a width, and that the col element requires a trailing slash: <col />.

EXAMPLE 4-14   Using the col element to apply attributes to a number of columns

```
<table width="90%" border="1" cellspacing="5" cellpadding="5" summary="This table
explores column grouping">
<caption>Column Grouping</caption>
<col span="2" width="100" />
<tr>
<th>Table Head</th>
<th>Table Head</th>
<th>Table Head</th>
</tr>

<tr>
<td>data</td>
<td>data</td>
<td>data</td>
</tr>

<tr>
<td>data</td>
<td>data</td>
<td>data</td>
</tr>
</table>
```

Figure 4-15 demonstrates how the first two columns are now grouped. The width I've defined in the col element of 100 pixels applies to both columns in the spanned group.

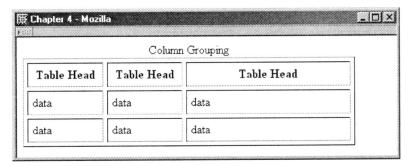

FIGURE 4-15   Grouping columns using the col element.

You can add other presentational attributes, too, including the `align` and `valign` attributes:

```
<col span="2" width="100" align="right" valign="bottom" />
```

This markup creates the results found in Figure 4-16.

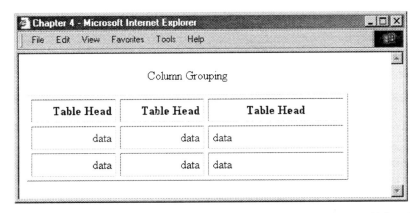

FIGURE 4-16   Using the col element to apply presentational attributes to multiple columns.

In this case, you'll notice that the headers within the group are right-aligned, as is the text in the group's data cells. If you look closely, you'll also notice that the text is slightly lower in the group than it is in the right column, which isn't part of the group.

Grouping Table Columns with *colgroup*

Another means of grouping columns is to the `colgroup` element, which performs essentially the same task as `col`. Example 4-15 takes the basic three-column, three-row table used in Example 4-14 and applies different features to two of those columns.

EXAMPLE 4-15   Using the `col` element to apply attributes to a number of columns

```
<table width="90%" border="1" cellspacing="5" cellpadding="5" summary="This table
explores column grouping">
<caption>Column Grouping</caption>
<colgroup align="right" valign="bottom" />
<colgroup align="right" valign="bottom" />
<tr>
<th>Table Head</th>
<th>Table Head</th>
<th>Table Head</th>
</tr>

<tr>
<td>data</td>
<td>data</td>
<td>data</td>
</tr>

<tr>
<td>data</td>
<td>data</td>
<td>data</td>
</tr>
</table>
```

This then applies the `align` attribute value to the entire group of table cells, rather than having to add the individual attribute to each of those cells. The visual results are exactly the same as found in Figure 4-16.

Beware Browser Support for *col* and *colgroup*

You'll notice that for Figure 4-16, I switched over from my favored browser, Mozilla, to Internet Explorer. Even though Mozilla is generally considered a superior browser, standards-wise, than IE, in this case, Mozilla's support for `col` and `colgroup` and their associated attributes is somewhat lacking. The same is true of many other browsers. For this reason, the use of `col` and `colgroup` should be limited to situations in which you are aware that your visitors can see the desired results. Many designers prefer not to use `col` or `colgroup` at all.

Grouping Table Rows

You can also group table rows using three elements that define the row groups based on function. The elements include thead, tfoot, and tbody for table head, table foot, and table body, respectively (see Example 4-16).

EXAMPLE 4-16   Grouping table rows

```
<thead>
<tr>
<th>Table Head</th>
<th>Table Head</th>
<th>Table Head</th>
</tr>
</thead>
<tfoot>
<tr>
<td>Table Foot</td>
<td>Table Foot</td>
<td>Table Foot</td>
</tfoot>
<tbody>
<tr>
<td>Table Body</td>
<td>Table Body</td>
<td>Table Body</td>
</tr>
</tbody>
</tr>
</table>
```

Browser support is more consistent for these elements. Figure 4-17 shows the results.

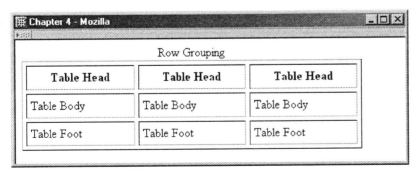

FIGURE 4-17   Grouping by row—you'll notice that I've defined the foot in the middle of the table, but the row defined as the table foot still appears at the foot of the table.

The Table's Set...

Whether you're a doctor, scientist, professional assistant, instructor, student, or legal clerk, you're going to find a need at some point to place information into tables. Think about all the uses you might find for using tables on public or private websites:

- Medical charting

- Research results from scientific studies

- Calendar of events

- Grade and attendance tracking

- Task management

- Court case information

And the list can go on for as long as you can imagine. It becomes quite easy to see why tables are so important for managing content appropriately.

Of course, another use for tables is to display information that is collected in databases. One way such information can be collected is via a website. Let's say you're a real estate agent who wants to develop a database of people interested in buying and selling land in your area.

You can put up an interactive form to collect information from willing participants. The form would then be processed on the server using database technology and would return the data to your website, formatted in a table. Of course, this demands the interactivity of forms and server-side technology. Although database and server applications are beyond the scope of this book, the necessary elements for providing interactive forms are found within markup.

Coming up next, you'll learn all about forms and how to set up great interactive forms that will help enhance your site visitor's experience to your pages—and help you get the most feedback, in turn.

CHAPTER 5

Building Forms

Forms are an essential part of how the Web is made interactive and useful. Forms are interactive because a form demands that you, the user, interact with it to perform some task. That task might be any number of important ones:

- Entering information into your online banking system so you can manage funds online

- Submitting your name and information to become a member of an online dating service

- Making a purchase for an airline ticket and travel services

- Purchasing other goods and services online

Without forms, we'd have had none of these features available—and, in fact, the Web itself would never have moved along to become as efficient as it is in terms of providing interactive services. Today other technologies are being used with regularity to accomplish the same things HTML forms do.

Flash, for example, supports rich forms that are also very fast and update on the same page. This doesn't mean that HTML forms are falling out of favor: Although Flash forms can be very useful for some users, they cannot be made as searchable and accessible in the way that HTML-based forms can. So even sites using Flash forms often also provide an HTML alternative. Other technologies are beginning to emerge to help make forms more feature rich, but these technologies are preliminary, so HTML forms remain the conventional method to bring interactivity and functionality to websites.

Forms are relatively easy to work with—at least, from the HTML side of things. It's the programming for the form that makes the form behave in certain ways—and programming forms on the server side is beyond the scope of this book.

Here you'll learn how to build HTML forms and make them logical and accessible. I'll also provide resources along the way so you can become more aware of the options you have when it comes to server-side scripts to validate and process the forms that you build.

The *form* Element

All forms begin with the form element:

```
<form>

</form>
```

The form element has two required attributes you'll need to add to it for the form to function at all:

- method—This attribute defines which way the form is going to communicate with your web server. The value options are get and post.

- action—The action attribute provides the correct path to where the form script is processed (see Example 5-1).

EXAMPLE 5-1   Adding method and action attributes and values to a form element

```
<form method="get" action="http://www.myserver.com/cgi-bin/mailscript/">

</form>
```

QUANTUM LEAP

You'll need to check with your ISP to find out the preferred method with any form-processing scripts it provides. What's more, many ISPs provide a number of form-processing scripts, but not all scripts will be as robust as what your needs might require.

If you're looking to create a simple contact form, you shouldn't have any problems. However, if it's a shopping cart script, for example, that's going to require additional programming and customization. It's important to point out that not all service providers allow you to have advanced scripts, so you'll really need to do your homework in advance to get the service you require.

At this point, the markup you've created will not do anything in and of itself. Forms work based on the concept of *controls*. Controls are the default boxes and buttons that appear as a result of your HTML form markup.

Adding an Input Textbox

Input textboxes are used for a number of form needs, including any time you want some-one to type out his name, address, and so forth. To create a textbox, you use the `input` element along with the `type` attribute and a value of `text` (see Example 5-2).

EXAMPLE 5-2   Adding input textboxes

```
<form method="get" action="http://www.myserver.com/cgi-bin/mailscript/">

First Name: <input type="text" /><br />
Last Name: <input type="text" /><br />
Phone: <input type="text" />

</form>
```

As Figure 5-1 shows, using `input` with the type attribute for a text input generates a familiar-looking form.

First Name:
Last Name:
Phone:

FIGURE 5-1   Form inputs with text.

Of course, you can see that this isn't exactly orderly or attractive. That we'll fix with CSS later in the book, but a few technical issues need to be dealt with long before we get to that. Most important is how to distinguish one form field from another. The `input` element creates the input textbox, but you'll want to identify each form field as well as modify them in terms of how they look and behave. To identify input fields, you use a combination of `name` and `id` with associated values. This ensures that the form will be backward compatible and enables you to identify specific input areas for styling, script-ing, and accessibility purposes. Example 5-3 shows how this would work in our code sample so far.

EXAMPLE 5-3   Identifying text input with name and `id`

```
<form method="get" action="http://www.myserver.com/cgi-bin/mailscript/">

First Name: <input type="text" name="firstname" id="firstname" /><br />
Last Name: <input type="text" name="lastname" id="lastname" /><br />
Phone: <input type="text" name="phone" id="phone" />

</form>
```

The next step is to set the size of the textbox. Using the size attribute, you can provide a width for each field. You can also set the number of characters that the text input will accept, and this is accomplished using the maxlength attribute (Example 5-4).

EXAMPLE 5-4 Modifying text input with size and maxlength

```
<form method="get" action="http://www.myserver.com/cgi-bin/mailscript/">

First Name: <input type="text" name="firstname" id="firstname" size="25"
maxlength="40" /><br />
Last Name: <input type="text" name="lastname" id="lastname" size="25"
maxlength="40"/><br />
Phone: <input type="text" name="phone" id="phone" size="15" maxlength="0"  />

</form>
```

Wherever maxlength is set to 0, the number of characters that can be entered is not restricted; those that have specific integers will be limited to that number. Figure 5-2 shows the sized text fields, which are longer than those in 5-1.

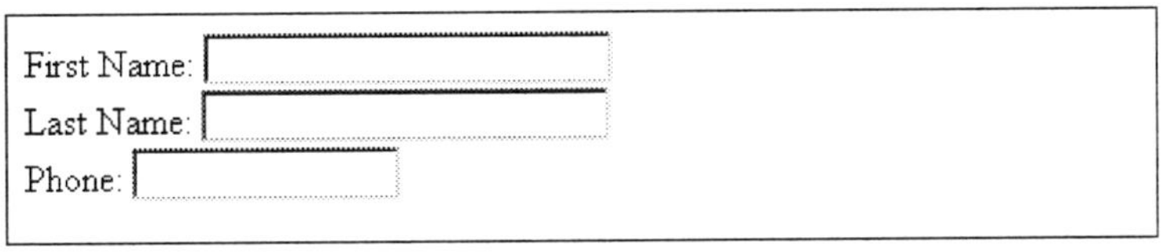

FIGURE 5-2 Sizing input fields and modifying character width.

Another input that works similarly to text input is the password field. This works the same exact way in all aspects, except that the results are echoed back using asterisks (see Figure 5-3).

```
<input type="password" name="password" id="password" size="15" />
```

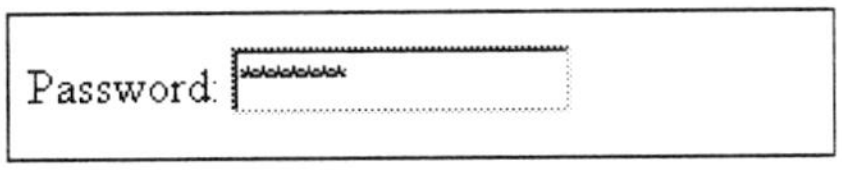

FIGURE 5-3 The password input field echoes back asterisks.

Adding Check Boxes and Radio Buttons

Check boxes are an excellent way to get information from a site visitor from a preset selection of choices. The advantage of check boxes is that visitors can select from more than one option, and that's the best time to use them—when the possibility of multiple answers exists. To create check boxes, you use the `input` element along with the `type` attribute and a value of `checkbox` (see Example 5-5).

EXAMPLE 5-5   Adding check boxes to the form

```
<p>Please choose your favorite way(s) to relax:</p>
<input type="checkbox" name="reading" id="reading" />Reading<br />
<input type="checkbox" name="sports" id="sports" />Sports<br />
<input type="checkbox" name="games" id="games" />Computer Games<br />
<input type="checkbox" name="tv" id="tv" />Television<br />
<input type="checkbox" name="movies" id="movies" />Go to the Movies<br />
<input type="checkbox" name="beer" id="beer" />Enjoy a cold beer<br />
<input type="checkbox" name="dogs" id="dogs" />Play with the dogs<br />
<input type="checkbox" name="music" id="music" />Listen to music<br />
<input type="checkbox" name="friends" id="friends" />Meet with friends and
                                                      hang out
```

Users can then make selections as they see fit (see Figure 5-4).

FIGURE 5-4   Users can select multiple options from a check box list.

You'll notice that the `name` and `id` attributes are set to logically relate to the associated option, and a `value` attribute is included in each option as well. This is necessary for the check boxes to work.

Radio buttons are similar to check boxes, in that they allow your visitor to make selections based on your preset options. However, in the case of radio buttons, the visitor is allowed to select only *one* option instead of one or more options. This is handled by using the same name value (in this case, gender) and then using the value attribute to distinguish the options. You *must* use the value attribute in radio buttons, or the unique selection feature will not work (see Example 5-6).

EXAMPLE 5-6 Adding radio buttons to the form

```
<form method="get" action="http://www.myserver.com/cgi-bin/mailscript/">

<h2>Gender:</h2>

<input type="radio" value="female" name="gender" id="female" />Female<br />
<input type="radio" value="male" name="gender" id="male" />Male<br />
<input type="radio" value="undisclosed" name="gender" id="undisclosed" />Prefer
not to say

</form>
```

Figure 5-5 shows the series of radio buttons described in Example 5-6.

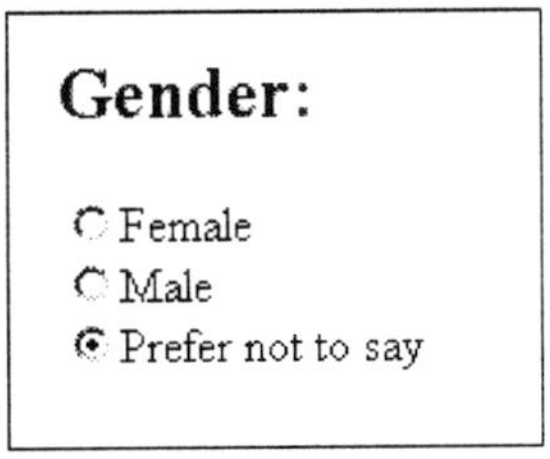

Gender:

○ Female
○ Male
◉ Prefer not to say

FIGURE 5-5 Choosing from a selection of radio buttons.

Check boxes and radio buttons can be used in any combination you require to best address the needs of your form. The main issue is to remember that check boxes can be used for multiple submissions, whereas radio buttons are limited to one choice only.

Preselecting Checked Items

In some instances you'll use radio buttons or check boxes and want to have items preselected. If your form is geared primarily toward female athletes for example, you can display your check boxes or radio buttons with preselected choices by using the checked attribute. This places a check or a dot in the preselected choice (see Example 5-7).

EXAMPLE 5-7   Adding radio buttons to the form

```
<form method="get" action="http://www.myserver.com/cgi-bin/mailscript/">

<p>Please choose your favorite way(s) to relax:</p>

<input type="checkbox" name="reading" id="reading" />Reading<br />
<input type="checkbox" name="sports" id="sports" checked="checked" />Sports<br />
<input type="checkbox" name="games" id="games" />Computer Games

<p>What is your gender?</p>

<input type="radio" value="female" name="gender" id="female" checked="checked"
/>Female<br />
<input type="radio" value="male" name="gender" id="male" />Male<br />
<input type="radio" value="undisclosed" name="gender" id="undisclosed" />Prefer
not to say

</form>
```

Figure 5-6 shows the preselected results.

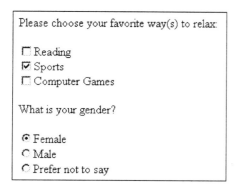

FIGURE 5-6   Preselecting check box and radio button options.

Using Form Menus

Two types of form menus exist: drop-down and list. Both are extremely useful and can be modified in numerous ways to suite a range of needs.

One of the most popular means of providing options in forms is the all-familiar drop-down menu. Menus of this sort are especially helpful when you have numerous options, and they are typically seen in standard menus for states, countries, pricing and so on.

Drop-down menus are created by combining your selections with the `select` and `option` elements (see Example 5-8).

EXAMPLE 5-8 A drop-down form menu

```
<form method="get" action="http://www.myserver.com/cgi-bin/mailscript/">

<p>State (U.S. Western Region):</p>

<select>
<option value="Arizona">Arizona</option>
<option value="California">California</option>
<option value="Colorado">Colorado</option>
<option value="Nevada">Nevada</option>
<option value="Texas">Texas</option>
<option value="Utah">Utah</option>
</select>

</form>
```

Figure 5-7 displays the drop-down menu.

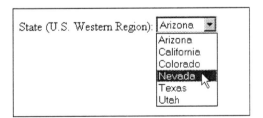

FIGURE 5-7 Selecting from a drop-down form menu.

You can add other features to your drop-down menu, including preselected choices. As with the `checked` attribute for check boxes, preselection can assist with your form's usability by providing a more custom approach. To preselect a specific option within a form menu, simply use the `selected` attribute:

```
<option value="Nevada" selected="selected">Nevada</option>
```

This causes Nevada to appear as the default selection in a drop-down form menu (see Figure 5-8).

State (U.S. Western Region): Nevada ▼

FIGURE 5-8 Use the `select` attribute to create a default selection in a drop-down menu.

You can also create a list menu. This is prepared exactly the same way a drop-down form menu is, but you add the `size` attribute with a numeric value that matches the number of options to the opening `select` tag:

```
<select size="6">
```

You can add a `selected` attribute to any option you'd like selected by default. An additional feature with list menus is to offer multiple selections.

Simply add the `multiple` attribute to the opening `select` tag:

```
<select size="6" multiple="multiple">
```

The menu now becomes a menu list, allowing your visitor to make multiple selections (see Figure 5-9).

FIGURE 5-9 A menu list with multiple options selected.

Working with Text Areas

In some instances, you want to provide an area for feedback or input that is more flexible than just a text input control, which supports only one line of text. Text areas are the perfect solution.

Text areas are created using the `textarea` element along with the `rows` and `cols` attributes to determine a visible field. Unlike tables, the rows and columns in the instance of text areas define how the text area is managed. Rows determine how many rows of text the resulting box will allow, and columns define how wide the box is (see Example 5-9).

EXAMPLE 5-9 Creating a text area

```
<form method="get" action="http://www.myserver.com/cgi-bin/mailscript/">

<p>Please let us know if you have any special requests:</p>

<textarea rows="10" cols="25">

</textarea>

</form>
```

The resulting text area will have 10 rows and 25 columns (see Figure 5-10). I've added some text so you can see how it will appear when a visitor types text into the text area.

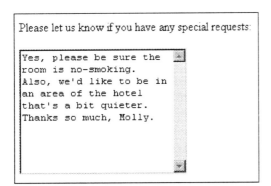

FIGURE 5-10 Text areas make it easy for visitors to input additional comments without the restrictions of textboxes, check boxes, radio buttons, or menus.

You can customize text areas a little more within the HTML, too. First, you might want to add the `name` attribute, which provides information that can be used by your form submission script to clarify its function.

Additionally, you can add an `id` attribute so you can attach scripts to the text area, if you so desire (see Example 5-10).

EXAMPLE 5-10   A text area with name and id attributes

```
<form method="get" action="http://www.myserver.com/cgi-bin/mailscript/">

<p>Please let us know if you have any special requests:</p>

<textarea rows="10" cols="25" name="requests" id="requestbox">

</textarea>

</form>
```

Additionally, if you want to customize the text area a little more, you can type text into the text area markup:

```
<textarea rows="10" cols="25" name="requests" id="requestbox">

Type your comments here.

</textarea>
```

Your visitors will now see the text within the box. When they click in the box, they can remove your text and add their own (see Figure 5-11).

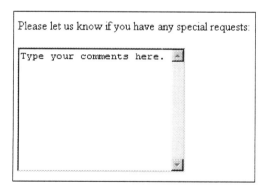

FIGURE 5-11   Text area with customized information to assist the site visitor.

Reset and Submit Buttons

The controls for reset and submit functions are built right into HTML, so you don't have to do much to get these working and even customized to a certain degree without ever touching images or style.

The reset button clears the form when it is clicked. The submit button submits the data in the form, which uses the information in the method and action attributes in the form element itself to send the data to the server for processing.

Example 5-11 shows how to create reset and submit buttons.

EXAMPLE 5-11   Creating reset and submit buttons

```
<form method="get" action="http://www.myserver.com/cgi-bin/mailscript/">

<input type="reset" value="reset" />
<input type="submit" value="submit" />

</form>
```

Figure 5-12 shows how the value attribute determines the information that appears within the buttons.

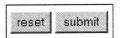

FIGURE 5-12   Reset and submit buttons are created automatically.

Because you can alter the values for the form buttons, you can customize them a bit in terms of what you'd like them to say (see Figure 5-13).

FIGURE 5-13   Customizing reset and submit buttons.

Using a Graphic Submit Button

If you'd like your submit button to look more integrated with your visual design, you can create an image and use it for the submit process instead. The caveat here is that this technique does not equally apply for the reset button unless you add JavaScript. But in terms of HTML itself, you can use a custom button for submit if you so desire.

For Example 5-12, I created a graphic submit button for my form and inserted it into the form using the `input` element with additional attributes for the image.

EXAMPLE 5-12   Using a graphical submit button

```
<form method="get" action="http://www.myserver.com/cgi-bin/mailscript/">

<input type="image" src="submit-button.gif" width="75" height="25" alt="submit!"
value="submit" />

</form>
```

You'll notice that the markup includes a value for the `type` attribute, `image`. Then you provide the image source for the button, its `width` and `height`, its `value`, and alternative text. Remember, it's an image, so you'll want to be sure you have that alternative text in there.

Figure 5-14 shows the stylized graphic button as the mouse passes over it. You'll notice that the mouse pointer turns to a hand, just as it would for any other link, and the alternative text is displayed, too.

FIGURE 5-14   Implementing a graphic submit button.

QUANTUM LEAP

In most contemporary web designs, images are used for submit buttons in tandem with CSS. You've certainly noticed that although the form controls described in the chapter so far are effective and straightforward in terms of implementation, they aren't exactly pretty. That will be repaired as soon as you begin styling form elements later in this book.

Making Forms More Accessible with *label*

By their very interactive nature, forms are a bit more demanding in the accessibility department than other HTML elements. This is largely because all the items we've been discussing in this chapter have to do with form controls, which are components built into browsers and invoked by the corresponding HTML.

For a visual person, all this makes sense. But for individuals who are having the form read to them instead of seeing it, context can be quickly lost.

The label element allows information to be attached to a given control. Using this along with the for attribute enables you to describe the form control being used in more detail (see Example 5-13).

EXAMPLE 5-13   Adding context using the label element

```
<form method="get" action="http://www.myserver.com/cgi-bin/mailscript/">

<label for="firstname">First Name:</label><input type="text" name="firstname"
id="firstname" /><br />
<label for="reading"><input type="checkbox" name="reading" id="reading"
/>Reading<br />

<label for="requestbox">Any special requests?</label> <br />
<textarea name="comments" id="requestbox" cols="25" rows="5">
</textarea>

</form>
```

You'll recall that earlier I mentioned that the use of the id attribute within the input was an important part of accessibility, and here you see why.

NOTE

You'll notice that the label always comes before the control it's describing. In every case in which you are labeling a form control, the value of the for attribute must match the exact value of the id attribute within the control itself. This enables screen readers to provide more descriptive information about the control.

Another important issue is that labels do not need to be applied to submit and reset buttons. This is because screen readers read the text you've supplied on the buttons, automatically providing the required context.

Grouping Form Fields

Another means of making your forms more accessible is to group form information. You'll recall that in Chapter 4, "Creating Tables," I showed you several ways to group table elements to make them more comprehensive. Well, the same concepts apply here, although different elements are used.

In the case of forms, you can break down areas of the form into specific sets of fields using the fieldset element. If you have a form with three contextual sections, such as Contact Information, Favorite Activities, and Reset or Submit, you can create fields around each of those. Then you can use the legend element to add a header for each of those sections, further providing context (see Example 5-14).

EXAMPLE 5-14   Breaking forms into logical fields using fieldset

```
<form method="get" action="http://www.myserver.com/cgi-bin/mailscript/">

<fieldset>
<legend>Contact Information</legend>
First Name: <input type="text" name="firstname" id="firstname" size="25"
maxlength="40" /><br />
Last Name: <input type="text" name="lastname" id="lastname" size="25"
maxlength="40"/><br />
Phone: <input type="text" name="phone" id="phone" size="15" maxlength="0"   />
</fieldset>

<fieldset>
<legend>Favorite activities</legend>
<input type="checkbox" value="reading" name="reading" id="reading" />Reading<br />
<input type="checkbox" value="sports" name="sports" id="sports" checked="checked"
/>Sports<br />
<input type="checkbox" value="games" name="games" id="games" />Computer Games
</fieldset>

<fieldset>
<legend>Reset or Submit Your Answers</legend>
<input type="reset" value="reset" />
<input type="submit" value="submit" />
</fieldset>

</form>
```

If you check your work in a browser, you'll see that each fieldset is separated by a line around the field, and the legend text appears within the top of that line.

You can see how this grouping of controls within a form can be helpful to bring logic and context to anyone, especially to those with learning disabilities and blindness.

With fieldset and legend, you can provide far more assistance to individuals who might not otherwise be able to understand the form as explicitly (see Figure 5-15).

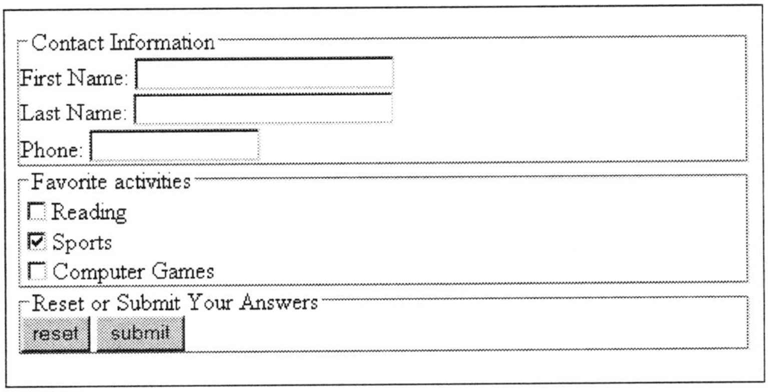

FIGURE 5-15   Using fieldset and legend to group and identify form fields.

QUANTUM LEAP

Remember, the default appearance of any HTML in a browser is just that—a default. You can modify any presentation that HTML itself causes using CSS. So, in the previous example, you can style the fieldset sections to have different colors, use a different border style, and have more space between each section.

You also can style the legend text to match other fonts within your design, change color, change size, and do whatever you'd like. However, to keep the integrity of fieldset and legend, it's wise not to deviate too far from the defaults (such as removing the borders around the fieldsets altogether), to ensure that the accessibility features remain available.

Grouping Menu Items

Still another means of bringing added clarity to your forms is grouping items within a menu. This is done using the optgroup element. Along with optgroup, you also use the label attribute in both the optgroup opening tag and each individual item within that group (see Example 5-15).

EXAMPLE 5-15   Using optgroup to group options in a form menu

```
<select name="regions" size="14">
<optgroup label="Western Region">
<option value="Arizona" label="Arizona">Arizona</option>
<option value="California" label="California">California</option>
<option value="Colorado" label="Colorado">Colorado</option>
<option value="Nevada" label="Nevada">Nevada</option>
<option value="Texas" label="Texas">Texas</option>
<option value="Utah" label="Utah">Utah</option>
</optgroup>
<optgroup label="Eastern Region">
<option value="Connecticut" label="Connecticut">Connecticut</option>
<option value="Maine" label="Maine">Maine</option>
<option value="New_Hampshire" label="New Hampshire">New Hampshire</option>
<option value="New_Jersey" label="New Jersey">New Jersey</option>
<option value="New_York" label="New York">New York</option>
<option value="Vermont" label="Vermont">Vermont</option>
</optgroup>
</select>
```

Figure 5-16 shows the results.

FIGURE 5-16   Grouping form menus into logical sections.

Customizing and Advancing Your Forms

You've learned everything in this chapter you need to know to create effective, useful, and accessible forms. Again, although they're not pretty just yet, you'll be able to spruce them up when you learn how using CSS.

For now, you'll want to take two important steps. The first is to build a complete form from start to finish, using as many text fields, text areas, check boxes, radio buttons, and menu lists as your needs require.

Then, of course, is the issue of how your form will be processed. Forms processing can be straightforward or fairly complex, depending upon your needs. Forms processing is also done on a number of server types, so technologies will vary—and what those technologies can do (and how far you can take them) with your forms will also vary. Fortunately, many free resources exist to help you understand and implement your forms more efficiently.

QUANTUM LEAP

To learn more about various aspects of forms processing, see the Web Authoring FAQ from the Web Design Group, http://www.htmlhelp.com/faq/html/forms.html.

For a list of numerous remote hosts for a range of form-processing needs, check out The CGI Resource, http://cgi.resourceindex.com/Remotely_Hosted/ Form_Processing/.

For PHP-based form scripts, see http://php.resourceindex.com/Complete_Scripts/ Form_Processing/

For forms processing on the Microsoft .NET platform, this article will be very helpful to you: http://www.ondotnet.com/pub/a/dotnet/2003/01/06/formsauthp1.html.

Now That You're Well-Formed...

I never feel very good about leaving readers without all the information necessary to tap into the true power of forms. But doing so is nearly impossible because forms can be used so effectively in so many different ways—and with a wide range of technologies, as you've seen.

In fact, in the world of professional web development, entire subspecialties exist in which individual developers spend the majority of their work developing the applications and databases that form-based, dynamic web pages require. You'll see the results of such complex specialties at many familiar websites. Anything with e-commerce, such as Amazon.com, requires this kind of complex development to properly process orders, credit card information, and shipping directions.

Portal sites are also very good examples of complex use of forms. Yahoo!, Excite, and even America online all use forms extensively to manage membership, personalization features, and so forth.

Still another excellent example of complex forms and data management comes via online banking. I don't know about you, but I'm sure at a loss these days without instant access to my accounts from anywhere in the world. It really helps a somewhat distracted person such as me stay on top of the practical side of life.

NOTE
Not using online banking yet? Check and see if your bank offers online banking options. My bank, Wells Fargo, which services the western United States, has an excellent website, http://www.wellsfargo.com/, and is even working toward making the site completely standards compliant and accessible.

Okay, have you had enough of forms? Great! It's time to move on to frames and learn their value in contemporary design. I'll also point out their many flaws and tell you why most people have eliminated frames from site designs altogether.

CHAPTER 6

Working with Frames

These days, it's a rare novelty to see someone using frames to create web pages. The reasons are numerous, including these fun facts:

- Frames modify the browser interface, which results in no consistency in how operating systems and individual browsers display the results.

- Frames are difficult for both blind and mobility-impaired users. Screen reader software has a hard time managing the altered interface. Mobility-impaired users also encounter difficulty moving from frame to frame.

- In older browsers, frame pages were difficult to bookmark. Bookmarking is improved in most modern browsers, but the user still has to know where to dig up this feature within the browser interface.

- Frames consume more server and client resources, for two reasons: First, frames-based designs rely on multiple documents just to build one page, so a server has to send each of these documents when each frame page is assembled. Second, browsers and the user's operating system have to work harder to manage them.

- Because multiple documents must be created for each single-frame page result, managing frames is an arduous, unhappy task when you're trying to manage, update, and modify a frame-based site.

So if frames aren't all that and a bag of chips, why on Earth would you want to learn them? I have two very specific reasons I want you to know about them:

1. Frames are a unique part of HTML. I want you to understand what you're looking at if you see frames and to also have them in your toolbox if you ever need them.

2. Frames can occasionally be *exactly the right choice* for a specific approach. Let's say you want to develop an application in which data loads into another location directly within the same interface. Frames can help you accomplish that kind of functionality; if you need it, you'll know how.

Finally, although iframes are not the same thing as conventional frames, they are in use. You might well want to tap into their unique functionality at some point.

The Power of Three

I often remember the way to build a frame-based page by thinking in threes. To create a single-frame page, you need *three* documents, at the minimum. What's more, you use *three* unique bits of HTML that are unused anywhere else in the language.

Frames are controlled by a master document known as a *frameset*. The frameset document is not displayed in the browser in and of itself, but it sets up all the controls for the resulting page.

Along with the frameset document, you need at least two HTML documents of content. These are displayed in the framed areas created by the frameset (see Figure 6-1).

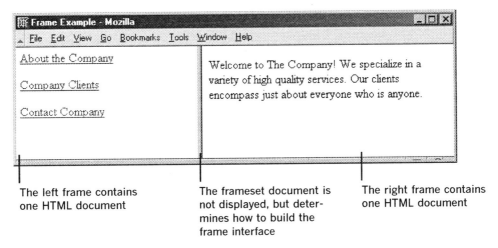

The left frame contains one HTML document

The frameset document is not displayed, but determines how to build the frame interface

The right frame contains one HTML document

FIGURE 6-1   A framed page example.

Of course, within your frameset, you can create as many frames as you desire. For each of those frames, however, you need to have a corresponding HTML content page.

As you can see, the number of documents required for a complex framed site can begin to add up—which as mentioned, causes extra demand on your server resources and your user's system resources, not to mention all the extra management issues that documents demand.

Creating a Frameset

First, I want you to focus on learning how to write frameset documents. They are definitely different from the HTML pages you've been exposed to in this book so far. For starters, they use a different DOCTYPE declaration (see Example 6-1). This is the first piece of unique markup for a frame-based page.

EXAMPLE 6-1   The frameset DOCTYPE declaration for XHTML 1.0

```
<!DOCTYPE html PUBLIC "-//W3C//DTD XHTML 1.0 Frameset//EN"
     "http://www.w3.org/TR/xhtml1/DTD/xhtml1-frameset.dtd">
```

Now things start to get really interesting! Instead of the conventional HTML structure you're by now familiar with, you won't be adding a head and a body; instead, you add a head and a frameset.

You'll be able to use the head portion the same way you would in any other document—for title, script, or style—but you won't have a body element because the frameset element takes its place for all framed documents. The frameset element (and its corresponding attributes, which we'll get to in just a bit) is the second piece of unique markup for a frame-based page (see Example 6-2).

EXAMPLE 6-2   Frameset document structure

```
<!DOCTYPE html PUBLIC "-//W3C//DTD XHTML 1.0 Frameset//EN"
     "http://www.w3.org/TR/xhtml1/DTD/xhtml1-frameset.dtd">

<html xmlns="http://www.w3.org/1999/xhtml">
<head>
<title>Frameset Document</title>
</head>
<frameset>

</frameset>
</html>
```

The third unique element is the frame element, which defines which HTML pages will be placed into the corresponding frames you're creating for your page (see Example 6-3). The number of frame elements corresponds directly to the number of frames in the page.

EXAMPLE 6-3   Frameset with the minimum required two frame elements

```
<frameset>
<frame />
<frame />
</frameset>
```

Adding Columns

Framesets support columns and rows. In this section, you'll add columns to your frameset. You begin by setting up the two-column frame page.

The cols attribute for the frameset element gives you three value options:

- Numeric value in pixels, such as cols="200". This results in a 200-pixel column.

- Percentage value, such as cols="75%". A percentage value results in the column being 75% of the available browser space.

- Dynamic value, represented by an asterisk, as in cols="*". This means that the column will dynamically resize to the available browser space.

Example 6-4 shows a frameset document used to create the two-column look we're after.

You'll note that I've also added frame elements.

To create a frame page, you need to have each column (or row, as you'll see in the next section) filled with a corresponding conventional HTML page. For these examples, I've created two very simple pages just for demonstration purposes, available for your use. You would, of course, add real content to these pages.

EXAMPLE 6-4   Creating a two-column frame page

```
<!DOCTYPE html PUBLIC "-//W3C//DTD XHTML 1.0 Frameset//EN"
    "http://www.w3.org/TR/xhtml1/DTD/xhtml1-frameset.dtd">

<html xmlns="http://www.w3.org/1999/xhtml">
<head>
<title>Frameset Document</title>
</head>

<frameset cols="200, *">

<frame src="lightgray.html" />
<frame src="darkgray.html" />

</frameset>
</html>
```

This results in the left, light-gray column being fixed at 200 pixels and the right, dark-gray column being dynamic (see Figure 6-2).

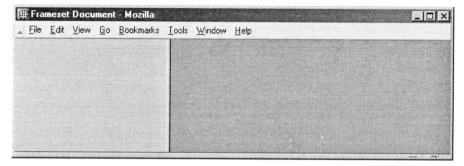

FIGURE 6-2   The left column is fixed at 200 pixels, whereas the right column will dynamically resize along with the browser.

Of course, you can have multiple columns—as many as you want. Just add more comma-separated values (and more frame elements to correspond). What's more, nothing says you can't mix and match the column values. Consider Example 6-5, which provides four total columns (see Figure 6-3).

EXAMPLE 6-5   Frame page with four columns

```
<frameset cols="25%, *, 100, 25%">
<frame src="lightgray.html" />
<frame src="darkgray.html" />
<frame src="lightgray.html" />
<frame src="darkgray.html" />
</frameset>
```

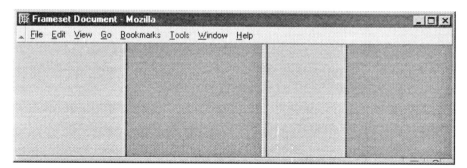

FIGURE 6-3   A four-column frame page; the far left and right columns will take up 25% of the browser space, the left center column is dynamic, and the right center is fixed at 100 pixels.

Working with Rows

Using the rows attribute, you can create rows in the same way you create columns. Example 6-6 defines a frame page with two rows, the top being 25% of the available space and the bottom being dynamically sized to the browser space.

EXAMPLE 6-6   Frame page with two rows

```
<frameset rows="25%, *">
<frame src="lightgray.html" />
<frame src="darkgray.html" />
</frameset>
```

Figure 6-4 shows the resulting rows.

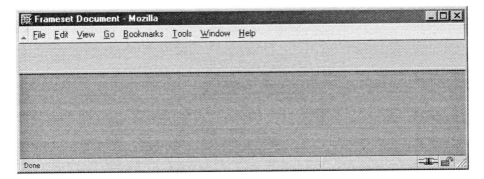

FIGURE 6-4   Rows in a frame page.

> **NOTE**
> By now, you are aware that the order of the frame pages must correspond with the columns and rows. Whichever comes first in the stack correlates to the first value for the `cols` or `rows` attributes.

As with columns, you can have as many rows as you like, and you can mix and match the value types, too.

> **NOTE**
> Want to have some fun with frames? Built back in 1996 (which shows you just how long ago frame-based sites were around—and also how long ago we pretty much stopped using them for most professional websites), the Crazy Netscape Navigator Frame Tricks Page is a source of real amusement. Give it a try, at http://www.geocities.com/Athens/3024/neatframes.htm.

Combining Columns and Rows

For a more complex approach to frame design, you can combine columns and rows to get the effect you're after. This is accomplished by nesting `frameset` elements (see Example 6-7).

EXAMPLE 6-7 Combining columns and rows

```
<frameset rows="100, *">
<frame src="top.html" />
    <frameset cols="200, *">
        <frame src="nav.html" />
        <frame src="main.html" />
    </frameset>
</frameset>
```

This results in a row along the top with two columns beneath it (see Figure 6-5).

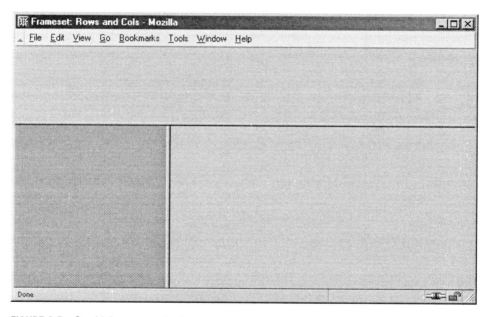

FIGURE 6-5 Combining rows and columns.

You can now try out numerous combinations. Again, we're using only dummy pages here, but you could see where this design might contain a masthead, the left column some navigation, and the right column the content.

Margin, Resize, and Scroll Controls

You can control the behavior of your frame pages with a number of attributes. These include attributes to manage margins, frame resizing, and scrolling within frames:

- The `marginheight` and `marginwidth` attributes allow a value in pixels to control the height and width of frame margins.

- The `noresize` attribute fixes the frame into position so the user can't move the frame edges.

- The `scrolling` attribute enables you to control the appearance of a scrollbar within a frame. This is important if you've fixed the size of your frame and the content within that frame is longer than the frame itself. There are three values for scrolling: yes (which forces a scrollbar at all times), no (which disallows a scrollbar completely), and auto (which automatically puts a scrollbar into the frame if it is necessary).

Example 6-8 shows a frameset document with margin, resize, and scroll controls in place.

EXAMPLE 6-8   Managing margins, resizing, and scrolling in frames

```
<frameset cols="200, *">
<frame src="menu.html" marginheight="5" marginwidth="5" noresize="noresize"
scrolling="yes" />
<frame src="main.html" marginheight="9" marginwidth="9"
noresize="noresize" scrolling="yes" />
</frameset>
```

Figure 6-6 shows the results.

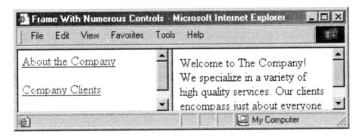

FIGURE 6-6   Note forced scrollbars in each of the frames.

Naming and Targeting Frames

Before you can ensure navigation within frames, you've got to first name the frames. Then you target them using the `target` attribute. There's also another target method you'll explore, referred to as *magic target names*.

Name targeting is done using the `name` attribute with a value that describes the frame. Typically, this value describes the function of that frame. So a navigation frame might be called `nav`, a content frame `content`, and so forth.

Example 6-9 describes a frameset document with all the frames properly named.

EXAMPLE 6-9 Naming frames

```
<!DOCTYPE html PUBLIC "-//W3C//DTD XHTML 1.0 Frameset//EN"
      "http://www.w3.org/TR/xhtml1/DTD/xhtml1-frameset.dtd">
<html xmlns="http://www.w3.org/1999/xhtml">

<head>
<title>Frames with Names</title>
</head>

<frameset cols="200, *">
<frame src="menu.html" marginheight="5" marginwidth="5" noresize=
"noresize" scrolling="auto" name="menu" />
<frame src="main.html" marginheight="9" marginwidth="9" noresize="noresize"
scrolling="auto" name="content" />
</frameset>

</html>
```

The document now sets up a frame page with a menu and a content area. Now that the specific frames are named, you can add targets to any links within the HTML so that the behavior works properly.

If you want to click a link in the menu frame and have the corresponding link page load into the content frame, you use the `target` attribute with a value of the page's name in the link (see Example 6-10).

EXAMPLE 6-10 Targeting frames with the `target` and `name` attributes

```
<ul>
<li><a href="about.html" target="content">About the Company</a></li>
<li><a href="clients.html" target="content">Company Clients</a></li>
<li><a href="contact.html" target="content">Contact Company</a></li>
</ul>
```

Now any time you click a link, the about, clients, or contact documents will load into the named content frame.

Magic Target Names

Magic target names are four predefined names within HTML that cause a specific behavior when a link is activated:

- `target="_blank"`—The _blank target name causes the targeted document to open in a completely new browser window.

- `target="_self"`—The targeted document will load in the same window where the originating link exists.

- `target="_parent"`—This loads the targeted document into the link's parent frameset.

- `target="_top"`—Use this attribute to load the link into the full window, overriding any existing frames.

If you want to break out of your frames and have a full, frameless document fill the window, do not use the name value you provided earlier in your target; use the magic target name, _top:

```
<li><a href="contact.html" target="_top">Contact Company</a></li>
```

This results in the contact.html page completely overriding the frameset document and all corresponding frames (see Figure 6-7).

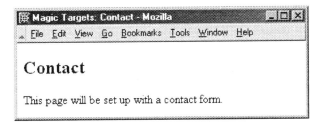

FIGURE 6-7 Using a magic target name, the contact page is now linked so that it completely overrides the frameset and loads into the original containing window.

NOTE

Do not try to force another person's site into your frames. This is considered problematic and possibly illegal. Also, be careful when naming targets yourself, avoid mixed case, and definitely avoid any symbols, such as the underscore, which is already reserved for the magic target name. Finally, using the _blank magic target name forces a new browser to open, which many people find troublesome.

Frames Without Frontiers

If you'd like to have a frame-based site with no borders, you can get rid of them. If you're following the rules, authoring borderless frames is easy. You simply add the attribute and value `frameborder="0"` within the `frame` tag (see Example 6-11).

EXAMPLE 6-11 Working with borderless frames

```
<!DOCTYPE html PUBLIC "-//W3C//DTD XHTML 1.0 Frameset//EN"
    "http://www.w3.org/TR/xhtml1/DTD/xhtml1-frameset.dtd">
<html xmlns="http://www.w3.org/1999/xhtml">
<head>
<title>Borderless Frames</title>
</head>
<frameset cols="200,*">
<frame frameborder="0" src="menu.html" name="menu" marginheight="5"
marginwidth="5" noresize="noresize" scrolling="auto" />
<frame frameborder="0" src="main.html" marginheight="9" marginwidth="9"
noresize="noresize" name="content" scrolling="auto" />
</frameset>
</html>
```

You can see the borderless results in Figure 6-8.

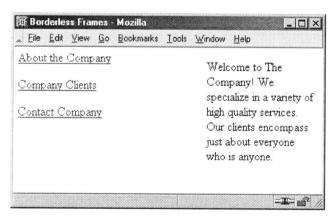

FIGURE 6-8 Look ma, no borders!

Of course, this works only in modern browsers because originally Netscape and Internet Explorer introduced their own, proprietary means of getting rid of frame borders.

Netscape browsers earlier than 6.0 allow for borderless frames in these circumstances:

- The `border` attribute is set, in pixels, to a numeric value of 0.

- The `framespacing` attribute is assigned a no value.

Older versions of Internet Explorer produce borderless frames under these conditions:

- The `frameborder` attribute is set, in pixels, to a numeric value of 0.

- The `framespacing` attribute is assigned a width, in pixels, to a numeric value of 0.

Each browser requires either a different attribute to control width or a different value to control spacing. It looks confusing, but if you stack attributes, you can easily create borderless frames that will be read by both browsers without difficulty. This technique results in two syntax options:

```
<frameset frameborder="0" framespacing="0" border="0">
```

or

```
<frameset frameborder="no" framespacing="0" border="0">
```

Example 6-12 shows how our example so far might look with the invalid syntax.

EXAMPLE 6-12   Supporting borderless frames in older browsers

```
<!DOCTYPE html PUBLIC "-//W3C//DTD XHTML 1.0 Frameset//EN"
"http://www.w3.org/TR/xhtml1/DTD/xhtml1-frameset.dtd">
<html xmlns="http://www.w3.org/1999/xhtml">
<head>
<title>Borderless Frames</title>
</head>
<frameset frameborder="0" framespacing="0" border="0" cols="200,*">
<frame src="menu.html" marginheight="5" marginwidth="5" noresize= "noresize"
scrolling="auto" />
<frame src="main.html" marginheight="9" marginwidth="9" noresize="noresize"
scrolling="auto" />
</frameset>
</html>
```

NOTE

I don't generally recommend breaking validation, but here's a case in point: If you want real backward compatibility with certain aspects of HTML, you have to sometimes break the rules. Fortunately, older browsers are becoming far less common, so support for them is becoming less necessary.

Making Frames Accessible with *noframes*

One of the most important considerations when designing with frames is, as mentioned earlier, ensuring that individuals who cannot use frames, such as the blind or mobility-impaired, still have access to important information on a website. One of the ways to achieve accessibility in a framed site is to employ the noframes element. This is placed in the frameset element. Critical information can then be provided at the same URL as the frameset page, and an entirely accessible site can be formed by using the same pages as the framed site (see Example 6-13 and Figure 6-9).

EXAMPLE 6-13 Making frames accessible with noframes

```
<!DOCTYPE html PUBLIC "-//W3C//DTD XHTML 1.0 Frameset//EN"
        http://www.w3.org/TR/xhtml1/DTD/xhtml1-frameset.dtd">
<html xmlns="http://www.w3.org/1999/xhtml">

<head>
<title>Frames with NOFRAMES Element</title>
</head>

<frameset cols="200*">
<frame src="menu.html" marginheight="5" marginwidth="5" noresize="noresize"
scrolling="auto" />
<frame src="main.html" name="right" marginheight="9" marginwidth="9"
noresize="noresize" scrolling="auto" />

<noframes>
<body>
<p>Welcome. We're happy to provide this non-frames access to our
Web site. If you prefer to view our site using frames, please
upgrade your browser to a recent one that fully supports frames.
Otherwise, please visit our <a href="index_noframes.html">
non-framed</a> version of this site.</p>
</body>
</noframes>

</frameset>
</html>
```

Are you ready for a kick?

Good!

Here's the markup as shown in Mosaic 1.0, a very early graphical browser. There's no frames support, of course, but simply using the noframes element ensures that I can get to the information, as can the blind and mobility-impaired.

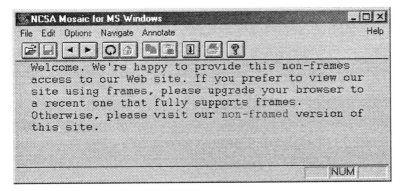

FIGURE 6-9 Even without frames support, older browsers and accessibility-related software can interpret the noframes information.

Because you can format an entire document within the noframes element, consider using the index page as the welcome page to your site. From there, link to internal pages that are external to the frame design.

NOTE

It's very important to remember that frameset documents do not support the body element, with this one exception: If the noframes element is in use, you use the body element as a means of creating the body information for the noframes version of your page. Otherwise, never use a body element in a frameset; use the frameset element instead.

Wonderful Inline Frames

Originally introduced by Internet Explorer 3.0, iframes, *inline* or *floating* frames, were officially adopted in HTML 4.0. This is good news because they're very effective when put to appropriate use. The bad news is that they aren't supported by Netscape 4.61 and many other browsers. Netscape 6.0+ does have inline frame support.

Iframes work a bit differently from standard frames. First, you don't create a separate frameset for the frame. You place the iframe information directly inline in any regular page.

Iframes are extremely handy in terms of being able to update specific windows within a browser. They are often used to manage web advertisements, which are often delivered from another server and updated regularly. This means that the main HTML page never gets touched—just the remote page does.

NOTE

You aren't limited to just HTML pages. You can link to any kind of source in an iframe, including images and multimedia objects.

Inline frames can be placed anywhere on a page. Unlike standard frames, they do not require a frameset. As with standard frames, iframes do require an additional page—in this case text.html, to work (see Example 6-14).

EXAMPLE 6-14   Inline frames

```
<!DOCTYPE html PUBLIC "-//W3C//DTD XHTML 1.0 Transitional//EN"
    "http://www.w3.org/TR/xhtml1/DTD/loose.dtd">
<html xmlns="http://www.w3.org/1999/xhtml">

<head>
<title>Inline Frames</title>
</head>

<body>
<iframe width="350" height="200" src="text.html" scrolling="auto" frameborder="1">
</iframe>

</body>
</html>
```

The browser will draw the iframe to your specifications. Here, I've got it set to a width of 350 pixels and a height of 200 pixels, with automatic scrolling and a frame border of 1 to help you visualize the results.

NOTE

I like to think of iframes a lot like images or objects. They really do work in a very similar way: The browser draws the area and then inserts the object—in this case, another HTML file—into the drawn area.

Figure 6-10 shows the results.

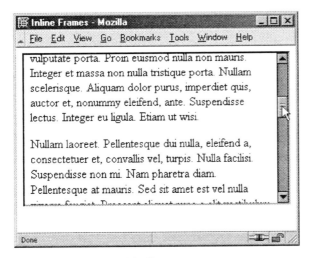

FIGURE 6-10   iframe in Mozilla.

NOTE

Frames have backward-compatibility issues. All modern browsers implement them, but older browser might not have support. Usually in those instances, the iframe is completely ignored. There is no method such as noframes for iframes, either. So, although their use is often very convenient, you'll want to limit it to instances in which you do not have to support older web browsers.

You're Framed!

Even though framed sites are not a sought-after concern these days, as you can tell from this chapter, it's important to understand them because they work in a very different way from regular HTML.

You might not choose to use frames for a site, but it's a good idea to practice their use and get a feel for how they can be put to good use.

You never know—it might be just the solution you find yourself looking for one day.

And, of course, iframes have a lot of very useful applications and are commonly used in contemporary design. It is important to understand the differences between frames and iframes, and to get comfortable with both approaches.

Finally, CSS can be used to not just style the information within framed sites or with iframes, but to actually create similar effects that frames do. You'll learn more about this in upcoming chapters.

And speaking of CSS, now that you've gotten through a lot of markup, it's time to move on to learning about CSS, and how it can take all the structural elements you've been working with and add lots of attractive, useful effects.

CHAPTER 7

Using CSS

ascading Style Sheets have been around since the end of 1996. Despite the relative longevity of the technology, its use in real-world web design has been limited to managing fonts and color, at least until recently. This limitation was imposed by the lack of consistent browser support. Because not all browsers managed CSS equally (if at all), it has been very difficult for designers to tap into the true power of style sheets. Instead, there's been a reliance on HTML for presentation.

Now we have far better support for CSS, so to tap into its many valuable features, web designers are moving away from HTML as a means of adding style and laying out pages, and into pure CSS design. Why is this so important? The reasons are many:

- Keeping presentation separate from the document means you can style that document for numerous media, including the screen, print, projection, and even hand-held devices.

- Separating presentation from the document means a lighter document, which, in turn, means the page loads and renders faster, making for happier visitors.

- CSS offers ways to control one document or millions of documents. Any time you'd like to make a change, you change that style in one location and automatically update to all the documents with which that CSS is connected. In HTML, this couldn't be done.

- CSS documents are cached. This means they are loaded into your browser's memory *one time*. As you move within a site, the browser never has to reinterpret the styles. The results are more fluid movement from page to page and faster-loading pages, which, of course, is always desirable.

- By separating presentation from structure and content, accessibility is easily achieved. Documents that don't have heavy tables and lots of presentational HTML are inherently more accessible than documents that do.

Clearly, CSS offers a lot. In this chapter, you'll learn how to set up CSS to be most efficient and flexible for your designs.

CSS Theory Simplified

Before you can actually put CSS to use, you need to know some important things about the language and how to use it effectively. I'll try to make this quick and painless because I know you want to get down to it.

CSS Rules

CSS rules are made up of a selector and at least one declaration. A selector is the code that selects the HTML to which you want to apply the style rule. We'll be focusing on common selectors in this book, but you can use more than a dozen selector types as you become more proficient at CSS. A declaration is made up of at least one CSS property and related property value. CSS properties define the style:

```
h1 {color: red;}
```

The h1 is the selector for your h1 headers, and the declaration is made up of the color property with a value of red. Simply said, this rule turns all h1 elements red. You'll note that the syntax of the style rule looks different from what you've seen in HTML. The curly braces contain the declarations, each property is followed by a colon, and a semicolon is used after each property. You can have as many properties as you want in a rule.

Applying CSS

Six types of style sheets exist:

- **Browser style**—This is the default style sheet within a browser. If you declare no style rules, these defaults are applied.

- **User style**—A user can write a style sheet and make it override any styles you create by changing a setting in the browser. These are used infrequently but can be helpful for individuals with special needs, such as low vision. In such a case, the user will create high-contrast, large-font styles that override your own.

- **Inline style**—This is style that is used right in the individual element and applied via the style attribute. It can be very useful for one-time styles by element, but it isn't considered ideal.

- **Embedded style**—This is style that controls one document and is placed inside the style element within the HTML document.

- **Linked style**—This is a style sheet that is linked to an HTML document using the link element in the head of the document. Any document linked to this style sheet gets the styles, and here's where the management power of CSS is found.

- **Imported style**—This is similar to linked styles, but it enables you to import styles into a linked style sheet as well as directly into a document. This is useful in workarounds and when managing many documents.

You'll see examples of these style sheets as we progress throughout the chapter.

The Cascade

People often wonder where the term *cascading* comes from. The cascade is an *application hierarchy*, which is a fancy term for a system of how rules are applied. If you examine the five types of style sheets just introduced, you'll notice that there are numerous means of applying style to the same document.

What if I've got an inline style, an embedded style sheet, and a linked style sheet? The cascade determines how the rules are applied. In the case of style sheet types, user style overrides all other styles; inline style trumps embedded, linked, and imported styles; embedded style takes precedence over inline style; and linked and imported styles are treated equally, applying everywhere any of these other style sheet types are not applied. Browser style comes into play only if no style for a given element is provided; in that case, the browser style is applied.

The cascade also refers to the manner in which multiple style sheets are applied. If you have three linked style sheets, the one *on the bottom* is the one that is interpreted if any conflicts exist among those styles.

Inheritance

Inheritance means that styles are inherited from their parent elements. Consider the following:

```
<body>
<h1>My header</h1>
<p>Subsequent Text</p>
</body>
```

Both the h1 and p elements are considered children of the body element. The styles you give to the body will be inherited by the children until you make another rule that overrides the inherited style. Not all properties, such as margins and padding, are inherited in CSS but almost all others are.

Specificity

Finally, if there are conflicts within any of your style sheets that aren't resolved by the cascade, CSS has an algorithm that resolves the conflict. This algorithm is based on how specific a rule is. It's a bit heavy for this discussion but worthy of mention.

Obviously, two pages can't really do justice to any of these topics, so if you're interested in learning more, be sure to look at the *Additional Resources* section.

Adding Style Inline

Okay, enough with the theory—let's get down to work! Here you'll learn to apply inline style. You'll use inline style infrequently because it styles only the element to which it is applied. This defeats the management power of CSS.

What's more, inline style can be equated with presentational HTML because it goes right into the document instead of being separated from it, defeating the primary benefits of CSS. I use inline style mostly for situations in which a quick fix for a single element is called for, or in rare cases when it's the only style for one unique element in an entire site.

Consider the following element:

```
<h1>Welcome!</h1>
```

If this header were part of a complete HTML document and you viewed it in a browser, the results would be equivalent to Figure 7-1.

Welcome!

FIGURE 7-1   Default size of an h1 as defined by browser styles.

Say you don't like the default color and size. You can add CSS rules directly to the element using the `style` attribute:

```
<h1 style="color: gray; font-size: 24px;">Welcome!</h1>
```

Now you've got a gray header sized at 24 pixels (see Figure 7-2).

FIGURE 7-2   Redefining color and size using inline style.

Using Embedded Style

Embedded style controls only the document in which it is embedded. As with inline style, this defeats the purpose of being able to apply styles site-wide. However, there are good uses for embedded style. One would be if that document is the only document in the site that takes those specific styles. Another is workflow related. I like to use embedded style while working on a design because it's all in the same document. This way, I don't have to switch between applications or windows to accomplish my tasks. Because the style rules are the same, I can simply cut out the final styles from the embedded sheet and link them, which you'll see how to do in just a bit.

Embedded style is added to the head portion of the document, within the style element, and it uses the required type attribute (see Example 7-1).

EXAMPLE 7.1   An HTML document snippet describing embedded style

```
<head>
<title>working with style</title>
        <style type="text/css">
        body {background-color: black; color: white;}
        h1 {font-size: 24px;}
        p {font-size: 12px;}
        </style>
</head>
<body>
<h1>Welcome!</h1>
<p>Paragraph one.</p>
<p>Paragraph two.</p>
</body>
```

Figure 7-3 shows the results.

FIGURE 7-3   Notice how the color from the body is inherited by all its children.

Creating a Linked Style Sheet

To truly tap into the power of CSS, you'll be using linked style sheets the majority of the time. A linked style sheet is a separate text file into which you place all your CSS rules (but *not* any HTML) and is named using the .css suffix. You then link any HTML file you want to have affected by that style sheet to the sheet using the link element in the head portion of the document.

Example 7-2 shows a style sheet ready for linking. In it, I've provided a range of style rules and then saved the file to my local folder, naming the file styles.css.

EXAMPLE 7-2 A style sheet ready for linking

```
body {
        background-color: #999;
        color: black;
        }
h1 {
        font-family: Verdana;
        font-size: 24px;
        color: #ccc;
        }
p {
        font-family: Georgia;
        font-size: 12px;
        color: white;
}
```

In Example 7-3, you'll find the complete HTML along with the required link to the style sheet within the same directory.

EXAMPLE 7-3 The HTML for the style sheet

```
<!DOCTYPE html PUBLIC "-//W3C//DTD XHTML 1.0 Transitional//EN"
        "http://www.w3.org/TR/xhtml1/DTD/xhtml1-transitional.dtd">

<html xmlns="http://www.w3.org/1999/xhtml">
<head>
<title>working with style</title>

<link rel="stylesheet" type="text/css" href="styles.css" media="all" />

</head>
<body>

<h1>Welcome!</h1>
```

```
<p>Paragraph one.</p>

<p>Paragraph two.</p>

</body>
</html>
```

The results can be seen in Figure 7-4.

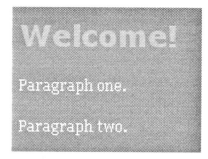

FIGURE 7-4   Results from a linked style sheet.

Of course, you can link as many documents you want to this style sheet using the link element.

You'll note several attributes in use with the link element, as follows:

- rel—This is the relationship attribute, and it describes the relationship of the link. In this case, the relationship is with a primary style sheet, so the stylesheet value is given.

- type—As with the style element in embedded styles, you must define the type of language and format in use—in this case, text/css.

- href—This is the familiar reference attribute. In this case, I've identified only the file because both documents are in the same directory. You might want to put your style sheets into a different directory; just be sure your href info is accurate. You can also use absolute linking to directly link to a style sheet.

- media—The media attribute enables you to define different styles for different media. If you wanted to create a separate style sheet for this document that's for handheld devices only, you would link to that and use the media="handheld" attribute. Similarly, a media="print" attribute would send that style sheet only to print. In this case, the media is defined as screen. The default is all, so if you want the same styles to apply to all media, you can use that or simply leave out the media attribute.

As mentioned, you can link as many style sheets to the same document as you want.

Importing Style Sheets

Imported style sheets are a lot like linked style sheets, in that you create a separate file for the styles you want to import. Then you can either import those sheets into a primary style sheet that is then linked to the document, or import directly into the document.

Importing Directly into a Document

Importing into a document actually involves two types of style sheets: the separate style sheet that's to be imported (I'll call that import.css) and an embedded style sheet in the document. This is because importing isn't done with an element such as link; instead, the CSS directive @import is used (see Example 7-4).

EXAMPLE 7-4   Importing style with an embedded sheet

```
<head>
<head>
<title>working with style</title>
<style type="text/css">

@import url(import.css);

</style>
</head>
```

The style sheet @import.css will be imported directly into the document. Imagine the style element being filled with all the style rules within the import.css file—that's exactly what happens. So now the style is actually embedded in this file.

You can use this technique for as many documents as you want, but typically this technique is used primarily in workarounds. A number of browsers, particularly Netscape 4 versions, do not support the @import directive, yet they do support the link element. Because Netscape 4.x has limited support for CSS and you have to take care to send styles to it, separating out those styles that you don't want it to misinterpret and those styles you know it can support into linked and imported allows Netscape users to see some, but not all, styles. This is very effective as a workaround when you must support Netscape 4 versions.

Another workaround using the @import directive is to simply place all styles into the imported sheet. Then any browser that doesn't support the @import simply won't read the styles, and a plain, unstyled document gets sent to the browser instead.

Most of the time, you won't be using the @import in an embedded sheet unless you have a very specific reason to do so.

Importing Style into a Linked Style Sheet

Another use for the @import directive, and the real reason @import exists, is to be able to modularize your styles and then import them into the primary style sheet. Consider Figure 7-5.

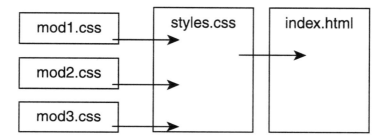

FIGURE 7-5   Importing styles into a main sheet.

Imagine that each module file (mod1.css, mod2.css, and mod3.css) contains styles specific to a feature or function within your site. As an example, you might have styles set to manage ads, styles specific to tables, and styles specific to forms. You could place these in separate module files and then import them into the styles.css file, which is then linked to index.html. The rationale behind this approach is that you could make modifications to the modules independently or cut them out easily when they are no longer needed. This technique is most effective when you have very large sites with lots of styles to manage.

Commenting and Formatting CSS

Just as you can add comments to your HTML files to describe sections, hide markup and content from the browser, or add directives to fellow document authors, you can comment your CSS documents. And just as HTML can be written with indentations or other personal formatting preferences, so can CSS.

Commenting CSS

CSS comments are different than HTML comments. CSS comments open with a forward slash and an asterisk, and close with an asterisk followed by a forward slash. Any content within that area is *not interpreted* by the browser (see Example 7-5).

EXAMPLE 7-5 Commenting CSS

```
/* global styles */

body {
        background-color: orange;
        font-family: Arial, Helvetica, sans-serif;
        color: white;
        }

/* layout styles */

#nav {
         position: absolute;
         top: 0;
         left: 0;
         width: 150px;
         }

/* hide this style and comment temporarily

.warning {
        color: red;
        }

John: please unhide the warning style when you're ready to launch */
```

Everything in bold will not be interpreted by the browser, but all the styles outside of comments will. As you can see, this can help you chunk your style sheets into logical groups, to aid both you and others to find given styles quickly. Additionally, you can hide styles you don't want for use later, and you can leave commentary for other people working with the style sheet.

You will sometimes see HTML comments surrounding CSS within an embedded sheet (see Example 7-6).

EXAMPLE 7-6   HTML comments to hide CSS

```
<head>
<title>working with style</title>
<style type="text/css">
<!--
        body {
                        background-color: #999;
                        color: black;
                        }
        h1 {
                        font-family: Verdana;
                        font-size: 24px;
                        color: #ccc;
                        }
        p {
                        font-family: Georgia;
                        font-size: 12px;
                        color: white;
                        }
-->
</style>
</head>
```

In this case, the HTML comments are being used to hide the CSS from older browsers that do not interpret CSS. Many of those browsers would try to display the CSS rules in the browser window. Using HTML comments in this manner is still in widespread use today, although for contemporary browsers the technique is unnecessary.

Formatting CSS

You might have noticed that I've used two formatting approaches in this chapter (sneaky, aren't I?). The first is to follow the selector with the declaration, all on the same line:

```
body {background-color: #999; color: black;}
```

The other is to break up the rule:

```
body {
                background-color: #999;
                color: black;
                }
```

Either approach is correct; it's just a matter of personal preference. Many CSS designers are of the mindset that every bit and byte counts, so they opt for the first approach. Others argue that breaking up the rule makes it easier to find the styles you want to modify. Either way, as long as all the required syntax is intact, the formatting of your style sheet is a personal choice.

Time to Put Your Imagination to Work!

If you're thinking at this point that working with markup and CSS is no play, well, your frustration is well founded. It's imperative that you get the complexities down, and I assure you that if you've made it through thus far, you're grasping complex ideas.

But no doubt you want to put those ideas to work and really get a feel for how to use CSS to make things look good. After all, that's what I keep promising, right?

Fortunately, the next chapter sets you up for a little fun: putting your imagination to work.

You'll be using images and color to spruce up your documents, and exploring the fine control that CSS offers you when it comes to working with imagery and color in your designs.

CHAPTER 8

Working with Color and Images Using CSS

olor is one area where CSS has long been our friend. Because color is determined by a combination of the computer's hardware capabilities, the operating system, and the browser, we've been able to use CSS to color backgrounds and text since relatively early in the life of style sheets. Here you'll learn to apply color to page backgrounds and element backgrounds, and even spice up tables with color.

Color options in CSS are more numerous than what was available to us in HTML. In CSS, you can choose among hexadecimal color, hexadecimal shorthand color, RGB color, color percentages, and the 17 color names supported by CSS 2.1.

CSS provides terrific control for images, too. In fact, the capability to place images into the background of any element is helping today's web designers create beautiful designs free of the constraints of tables. In this chapter, you'll learn how to apply images to backgrounds and elements, and you'll learn about methods of using images for a range of visual techniques.

Image options are numerous in CSS. You can control the way images tile (or don't tile), fix them to a location within an element's background, scroll the image or fix the image so text scrolls over it—lots of choices. You'll get to try out all these techniques and really get a feel for how CSS not only enables you to use images in ways never available in HTML, but does so with a range of control you'll really appreciate.

So far, you've been focusing on structuring your content with HTML, adding images and media, and working with tables, frames, and forms. Everything you've done so far has been about creating the canvas. Now you'll get a chance to splash some color and life onto that canvas, making your seemingly bland documents come to life.

NOTE

The figure examples of color in this book have been limited to grayscale. However, you should feel free to try using any of the rules I describe with any range of colors to get the results best suited to your needs.

Color and CSS

To use color well in CSS, you'll want to know about the various ways color can be defined. Although color can be applied using any number of properties, there are specific value options that you'll want to know about.

Hexadecimal Color

Hexadecimal (hex) is a base 16 number system, useful in computing because 8 bits (1 byte of memory) can be represented by a single number or letter. The system uses numbers from 0 to 9 and letters from a to f in any combination of six (and starting with an octothorpe) to represent the correlating red, green, and blue colors (#RRGGBB).

```
#FFFFFF = 255, 255, 255 = white
```

Any hexadecimal combination is allowed in HTML and CSS to represent color (see Example 8-1).

EXAMPLE 8-1   Hexadecimal color in style

```
body {color: #FFCC99; background-color: #808080;}
a {color: #66CC33;}
```

If you applied these styles to a document, the background color would be gray, the text color peach, and the link color bright green.

Hexadecimal Shorthand

Hex shorthand enables you to shorten any hex color that has value pairs. This means that each RR, GG, and BB values have to be the same, such as #00CC33 or #888888. In hex shorthand, you take one digit from each value pair, so the results would be #0C3 and #888. In a case as in #808080, the values are not paired, so you can't make it into shorthand (see Example 8-2).

EXAMPLE 8-2   Hexadecimal shorthand color

```
body {color: #FC9; background-color: #808080;}
a {color: #6C3;}
```

> **NOTE**
> You can use hex shorthand in any CSS document, but not in presentational HTML.

RGB Values

Another means of representing color in CSS is using the actual RGB values. These can be found in an imaging program such as Photoshop (see Figure 8-1).

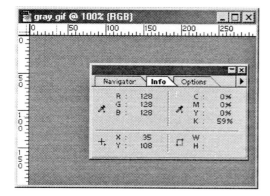

FIGURE 8-1   Finding the RGB values of a gray color using Photoshop.

In this case, the color would be presented using the following syntax:

```
color: rgb(128, 128, 128);
```

RGB Percentages

You can also use percentages of red, green, and blue. A 0% value is black, and a 100% value is white. So, if you set a color as follows:

```
color: rgb(50%, 100%, 30%);
```

the color applied will be a bright green.

Color Names

You can use 17 color names to describe color. The colors are aqua, black, blue, fuchsia, gray, green, lime, maroon, navy, olive, purple, red, silver, teal, white, yellow, and orange (orange was just introduced in CSS 2.1):

```
color: orange;
```

You're probably wondering which color value type you should use. The honest answer? All of them! You'll probably find yourself using combinations of keywords, shorthand hex, and hexadecimal most frequently.

NOTE

In the upcoming CSS 3.0, many additional colors have been added, but they aren't available for widespread, valid use at the time of this writing.

Adding Color to Backgrounds

Adding color to backgrounds is extremely easy and very useful. You can add color to your page background and any element background.

Color and the Document Background

Color is added to the document background by selecting the body element and using the `background-color` property and a color property value:

```
body {background-color: #999;}
```

Here you see I've chosen a background of dark gray to the entire body. When viewed in a browser, this turns the background color completely gray (see Figure 8-2).

FIGURE 8-2 Applying color to a document background.

> **NOTE**
> You should always set a page background color, even if you intend to use graphics and other element backgrounds in your design. This is because colors are interpreted by browsers very quickly and render before any graphics, providing a more streamlined visual experience for your visitors.

Color and Element Backgrounds

With CSS, you can add color to individual element backgrounds. To do this, simply select the element and create a rule. I'll do this for the h1 as I build a style sheet for our simple document:

```
body {background-color: #999;}
h1 {background-color: #ccc;}
```

Figure 8-3 shows the h1 element with the background color added.

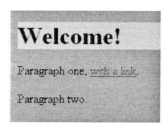

FIGURE 8-3   Adding color to the h1 element background.

I'll go ahead and add rules for the paragraph and anchor element color, too (see Example 8-3).

EXAMPLE 8-3   Document and background elements with color added

```
body {background-color: #999;}
h1 {background-color: #ccc;}
p {background-color: #fff;}
a {background-color: #ccc;}
```

Figure 8-4 shows how the background color is applied.

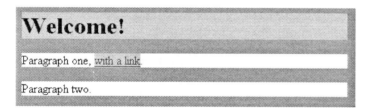

FIGURE 8-4   Background colors as applied to the document and element backgrounds; note that the element background colors stretch to the full width of the element.

Spicing Up a Table Using Background Color

In this section, I'll show you how to add a little spice to your tables using background colors. So far, you've used element selectors, which relate directly to a specific HTML element, such as body, h1, p, and a. In this section, you'll add what's known as a class selector.

Class selectors are custom selectors that you give a name to; you precede that name with a dot, as in .classname. Classes are then applied to an element in the HTML using the class attribute, with a value of the class name:

```
<tr class="classname"> . . . </tr>
```

Typically, you'll want to describe the function of the class rather than the presentation. So, if you're going to apply a background color to every other table row, you'll want to name your class something like .alternaterow instead of .gray. This way, if you want to change the color, you needn't change the class name throughout your documents, which defeats the management advantages of CSS.

Example 8.4 shows a modified table you first worked with in Chapter 4, "Creating Tables." You'll note that I made one change in the table markup: I took out all the table attributes except for cellspacing. This is because there is no effective means of providing cellspacing in CSS.

I've also added an embedded style sheet that includes the table width, border, and padding styles, along with element selectors and a class selector to style the table using background colors in the elements.

EXAMPLE 8-4   *Styling the table with element and class selectors*

```
<!DOCTYPE html PUBLIC "-//W3C//DTD XHTML 1.0 Transitional//EN"
         "http://www.w3.org/TR/xhtml1/DTD/xhtml1-transitional.dtd">

<html xmlns="http://www.w3.org/1999/xhtml">
<head>
<title>working with style</title>

<style type="text/css">
body {color: white;}
caption {background-color: #999; border: 1px solid black;}
table {background-color: #ccc; border: 1px solid black; padding: 5px; width: 90%;}
th {background-color: #333; border:}
tr {background-color: #999;}
td {background-color: #ccc; border: 1px solid black;}
.highlight {background-color: #fff; color: orange;}
</style>
```

```
</head>

<body>

<table cellspacing="5">
<caption>Comparing weather and time zones</caption>
<tr>
<th>Location</th>
<th>Tucson, Arizona</th>
<th>Las Vegas, Nevada</th>
</tr>
<tr>
<th>Weather</th>
<td>Warm to Hot</td>
<td>Warm to Hot</td>
</tr>
<tr>
<th>Time Zone</th>
<td>No Daylight Savings</td>
<td  class="highlight">Mountain Standard Time</td>
</tr>
</table>

</body>
</html>
```

Figure 8-5 shows the results.

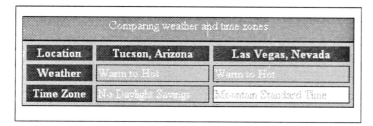

FIGURE 8-5   Styling a table with element and class selectors.

NOTE

You'll also notice I added borders to spice things up a bit. You can learn more about styling borders in Chapter 11, "Margins, Borders, and Padding."

As you are beginning to find out, you can do a lot with CSS to enhance your documents. Here we've turned a plain-vanilla table into something with a little style.

Attaching a Background Graphic

You can attach a background graphic to the document or any element, just as you can with background color. There are more ways to control backgrounds with CSS, though, giving you a broad range of options when it comes to applying visual design to your site. By combining a page background with element backgrounds, you can create layers of images and numerous special effects.

Background graphics are typically either small tiles used to repeat to create a wallpaper pattern, or horizontal or vertical graphics with sections of color, imagery, and even typographic features. You can find many predesigned backgrounds online (see Figure 8-6), or you can create your own.

FIGURE 8-6   A background texture for a wallpaper effect I found at http://www.grsites.com/textures/.

First, let's have a go at attaching the background graphic to the document. This is done by selecting the body and creating a rule using the `background-image` property with a value of the image's location and name:

```
body {background-image: url(gray.jpg);}
```

Figure 8-7 shows the results of the tiled background within a web browser. You'll notice how the image tiles into the entire viewable area, creating an intriguing look.

NOTE

Tiling images in a background is normal behavior for the browser. With HTML, you have no control over how an image tiles. As you'll soon see, CSS gives you far more control over how background images can be manipulated.

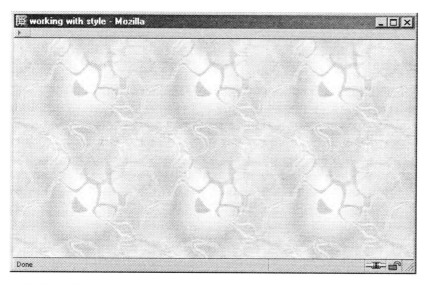

FIGURE 8-7 Tiling a background in the body.

You can also add images to elements. If you wanted this image to appear in the background of all your headings, you could create the following rule:

```
h1, h2, h3, h4, h5, h6 {background-image: url(gray.jpg);}
```

In this case, all header backgrounds would use the background tile.

QUANTUM LEAP: GROUPING SELECTORS

The rule I just wrote with all headers separated by commas is a means of grouping selectors that all take the same rules. This way, I can group any selectors that share rules by naming the selector and following it with a comma:

```
h1, p, .footertext {color: teal;}
```

This way, h1, p, and the class of footertext will all be colored teal. You can continue writing additional rules for unshared styles:

```
h1 {font-size: 24px;}
```

With both of these rules in the same style sheet, both styles would be applied, resulting in the h1 being 24 pixels with a color of teal.

Controlling How Backgrounds Tile

CSS enables you to control the way backgrounds tile. This is done using the `background-repeat` property along with the appropriate value.

Tiling Along the Horizontal Axis

The horizontal axis, also referred to as the x-axis, enables you to tile a background along the element's horizontal axis, but not the vertical one:

```
body {background-image: url(gray.jpg); background-repeat: repeat-x;}
```

Figure 8-8 shows the results.

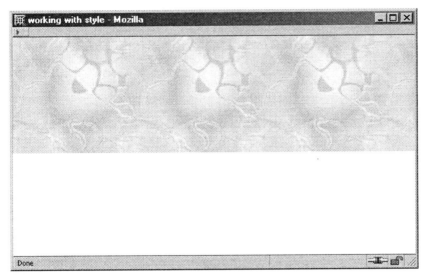

FIGURE 8-8   Controlling horizontal tiling with the `background-repeat` property.

Tiling a Background Along the Vertical Axis

Similarly, you can repeat a background tile along the vertical axis only. To do this, you use the `background-repeat` property along with a value of `repeat-y`:

```
body {background-image: url(gray.jpg); background-repeat: repeat-y;}
```

You can see that the image is now tiled along the vertical axis only in Figure 8-9.

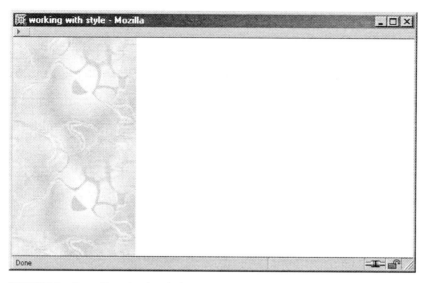

FIGURE 8-9   Repeating a background along the vertical axis.

You can also set the image to not repeat using a value of no-repeat:

body {background-image: url(gray.jpg); background-repeat: no-repeat;}

This results in the tile showing up in the top-left corner one time, with no repeating.

QUANTUM LEAP: OTHER AVAILABLE PROPERTIES

Two other values are available for the background-repeat property. The first is simply repeat. Using it causes the tile to repeat on both the horizontal and vertical axes, which is default behavior for backgrounds; you probably won't use it unless you are specifically overwriting a previous rule. Many CSS properties offer a default value of this nature for precisely that reason.

The second available value is inherit. This value is available for most all properties, and because most properties are inherited, it simply strengthens the case that the property will be inherited by its descendents. You will likely not use inherit too frequently, either, unless you are specifically undoing another rule or you are applying the value to a property that is not normally inherited but that supports the value, such as background-position.

Positioning a Background Graphic

Along with tiling, you can position a background graphic into the document or any element you like. To position a background graphic, you have to set the `background-repeat` value to `no-repeat` first. Then you can position it using any one of the values described in Table 8-1.

TABLE 8-1   Background Position Property Values

Value Type	Example	Placement
Percentage	background-position: 0% 0%;	Top-left corner
	background-position: 100% 100%;	Bottom-right corner
	background-position: 14% 80%;	14% across, 80% down
Length	background-position: 20px 20px;	20px from left, 20px down
Keywords	background-position: top left;	
	background-position: left top;	0% 0%
	background-position: top center;	
	background-position: center top;	50% 0%
	background-position: right top;	
	background-position: top right;	100% 0%
	background-position: left;	
	background-position: left center;	
	background-position: center left;	0% 50%
	background-position: center;	
	background-position: center center;	50% 50%
	background-position: right;	
	background-position: right center;	
	background-position: center right;	100% 50%
	background-position: bottom left;	
	background-position: left bottom;	0% 100%
	background-position: bottom;	
	background-position: bottom center;	
	background-position: center bottom;	50% 100%
	background-position: right bottom;	
	background-position: bottom right;	100% 100%

Confused yet? So was I, until I started playing around with positioning backgrounds. The important thing to remember is that for percentage and length values, the first value is the horizontal value and the second is the vertical value. With keywords, the behavior is as described in the table.

NOTE

You can combine percentages and length values with `background-position` but not keywords, so you can have a value of 100% 20px but you cannot have a value of 100% left.

If only one percentage or length value is given, it is applied to the horizontal position, and the vertical position defaults to 50%.

Example 8-5 sets up the style sheet for a sample of each value type.

EXAMPLE 8-5 Positioning a background graphic with percentage, length, and keywords

```
h1 {background-image: url(tile.gif); background-repeat: no-repeat; background-
position: 0% 0%;}
h2 {background-image: url(tile.gif); background-repeat: no-repeat; background-
position: 100px 4px;}
h3 {background-image: url(tile.gif); background-repeat: no-repeat; background-
position: bottom right;}
```

Note that I've defined not only the image, but also the repeat value of no-repeat, to ensure that the background-positioning values work properly. Figure 8-10 serves up the resulting background graphic positions.

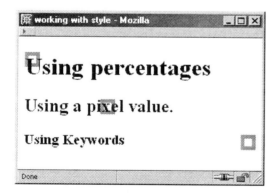

FIGURE 8-10   The small gray-lined tile being positioned within the background of header elements.

Fixing and Scrolling Background Images

You can have your background image fixed to the browser's viewport, or allow it to scroll along with the document by using the `background-attachment` property along with a value of either fixed or `scroll`.

Typically, this is used for either the entire body or content areas within the document. However, as you've seen so far, you can use it in any element where it makes sense to do so.

Consider the following rule:

```
body {background-image: url(arrows.gif); background-position: right; background-repeat: no-repeat; background-attachment: scroll;}
```

Here, I've attached a background image, positioned it to the right with no repeat, and scrolled the background. This actually creates a rule that mimics default browser behavior, which is to scroll the background with the content (see Figure 8-11).

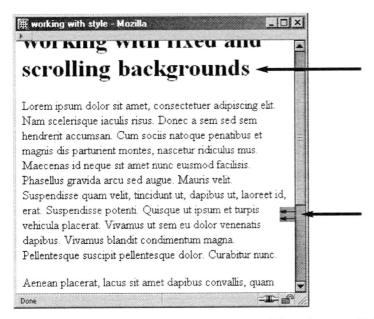

FIGURE 8-11   When a background graphic is set to scroll, it scrolls along with the element to which it's attached—in this case, the body.

Now, if you were to write the same rule with a value of fixed, the results would be quite different (see Figure 8-12).

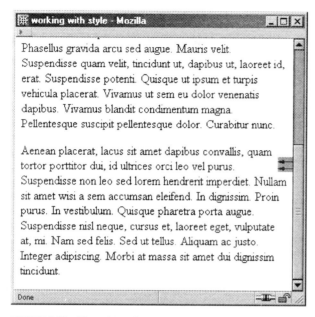

FIGURE 8-12   No matter where I scroll, the background image remains fixed in this case.

You can achieve a range of interesting effects using scrolling with backgrounds. Of course, you'll want to try it for yourself, to really see how scrolling works in a browser. Try a range of options: Set the image to repeat, for example, or position your image in different locations and try out both the fixed and scroll values to compare how each works.

NOTE

Some accessibility advisors suggest that using scrolling text over backgrounds is more difficult to see. I know this much: I get motion sensitivity fairly easily, and if I'm trying to scroll through text over a textured background, it will make me a little woozy. So use this technique with care!

Making a Background Color Transparent

One thing I didn't introduce while discussing background colors is the value of trans-parent for the background-color property. There's a method to my madness, of course: I wanted to introduce background images so you could get the full value of this very important CSS option.

Example 8-6 describes the table used earlier, this time with a background image set for the body. You'll also notice that I've changed the .highlight class to have a background-color property value set to transparent.

EXAMPLE 8-6 Setting up a transparent background color

```
<!DOCTYPE html PUBLIC "-//W3C//DTD XHTML 1.0 Transitional//EN"
          "http://www.w3.org/TR/xhtml1/DTD/xhtml1-transitional.dtd">

<html xmlns="http://www.w3.org/1999/xhtml">
<head>
<title>working with style</title>

<style type="text/css">
body {background-image: url(gray.jpg); color: white;}
caption {color: black; border: 1px solid black;}
table {border: 1px solid black; padding: 5px; width: 90%;}
th {background-color: #333;}
tr {background-color: #999;}
td {background-color: #ccc; border: 1px solid black;}
.highlight {background-color: transparent; color: orange;}
</style>

</head>

<body>

<table cellspacing="5">
<caption>Comparing weather and time zones</caption>
<tr>
<th>Location</th>
<th>Tucson, Arizona</th>
<th>Las Vegas, Nevada</th>
</tr>
<tr>
<th>Weather</th>
<td>Warm to Hot</td>
<td>Warm to Hot</td>
</tr>
<tr>
```

```
<th>Time Zone</th>
<td>No Daylight Savings</td>
<td  class="highlight">Mountain Standard Time</td>
</tr>
</table>

</body>
</html>
```

As you can see, this allows the background behind the element to show through (see Figure 8-13).

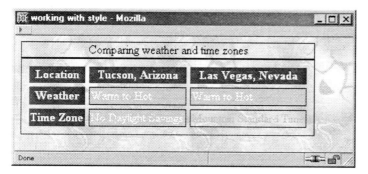

FIGURE 8-13   The `transparent` value allows the background to show through the element—in this case, the table cell with the highlight class shows.

CSS Shorthand for Backgrounds

Another interesting piece of CSS is that certain properties have a shorthand equivalent. This occurs only with a handful of properties; background is one of them.

Shorthand properties combine the features of all related properties. In the case of background, this means that color, image, repeat, and attachment can all be combined into one rule using the background property.

To help you compare, Example 8-7 describes the styles for all the background properties.

EXAMPLE 8-7   Longhand background styles

```
body {
          background-color: white;
          background-image: url(images/lemon-slice.gif);
          background-repeat: no-repeat;
          background-attachment: scroll;
          background-position: right bottom;
}
```

The shorthand version equates to this:

```
body {background: white url(images/lemon-slice.gif) no-repeat scroll right bottom;}
```

I created an HTML page with some mock text and applied the background styles using the shorthand version (see Figure 8-14).

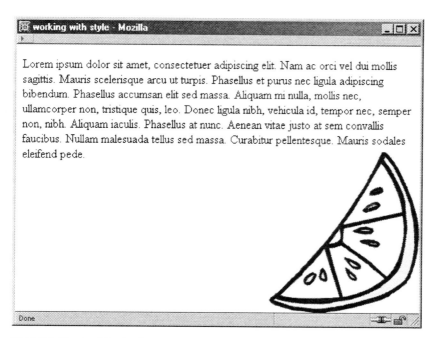

FIGURE 8-14 Applying background properties using CSS shorthand.

Of course, either the longhand or the shorthand versions would have worked to achieve the same end.

QUANTUM LEAP: WHEN TO USE SHORTHAND

Shorthand CSS is extremely useful when you're trying to conserve file size. It also can make general management of your CSS easier. I tend to use it wherever I can, with few exceptions.

However, I have heard people (particularly those who work in professional web-development team environments) point out that shorthand is harder for novices to work with. Some team managers choose to author their CSS in longhand no matter what because they find that it can help cut down on errors and confusion when diverse skill levels exist within a team.

Having Fun Yet?

Hopefully, you're having a bit more fun now that you can use color and images to spruce up your pages.

As you can see, CSS gives you so many more options for color management that it's not funny. Even more flexible is the way in which you can now manipulate images to create your designs via CSS, yet keep them separate from any inline images.

The CSS Zen Garden (http://www.csszengarden.com/) is a fantastic place to check out how images aren't used *anywhere* inline. All the fabulous images within that site are placed into element backgrounds and managed with the techniques learned in this chapter.

Moving along, you're going to learn how to style your text effectively. I waited until after color and imagery because you can integrate both with your text.

I can't wait to see what you come up with!

CHAPTER 9

Styling Text

Now that you have a taste of what CSS can do, you'll take it further and begin to style your text. Historically, CSS has been used more to style text than just about anything, largely because of good support for much of the text-related styles that were in CSS 1.0. Some new options have appeared since then, giving you even more control over the way you manage text for web documents. The basic principles for how text is styled in CSS come from traditional typography, although limitations based on both CSS and browser support have prevented certain growth in the area of web-based type.

A warning from the start, though: Working with fonts can be complicated. First, you must understand that, in terms of available fonts for text-based type on the Web, there's dependence upon a person's operating system and installed font base. If a specific font is not installed on someone's machine, that person will *not* be able to view the font. The same limitation existed for presentational HTML, too, and not much has changed since then. Then there is a major browser flaw in font sizing that makes using font sizes a real pain. Over these concerns you are essentially powerless, except in what you can learn in terms of how to manage them. So bear with me through the details, okay?

The good news is that you do have some choice over fonts, and CSS expands the way you use the fonts by being able to add color, weight, height, spacing—all kinds of features that add visual interest to the fonts you do choose. As you become more adept with CSS in general, you'll learn to combine graphics and text-based type to come up with increasingly sophisticated type designs.

Within the CSS specification, properties for managing typography are found in two primary places. The first is in font-related properties, which are all specific to the way a font is chosen and then displayed. The second is text-related properties, in which text is further managed, usually without some manipulation to the actual font. Some font features come from the more general visual category of styles and can be used with (but are not limited to) text.

In this chapter, you'll learn about font and text styles, along with some of the additional style properties that will affect your text but not necessarily be limited to use with text. You'll also learn about additional selector types that have not yet been introduced to you.

Choosing Fonts

Choosing fonts for document design can be confusing for those who have little exposure to design or typography. Fortunately, there are some good rules of thumb to fall back on.

Fonts have traditionally been broken down into groups, referred to as *font categories* or, as in CSS, *font families*. Fonts are grouped based on like characteristics. In CSS, there are five general categories:

- **Serif**—A serif font is one that has flourishes on the letter, referred to as, you guessed it, serifs. These fonts are thought to be excellent for body text, especially in print, and are very suitable for header and other text such as captions. Serif fonts that might be familiar to you include Times and Georgia, both of which are widely used on the Web.

- **Sans-serif**—The term *sans-serif* means "without serif" and describes, quite literally, fonts that have no flourishes. Instead, sans-serif fonts tend to have rounded, wider letters. Typically thought to be best for headers in print, they are anecdotally thought by many to be the better choice for body text onscreen. They aren't always the best choice for very small text or for italicized text, however. Familiar fonts within this category include Arial, Helvetica, and Verdana.

- **Monospace**—Monospace fonts are fonts whose letters are all the same width. They are typically used to describe programming code samples. In recent years, they've been popular in design, giving a very "grunge" look to the designs in which they are used. However, you'll typically limit use of monospace fonts to code samples. The most common monospace font in computing is Courier.

- **Fantasy**—Fantasy fonts, also known as *decorative* fonts, are fonts with unusual features. They tend to be elaborate and useful for headers or small areas of text, and not very useful for body text because their decorations make them difficult to read. You will rarely, if ever, use a fantasy font in CSS because they are very numerous and are not found with any consistency on most computers. An example is the Western font.

- **Cursive**—Cursive fonts are also referred to as *handwriting* fonts. They mimic cursive handwriting and are often filled with flourishes. As with fantasy fonts, cursive fonts are rarely applied with CSS. Many designers set fantasy or cursive fonts on graphics and use them as decorative typographic elements within a design. A common cursive font is Lucida Handwriting (see Figure 9-1).

FIGURE 9-1 I used inline CSS to style each line of text with the font specified.

Fonts that are common to almost everyone's system these days include Arial, Helvetica, Verdana, Times, Georgia, and Courier. Tahoma, Trebuchet, and Lucida fonts are fairly widespread because they ship with all Windows versions and were originally included in Microsoft's Web Font Pack, a free set of fonts that Microsoft distributed in the relatively early days of the Web.

If you're just starting out, it's best to stick to a very simple scheme with fonts. You can do one of the following:

- Choose one font, a common serif or sans-serif, and use that same font for everything. Modify size, weight, color and other styles to gain interest.

- Choose two fonts, a common serif and a common sans-serif. Use the serif for all headings, captions, and other text; use the sans-serif for body text. (This option is very common on the Web.)

- Choose two fonts, a common sans-serif and a common serif. Use the sans-serif for all headings, captions, and other text; use the serif for body text. (Also a common option for the Web, this technique has long been used in the print world; look at any newspaper or book, and you're likely to see this combination in use.)

As you become more adept at using fonts, you might want to get more creative, but, typically, sticking to one of these options will make your documents look more professional and consistent.

Applying Font Families to Text

With an idea of what you can reasonably choose from, it's time to go ahead and apply font families to your text. To do this, you select the text in question, and then use the font-family property and an associated value.

The value you use for the font-family property can be a single font name, a font family keyword, or a series of names followed by a font family keyword.

Single Font Names

Choose this technique only when you are absolutely certain that your audience has the font in question.

```
body {font-family: Arial;}
```

This sets the default font for all documents to Arial. The problem with this technique is that if the user doesn't have Arial installed on his or her machine, the browser will use the default font—this is typically Times and might be quite a different look than what you're after.

Font Family Keywords

Font family keywords in CSS match the family names described in the last section: serif, sans-serif, monospace, fantasy, and cursive.

```
h1 {font-family: fantasy;}
```

This would apply the default fantasy font on your visitor's machine to all h1 headers. The problem with using keywords is that you have no control over which font that will be. As a result, keywords are typically used as a fallback method. So, if you're choosing a single font name, you can also add the related keyword *after* the font you've chosen:

```
h1 {font-family: Arial, sans-serif;}
```

In the fairly unlikely event that Arial isn't installed on your user's machine, it defaults to a sans-serif font on the user's machine.

Multiple Names

A technique that affords more control is using multiple family names. This means choosing fonts from the same family used in a specific order:

```
body {font-family: Arial, Helvetica, Verdana, sans-serif;}
```

The browser will look for the first named font; if it doesn't exist, it will apply the second, or third. Additionally, you'll note that I've added the family keyword name.

In Example 9-1, I've created a style sheet to demonstrate using the `font-family` property.

EXAMPLE 9-1   Applying fonts to page elements

```
body {font-family: Georgia, Times, serif;}
h1, h2 {font-family: Arial, Helvetica, sans-serif;}
```

You'll notice that I've declared a font for the body but not the paragraphs. This provides a default for all text that falls into the body of a document.

In this example, the paragraphs simply inherit the font family from the body element. Notice also that I've grouped the h1 and h2 because I want them to have the same font. Figure 9-2 shows the results.

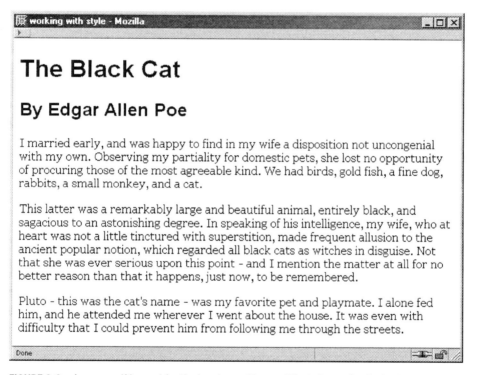

FIGURE 9-2   A sans-serif is used for the headers, with a serif font chosen for the body.

Of course, I haven't defined any other sizes or styles just yet. As a result, the browser styles are applied, so the default size for h1, h2, and paragraphs is determined by my browser until I create additional rules to control those styles.

Sizing Fonts

In this section, you'll learn to size fonts using the `font-size` property along with an absolute, relative, length, or percentage value.

Absolute and Relative Keywords

Absolute keywords size fonts based on the way that the browser computes their size. The keywords available are `xx-small`, `x-small`, `small`, `medium`, `large`, `x-large`, and `xx-large`. Here, I've applied an absolute keyword to paragraph text:

```
p {font-size: medium;}
```

The `medium` size is typically equivalent to the browser's default size for that element. Figure 9-3 shows all the keywords as applied to default browser text.

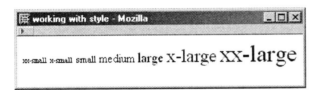

FIGURE 9-3   Absolute keyword sizing within a web browser.

Where absolute keywords are dependent upon the browser's computation of fonts, the relative keywords of `larger` and `smaller` relate to the size of the parent element. So, if I've set my body font size to `medium`, I can use the relative keyword of `larger` to change the size to `large`, or `smaller` to change the size to `small`. Just remember that relative keywords always relate to an already defined size, whether it's defined by a keyword, length, or percentage value.

Length Values

Length values are used with many properties. They include three relative and five absolute values. Relative values are `em`, `ex`, and `px`; absolute values are `pt`, `pc`, `in`, `mm`, and `cm`. Absolute values should not be used for the screen, although they are useful when creating print style sheets.

The most commonly used length values for type on the Web are pixels and ems because, technically, they are both scalable, which is appropriate for screen. There's a major problem, however: Microsoft Internet Explorer for Windows does not scale pixels. This is a terrible oversight that has caused real problems, especially because you want to offer your vision-impaired users scalable sizing. Compare the values on the left to the values on the right, where I've bumped up the browser text (in IE, View > Text Size) from its default size of `medium` to `larger` (see Figure 9-4).

0.5 em 1 em 1.5 em	0.5 em 1 em 1.5 em
12 px 16 px 22 px	12 px 16 px 22 px
12 pt 22 pt	12 pt 22 pt

FIGURE 9-4 Comparing font sizes in Internet Explorer 6.0.

You'll note that the em values scale, but the pixels and points do not. The pixels *should* scale—and they do in browsers with correct font-sizing support. The points (which I advise you not to use for screen) remain the same size because they are absolute values, meaning they should never scale. As a result, many web designers advocate the use of ems over pixels. You'll note, however, the teeny text on the left. This can also cause serious problems if people have their browsers set to a smaller font size than `medium`.

Percentages

Percentage values in font sizing are *always* relative to another value, such as a keyword or length value. So, if I set my `body` font size to `1em` and then set my `h1` header to `150%`, I'll end up with a larger `h1` than the `body` font size, which is relative to the browser default:

```
body {font-size: 1em;}
h1 {font-size: 150%}
```

Percentages are particularly helpful in working around browser limitations in font sizing. The reason is that percentages are also scalable. As a result, many workarounds for the pixel problem in IE have been achieved by combining ems and percentages. Still, many designers prefer to go with pixels because of their more consistent rendering, at the cost of better accessibility.

NOTE

You'll use a variety of sizing options throughout this book, to get the hang of it. For more information on font sizing problems, see Owen Briggs's article "Text Sizing," at http://www.thenoodleincident.com/tutorials/box_lesson/font/index.html.

Font Weight and Style

Whew! That was a *lot* of detail for a book that's supposed to be straightforward. But to be fair to you and ensure that you've got a solid foundation, I had to do it. Now let's get on with the show!

Along with their family and size, fonts can have weight and style. Font weight refers to how bold (or not bold) a font is. Font style refers to different faces that might exist within a given family.

Font Weight

Defining the weight of the font is done by using the `font-weight` property combined with an associated value. Values for weight include numeric (100-900, where 100 is very light, 900 is the darkest, and 400 is normal), the keyword `normal` (corresponding to a weight of 400), the keyword `bold` (equivalent to a weight of 700), the keyword `bolder` (specifies the next higher weight), and the keyword `lighter` (specifies the next lighter weight).

Example 9-2 shows a style sheet with a variety of weights applied.

EXAMPLE 9-2   Styles describing font family, size, and weight

```
body {font-family: Georgia, Times, serif; font-size: 1em; font-weight: normal;}
h1, h2 {font-family: Arial, Helvetica, sans-serif;}
h1 {font-size: 150%; font-weight: bold;}
h2 {font-size: 130%; font-weight: lighter;}
.accent {font-weight: 700;}
```

Figure 9-5 shows the text used earlier in the chapter with these styles applied.

FIGURE 9-5   Applying weight to the body, headers, and an accent class.

Font Style

Font styles help alter the face. To apply a font style, you use the `font-style` property with a value of `normal`, `italic`, or `oblique`.

The `normal` value is used only when you're specifically concerned about text being rendered in its normal weight. Otherwise, it's the default and unnecessary to use.

Oblique faces are slanted faces that are appropriate for electronic text. The `oblique` value is truly useful only when a font has an oblique face resident on a user's computer, which doesn't apply to the majority of fonts with which you will be working. If there is no oblique face for the font, the font will appear as italic.

The `italic` value italicizes the font. Bottom line? Your best value for the `font-style` property will be `italic` in almost all cases (see Example 9-3).

EXAMPLE 9-3   Styles describing font family, size, weight, and style

```
body {font-family: Georgia, Times, serif; font-size: 1em; font-weight: normal;}
h1, h2 {font-family: Arial, Helvetica, sans-serif;}
h1 {font-size: 150%; font-weight: bold;}
h2 {font-size: 130%; font-weight: lighter; font-style: italic;}
.accent {font-weight: 700;}
```

Figure 9-6 shows how the italics are applied to the h2 header.

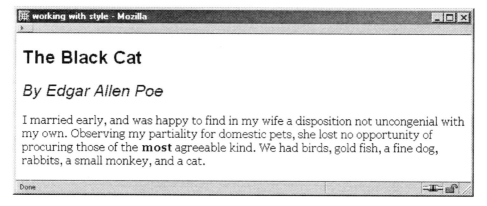

FIGURE 9-6   Adding a font style to the h2 element.

Coloring Text

This is the easy part! Text color uses the `color:` property, which, as you can see, does not have a font or text prefix.

To apply a color to a font, simply use the `color` property along with an appropriate color value. You can refer to Chapter 8, "Working with Color and Images Using CSS," where I applied the `color` property in numerous cases and discussed color values at length.

I want to color up the text a bit, so I'm going to apply color to my existing styles (see Example 9-4).

EXAMPLE 9-4 Coloring the text

```
body {font-family: Georgia, Times, serif; font-size: 1em; font-weight: normal;
color: black;}
h1, h2 {font-family: Arial, Helvetica, sans-serif;}
h1 {font-size: 150%; font-weight: bold; color: #999;}
h2 {font-size: 130%; font-weight: lighter; font-style: italic; color: #333;}
.accent {font-weight: 700; color: red;}
```

You can see the headers change color in Figure 9-7.

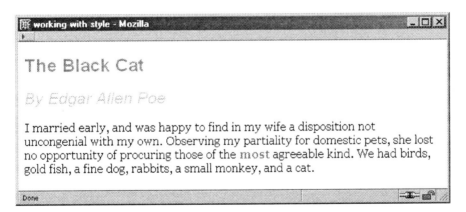

FIGURE 9-7 Applying color to the body, h1, h2, and class selectors.

Of course, you can't see the red accent color applied to the accent class because of the nature of this book, but be sure to write up your styles and fire up your browser to check it out for yourself.

Aligning Text

Back in the days of presentational HTML, text was aligned using the `align` attribute and a corresponding justification value. CSS uses the exact same premise, but, of course, it's done outside the HTML using the `text-align` property. The values are the same and should be familiar to anyone who's ever used a word processor:

- `left`—Also referred to as *ragged right*, left justification sets the text flush left with lines breaking to the right. This is default behavior for all browsers and is the preference for all body text. `text-align: left;`

- `center`—This centers the text. Centered text is useful for styling headers, captions, and other accent text. It is very difficult to read long sections of centered text, so it's not best to use for body text. `text-align: center;`

- `right`—This places all text flush right, leaving a ragged left edge. `text-align: right;`

- `justify`—Justifying text means having the left and right edges be equally flush. This is done by calculating words and spacing within the available line length. It's commonly seen in print newspapers and magazines. It can create a very uniform, attractive look, but most people avoid it because the spacing can appear to be very awkward and, therefore, more difficult to read. `text-align: justify;`

Figure 9-8 compares a paragraph with each alignment option applied.

This latter was a remarkably large an beautiful animal, entirely black, and sagacious to an astonishing degree.	This latter was a remarkably large and beautiful animal, entirely black, and sagacious to an astonishing degree.	This latter was a remarkably large and beautiful animal, entirely black, and sagacious to an astonishing degree.	This latter was a remarkably large and beautiful animal, entirely black, and sagacious to an astonishing degree.

FIGURE 9-8   Left, center, right, and justified text.

Text Decoration

You can "decorate" text with CSS—that is, apply or remove a particular decorative value. This is done using the `text-decoration` property, with values as follows:

- `none`—This is used primarily to remove the default underlines from links. See Chapter 10, "Link Effects, Lists, and Navigation."

- `underline`—This places a line underneath the selected text. Usability specialists tend to shun underlined text because it can be confused with linked text.

- `overline`—This places a line above the selected text.

- `line-through`—This places a line through the selected text.

- `blink`—Yep, you read that right. This causes text to blink, a feature that was introduced (and used to the point of pain) by Netscape in the early days. It works in all contemporary browsers but Internet Explorer.

Example 9-5 serves up an inline CSS sample for decorating text.

EXAMPLE 9-5   Decorating text with CSS

```
<p style="text-decoration: underline;">This text is underlined</p>
<p style="text-decoration: overline;">This text has an overline</p>
<p style="text-decoration: line-through;">This text has a line-through</p>
<p style="text-decoration: blink;">This text blinks</p>
```

Figure 9-9 shows the results, with the exception of the blink.

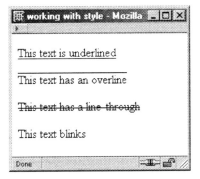

FIGURE 9-9   Decorating text with CSS—try out the sample CSS to see the blink.

Indenting Text

Another very useful text property is text-indent. This enables you to indent text with CSS instead of spacer graphics or numerous nonbreaking space characters in your HTML.

You can use any length value (described earlier this chapter) that is fixed.

```
p {text-indent: 45px;}
```

This results in each paragraph having an initial indentation of 45 pixels (see Figure 9-10).

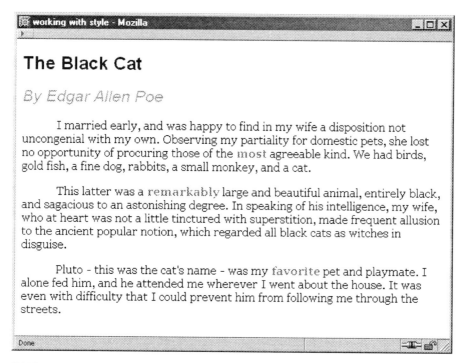

FIGURE 9-10   Indenting paragraphs with a 45-pixel indent.

You can use percentage values, too, which will be relative to the element's containing box (more on that in Chapter 12, "Positioning, Floats, and Z-Index"):

```
p {text-indent: 40%;}
```

This results in a deep indentation, which you can use from time to time for an unusual look (see Figure 9-11).

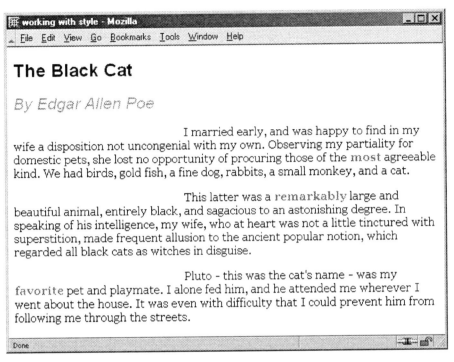

FIGURE 9-11 Indenting using percentages.

You can use negative length values to *outdent* text (see Figure 9-12).

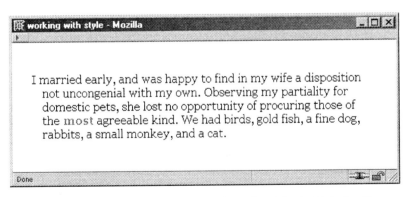

FIGURE 9-12 Outdenting text by setting margins and applying text-indent: -20px;.

Transforming and Varying Text

You can style the case of text and vary its font using two different properties.

To transform case, you use the `text-transform` property and a value of `capitalize`, `uppercase`, `lowercase`, or `none`.

To vary text, you use the `font-variant` property and a value of `small-caps` or `normal` (which is the default).

Example 9-6 shows a document employing transformation and variants.

EXAMPLE 9-6   Transforming and varying text with CSS

```
<!DOCTYPE html PUBLIC "-//W3C//DTD XHTML 1.0 Transitional//EN"
          "http://www.w3.org/TR/xhtml1/DTD/xhtml1-transitional.dtd">

<html xmlns="http://www.w3.org/1999/xhtml">
<head>
<title>working with style</title>
<style type="text/css">
body {font-family: Georgia, Times, serif; color: black;}
h1 {font-family: Arial, Helvetica, sans-serif; font-size: 24px;
font-variant: small-caps;}
h2 {font-family: Georgia, Times, serif; color: #999; font-size: 18px; font-style:
italic; text-transform: lowercase;}
.accent {font-weight: 700; color: red; text-transform: uppercase;}
p {font-size: 16px; text-transform: capitalize;}
</style>
</head>
<body>
<h1>The Black Cat</h1>
<h2>By Edgar Allen Poe</h2>
<p>I married early, and was happy to find in my wife a disposition not
uncongenial with my own. Observing my partiality for domestic pets, she
lost no opportunity of procuring those of the <span class="accent">most</span>
agreeable kind. We had birds, gold fish, a fine dog, rabbits, a small monkey,
and a cat.</p>
<p>This latter was a <span class="accent">remarkably</span> large and beautiful
animal, entirely black, and sagacious to an astonishing degree. In speaking of his
intelligence, my wife, who at heart was not a little tinctured with superstition,
made frequent allusion to the ancient popular notion, which regarded all black
cats as witches in disguise.</p>
<p>Pluto - this was the cat's name - was my <span class="accent">favorite</span>
pet and playmate. I alone fed him, and he attended me wherever I went about the
house. It was even with difficulty that I could prevent him from following me
through the streets.</p>
</body>
</html>
```

You can see how `text-transform` and `font-variant` work in Figure 9-13.

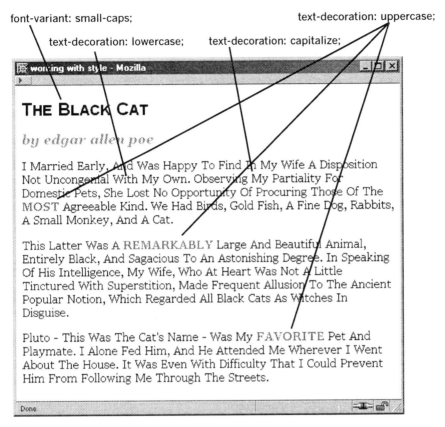

font-variant: small-caps;

text-decoration: lowercase;

text-decoration: capitalize;

text-decoration: uppercase;

FIGURE 9-13 Transforming and varying text.

Browsers that provide full support for transforming and varying text will apply the styles *regardless* of the case your text is actually composed in. Of course, for sensible reasons, you'll want your text content to be treated normally in the document. This way, you can always change the styles without having to reauthor the document.

NOTE
Browser support for `text-transform` and `font-variant` is pretty good overall, but one known issue in contemporary browsers is that `font-variant: small-caps;` does *not* work in certain early versions of the popular Safari browser from Apple. The style simply won't be applied in any way, and the text will pick up only those styles that Safari does support.

Setting Line Height

Referred to in traditional typography as *leading*, line height is the space between each line in a section of text. CSS enables you to control this using the `line-height` property, with length, number, or percentage values (see Example 9-7).

EXAMPLE 9-7 Adding line height to paragraphs with length, number, and percentage

```
<p style="line-height: 20px;">I married early, and was happy to find in my wife a
disposition not uncongenial with my own. </p>
<p style="line-height: 2;">Observing my partiality for domestic pets, she lost no
opportunity of procuring those of the most agreeable kind. We had birds, gold
fish, a fine dog, rabbits, a small monkey, and a cat.</p>
<p style="line-height: 65%;">This latter was a remarkably large and beautiful
animal, entirely black, and sagacious to an astonishing degree.</p>
```

In the complete document, I set a body font to 14 pixels and then applied `line-height` inline for each paragraph I wanted to modify (see Figure 9-14).

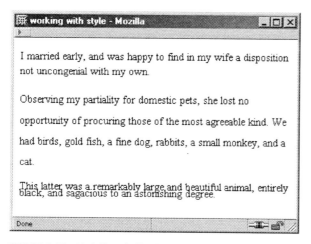

FIGURE 9-14 Variations in line height can lead to interesting effects.

Typically, it's a good idea to stick to the font's default `line-height` for best readability.

Spacing Letters and Words

Another aspect of typography that CSS has picked up on is letter spacing and word spacing, handled by the `letter-spacing` and `word-spacing` properties, respectively. Values for each are lengths (see Example 9-8).

EXAMPLE 9-8   Letter and word spacing

```
<p style="letter-spacing: 10px;">I married early, and was happy to find in my wife
a disposition not uncongenial with my own. </p>
<p style="word-spacing: 0.5em;">Observing my partiality for domestic pets, she
lost no opportunity of procuring those of the most agreeable kind. We had birds,
gold fish, a fine dog, rabbits, a small monkey, and a cat.</p>
```

The first paragraph will have 10 pixels between each letter, and the second will have 0.5 ems between each word (see Figure 9-15).

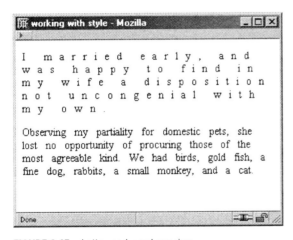

FIGURE 9-15   Letter and word spacing.

The results are unusual. Although you wouldn't normally use these styles in conservative documents, you can begin to see how using such styles can provide sophisticated design options.

Modifying First-Letter and First-Line Text

You can style the first letter of text (a drop cap) and the first line of text using the pseudo element selectors. You haven't seen these yet, so here's a look:

```
:first-line
:first-letter
```

These get attached to the element to which you'd like the style to apply (see Example 9-9).

EXAMPLE 9-9   Using pseudo element selectors to style

```
p:first-line {font-weight: bold; color: #333;}
p:first-letter {font-style: italic; color: #999;}
```

In Figure 9-16, I've applied these styles to text.

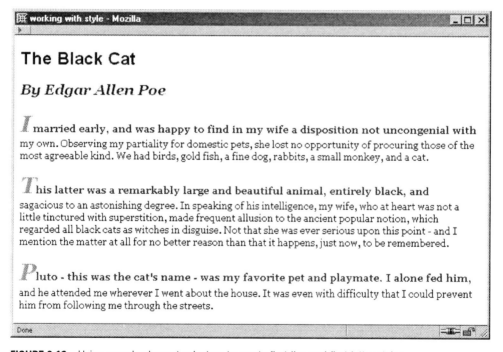

FIGURE 9-16   Using pseudo element selectors to create first-line and first-letter styles.

Using Shorthand for Font Styles

As with backgrounds, there's a shorthand property for font styles. These incorporate some of the font properties and the line-height property, but none of the text properties. What's more, you have to pay close attention to order when you use shorthand with fonts.

The shorthand property is font: and the order of its values is as follows: font-style, font-variant, font-weight, font-size/line-height, font-family.

```
p {font: italic small-caps bold 14px/15px Arial, Helvetica, sans-serif;}
```

This will result in all paragraphs being italic, small-capped, and bold, with a font size of 14 pixels, a line height of 15 pixels (note the slash between them, the only time this symbol is ever used in CSS) and text in Arial, Helvetica, or a default sans-serif font.

If you want to leave out any value, just keep the integrity of the rest of the order:

```
p {font: bold 14px Arial, sans-serif;}
```

This results in a 14-pixel bold Arial font. You can use shorthand any time you like; just be aware that, with fonts, order is imperative or your style sheet might not work.

QUANTUM LEAP: UNSUPPORTED AND POORLY SUPPORTED FONT AND TEXT PROPERTIES

Several poorly or completely unsupported styles are available in the current specification for fonts and text. I'd like to take a moment to mention them here, mostly because they're really cool. Also, I bring this up because eventually support for these properties will likely be more widespread.

The font-size-adjust property enables you to set an adjustment value so that all your fonts appear relatively uniform in terms of their sizing. This would come in very handy because different fonts have different native sizing: Surely you've noticed that a 12-pixel Times font is smaller than a 12-pixel Arial font. Well, as soon as you begin to have multiple fonts, you might want to make them more visually uniform. By setting a font-size-adjust value, you normalize the size of the fonts so that all fonts within the style are sized consistently. You can see why this would be useful.

The font-stretch property enables you to condense or expand text. This is helpful when you want to get some interesting effects.

Finally, the text-shadow property enables you to create a drop shadow effect for your text. Won't this be cool when you can actually use it? The property allows for color and offset values, and will eliminate the need for graphics when the goal is simply to add a shadow effect to the text.

Now You're Getting Fancy!

I just know you're having fun now! You've got enough skill with images, color, and text to really create a nice-looking page or site.

But, of course, there's lots more to learn with CSS. In the next chapter, you'll take a look at the ways links are used in today's web design. Once we could style links with only limited options, but now we can have multiple styles of links, including multiple colors for all states, even hovers.

You'll also learn about lists and how the combination of lists and links has become a mainstay of approaching contemporary navigation—both vertical *and* horizontal, helping you to create awesome and interactive interfaces with minimal or even no use of images.

CHAPTER 10

Link Effects, Lists, and Navigation

As you learned in Chapter 2, "Adding Text and Links," the link is really what empowered the Web as a medium. The capability to move from page to page and site to site based on choice created the opportunity for websites to get noticed, which, in turn, allowed the Web to grow so quickly.

CSS has been used to style links for as long as CSS has been available. In fact, along with text styles, link styles are by far the most common use of CSS to date. Of course, as we learn more about CSS and how to use it as a means of managing most, if not all, of our visual presentation, that truth becomes somewhat diluted. At this point, though, styling links with CSS remains one of the most widespread applications of the technology.

With CSS, you can create beautiful effects for links, including hover effects that, before CSS, had to be managed with JavaScript and numerous images or with a Java applet. Using color and images, you can reproduce the effects that demanded so many resources with much greater efficiency and control, and no reliance on anything but clean markup and savvy styling, resulting in beautiful designs that degrade well in older browsers and are completely accessible to those with disabilities.

Lists help you organize your content, and with CSS, you can do a great deal with lists. Along with styling the way list text is managed, you can use CSS to change the way the numbers or bullets are displayed, replace them with an image, or remove the list markers completely.

A very exciting opportunity comes about when you merge lists and links. You end up with a means of navigation. For, after all, what is navigation other than a list of links? Whether managed vertically in a side column or horizontally along the top of the page, using CSS, lists and links can be manipulated to create very richly featured navigation with a minimum of fuss.

In this chapter, you begin by creating simple styles for links and then progress to multiple link styles. You'll then learn to manage lists with CSS. Finally, you'll work with lists and links for both vertical and horizontal navigation. Along the way, you'll be introduced to new CSS properties, as well as a number of selector types you've not worked with just yet.

Working with Link States

First things first! Several states for links are considered standard for all browsers:

- link—The link state is the state of the link before being activated.

- visited—The visited state occurs after the link has been visited.

- hover—Hovering is the state of the link as you hover the mouse pointer over the link.

- active—The active state occurs as you are clicking on the link to activate it.

NOTE

There is another state, focus. This is used whenever an element is capable of receiving keyboard input, such as with a form. This is not typically used with links, but it's good to be aware of.

CSS categorizes the link and visited states as *pseudo classes*, and the hover and active states as *dynamic pseudo classes*. You can see how hover and active are dynamic: They require some kind of action from the user to work. The link and visited states occur before and after interaction.

You might also remember from the discussion in Chapter 9, "Styling Text," the pseudo element selectors :first-child and :first-line. All pseudo selectors take the preceding colon. So, the corresponding selectors available to style links are :link, :visited, :hover, and :active.

Example 10-1 sets up some general styles for the document, as well as styles for all link states.

EXAMPLE 10-1 Styling links using pseudo class and dynamic pseudo class selectors

```
body {font: 14px Georgia, Times, serif; color: white; background-color: black;}
h1 {font: 22px Arial, Helvetica, sans-serif; color: orange; text-decoration:
underline;}
h2 {font: italic 20px Georgia, Times, serif; color: #ccc; background-color: black;
text-transform: lowercase;}
a {color: orange;}
a:link {color: orange;}
a:visited {color: yellow;}
a:hover {color: fuchsia;}
a:active {color: red;}
```

You'll notice that I've styled the anchor element, too. Because the a is an element selector, you can use it to set defaults that will then be inherited. Pseudo classes are not inherited, for logical reasons: The whole point is to be able to make changes in each state. However, there will be commonalities, so those common styles can be set in the anchor, with the independent styles in the selectors for each state.

Figure 10-1 shows the document to which I've applied these styles. You'll notice my cursor hovering over a link so you can visualize the change.

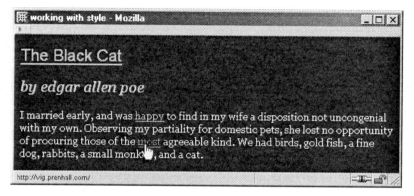

FIGURE 10-1 Viewing link and hover states in the context of a document.

NOTE

For link effects to work properly, they must appear in this order: link, visited, hover, active. Any other order will cause inconsistent behavior. Just remember the order of LVHA, or, as a popular mnemonic in the industry goes, LoVe/HAte.

I enlarged the link text to demonstrate more clearly the appearance of each state (see Figure 10-2).

FIGURE 10-2 Link, visited, hover, and active states.

You might not be able to see the color until you try it out in a browser, but you will notice the changes—especially note the marquee surrounding the activated link.

Modifying Link Styles

Simple, wasn't that? You'll dig a little deeper now and make some changes to the way your links look. Typically, most modifications are made for the hover state, but you can style for all states.

A popular approach is to add a background color on hover (see Example 10-2).

EXAMPLE 10-2   Adding a background color to the hover state

```
a {color: orange;}
a:link {color: orange;}
a:visited {color: yellow;}
a:hover {color: fuchsia; background-color: white;}
a:active {color: red;}
```

As the mouse passes over the link, the background turns white (see Figure 10-3).

FIGURE 10-3   Changing the background color in a hover state.

You can also modify the text weight by making it bold, or change its style and make it italic (see Example 10-3).

EXAMPLE 10-3   Adding a background color to the hover state

```
a {color: orange;}
a:link {color: orange;}
a:visited {color: yellow;}
a:hover {color: fuchsia; font-style: italic;}
a:active {color: red;}
```

NOTE

Many usability specialists suggest avoiding major changes in link state styles because they feel it's disconcerting. Some very rigid usability experts advocate not even styling links and leaving them with their default colors and underlines. Most designers do not agree with the more rigid approach, though, and prefer to use link styles to enhance their design work. The main concern is ensuring that there's some way for a visitor to know that the link is, in fact, a link.

As the mouse passes over the link, the background turns italic (see Figure 10-4).

FIGURE 10-4   Modifying the text style to italic in the hover state.

Perhaps the most popular modification is removing the link underline. You can do this for all states with the `text-decoration: none;` declaration:

```
a {color: orange; text-decoration: none;}
```

As I mentioned, common styles to all states should be placed in the anchor element so you can tap into inheritance. There's no need to add this declaration to any of the pseudo selectors because they'll inherit the rule (see Figure 10-5).

FIGURE 10-5   Look, Ma—no underlines!

You can mix and match rules, too. Some designers like to have the underline appear only in the `hover` state. To do that, you simply add the `text-decoration: underline;` declaration to the `:hover` selector, which overrides the inherited value in the anchor because of the *specificity* of the selectors (see Chapter 7, "Using CSS," for more details on specificity). Figure 10-6 shows the links without underlines until the hover state is activated.

FIGURE 10-6   The `link`, `visited`, `hover`, and `active` states, with underlining in the hover state.

Multiple Link Styles Using Class Selectors

Another fantastic option made available via CSS is the capability to have more than one style of links per document. This is especially helpful when you have areas on a page with distinctly different features than other areas of the page. A perfect example is a navigation area with a blue background, and a content area with a white background. If you wanted white links on the blue background, it clearly couldn't work within the white content because the links would be invisible.

You can approach multiple link styles in a few ways, including creating separate classes. You could have basic link styles for the default and content areas, and you could set up a special class for the navigation area (see Example 10-4).

EXAMPLE 10-4   Using classes to create multiple link styles

```
/* default link styles, appropriate for content area */
a {color: orange; text-decoration: none;}
a:link {color: orange;}
a:visited {color: yellow;}
a:hover {color: fuchsia;}
a:active {color: red;}

/* classed link styles, appropriate for navigation area */
a.nav {color: white; text-decoration: none;}
a.nav:link {color: white;}
a.nav:visited {color: yellow;}
a.nav:hover {color: orange;}
a.nav:active {color: fuschia;}
```

You would then apply the `class="nav"` attribute within those links that you'd like to apply the class to:

```
<a class="nav" href="http://www.molly.com/">Molly.Com</a>
```

I've created an HTML file with two sections to represent content and navigation areas, and applied the class to the link in the navigation area (see Figure 10-7).

FIGURE 10-7   Applying multiple link styles using classes.

Styling Links Using Descendant Selectors

Of course, using a lot of classes means not only writing more CSS rules, but also adding numerous class attributes to the HTML. If you have a lot of content to style and you rely too much on classes, it'll result in what industry specialists refer to as "class-it is," the overuse of classes. You can avoid this by tapping into other kinds of selectors.

Elements can be uniquely identified using what's known as an *ID selector*. These selectors start off with an octothorpe followed by a custom name—very similar to what you do when creating a class:

```
#id-name
```

> **NOTE**
> The difference between class and ID selectors is a critical one. Class selectors can be used as many times in a document as you desire, whereas an ID can be used only *once per document*. Therefore, IDs are particularly useful when identifying unique divisions of a document, such as navigation, content, masthead, and footer. You'll see this at work a great deal in upcoming chapters, particularly when we get into CSS layouts.

After a division is identified, you can tap into *descendant* selectors. These are selectors that select based on the defined parent element. First you use the selector for the parent, then a space, and then the element you want to pass the styles along to: #nav a. This declaration selects any child anchor of the parent element identified as nav. Example 10-5 shows this at work in the context of multiple linking.

EXAMPLE 10-5   Multiple links using ID and descendant selectors

```
<!DOCTYPE html PUBLIC "-//W3C//DTD XHTML 1.0 Transitional//EN"
          "http://www.w3.org/TR/xhtml1/DTD/xhtml1-transitional.dtd">
<html xmlns="http://www.w3.org/1999/xhtml">
<head>
<title>working with style</title>
<style type="text/css">
body {font: 14px Georgia, Times, serif; color: white; background-color: black;}
h1 {font: 22px Arial, Helvetica, sans-serif; color: orange; text-decoration:
underline;}
h2 {font: italic 20px Georgia, Times, serif; color: #ccc; background-color: black;
text-transform: lowercase;}
/* link defaults */
a {color: orange; text-decoration: none;}
a:link {color: orange;}
a:visited {color: yellow;}
a:hover {color: fuchsia; text-decoration: underline;}
a:active {color: red;}
```

```
/* link styles for all descendant links of the example2 division */
#example2 {background-color: white; color: black;}
#example2 a {color: lime;}
#example2 a:link {color: lime;}
#example2 a:visited {color: red;}
#example2 a:hover {color: aqua; text-decoration: underline;}
#example2 a:active {color: fuchsia;}
</style>
</head>
<body>
<div id="example1">
<p>I married early, and was happy to find in my wife a disposition not uncongenial
with my own. Observing my partiality for domestic pets, she lost no opportunity
of procuring those of the <a href="http://www.prenhall.com/">most</a> agreeable
kind. We had birds, gold fish, a fine dog, rabbits, a small monkey, and a cat.</p>
</div>
<div id="example2">
<p>This latter was a <a href="http://wwwprenhall.com/">remarkably</a> large and
beautiful animal, entirely black, and sagacious to an astonishing degree. In
speaking of his intelligence, my wife, who at heart was not a little tinctured
with superstition, made frequent allusion to the ancient popular notion, which
regarded all black cats as witches in disguise. Not that she was ever serious
upon this point - and I mention the matter at all for no better reason than that
it happens, just now, to be remembered.</p>
</div>
</body>
</html>
```

In this case, two divisions have IDs. Because there are no link styles defined for the example1 division, those links will take the defaults. But because I've created link styles specifically for example2, those styles are then applied to all descendant links within that division (see Figure 10-8).

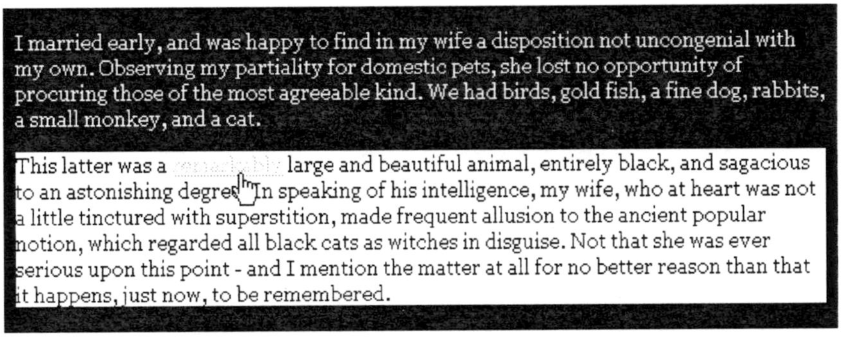

FIGURE 10-8 Applying multiple links using descendant selectors, which streamlines both the CSS and the markup by avoiding classitis.

Styling Ordered Lists

Moving on to lists, you'll begin by styling an ordered list. You'll modify the marker type and then replace the marker altogether with an image. I began with some text and background styles along with an unstyled ordered list, resulting in Figure 10-9.

Directions To The Party!

1. From the corner of Broadway and 5th Avenue, take a right onto 5th.
2. Follow 5th North about three miles until you come to the Oak Road intersection.
3. Take a right on Oak Road. Stay on Oak about five miles.
4. You'll see an intersection at Oak and Vine. Stay on Oak two more blocks.
5. Take a left onto Broome Street. We're three houses in on the right.

FIGURE 10-9   A styled page with an ordered list.

If you want to use an alternate marker, you can do so using the list-style-type property with a corresponding value. There are numerous values (most supporting numerals in other languages), but the ones you'll likely want to swap in an ordered list are decimal-leading-zero (which starts the numbering at zero) and lower-roman or upper-roman (which use lower or upper Roman numerals, respectively). Simply add the value you want to the existing style sheet:

```
ol {list-style-type: lower-roman;}
```

This results in the numerals displaying in lowercase Roman (see Figure 10-10).

Directions To The Party!

i. From the corner of Broadway and 5th Avenue, take a right onto 5th.
ii. Follow 5th North about three miles until you come to the Oak Road intersection.
iii. Take a right on Oak Road. Stay on Oak about five miles.
iv. You'll see an intersection at Oak and Vine. Stay on Oak two more blocks.
v. Take a left onto Broome Street. We're three houses in on the right.

FIGURE 10-10   Styling the ordered list with lowercase Roman numerals.

If you'd like to replace the numerals with an image, create images for each number you require and apply classes to each list item to get the results (see Example 10-6).

EXAMPLE 10-6   Using classes to apply images to the ordered list

```
<!DOCTYPE html PUBLIC "-//W3C//DTD XHTML 1.0 Transitional//EN"
          "http://www.w3.org/TR/xhtml1/DTD/xhtml1-transitional.dtd">
<html xmlns="http://www.w3.org/1999/xhtml">
<head>
<title>working with style</title>
<style type="text/css">
body {font: 14px Georgia, Times, serif; color: black; background-image:
url(balloons.gif); background-position: right top; background-repeat: no-repeat;}
h1 {font: 22px Arial, Helvetica, sans-serif; color: orange; text-decoration:
underline; text-transform: capitalize;}
h2 {font: italic 20px Georgia, Times, serif; color: red; text-transform:
lowercase;}
.list1 {list-style-image: url(1.gif);}
.list2 {list-style-image: url(2.gif);}
.list3 {list-style-image: url(3.gif);}
</style>
</head>
<body>
<h1>Directions to the Party!</h1>
<ol>
<li class="list1">From the corner of Broadway and 5th Avenue, take a right onto
5th.</li>
<li class="list2">Follow 5th North about three miles until you come to the Oak
Road intersection.</li>
<li class="list3">Take a right on Oak Road. Stay on Oak about five miles.</li>
</ol>
</body>
</html>
```

You can see not only the relevant CSS here, but also see the rules I created for the rest of the page styles (see Figure 10-11).

FIGURE 10-11   Adding graphic numerals to the list using classes.

NOTE

You can also alter the position of ordered and unordered lists. You'll do that in the following section.

Styling Unordered Lists

As with ordered lists, you can change the marker, replace it with an image, and modify the list marker's position in relation to the text.

Unordered list markers can be styled using one of three keywords: disc, circle, or square (see Example 10-7).

EXAMPLE 10-7   Inline styles demonstrating the three marker keywords for unordered lists

```
<h2>What to Bring:</h2>
<ul>
<li style="list-style-type: disc;">A beverage of choice.</li>
<li style="list-style-type: circle;">Munchies.</li>
<li style="list-style-type: square;">Music and movies.</li>
</ul>
```

Figure 10-12 shows the shapely results.

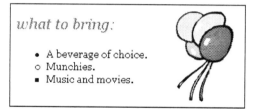

FIGURE 10-12   Showing off the disc, circle, and square options—note that some browsers will use slightly different markers, but the general features are retained.

If you'd like to replace the marker with a custom image, create the image and add it using the list-style-image property (see Example 10-8).

EXAMPLE 10-8   Viewing the complete document along with the image-based bullet

```
<!DOCTYPE html PUBLIC "-//W3C//DTD XHTML 1.0 Transitional//EN"
          "http://www.w3.org/TR/xhtml1/DTD/xhtml1-transitional.dtd">
<html xmlns="http://www.w3.org/1999/xhtml">
<head>
<title>working with style</title>
<style type="text/css">
body {font: 14px Georgia, Times, serif; color: black; background-image:
url(balloons.gif); background-position: right top; background-repeat: no-repeat;}
h1 {font: italic 20px Georgia, Times, serif; color: red; text-transform:
lowercase;}
ul {list-style-image: url(bullet.gif);}
</style>
</head>
```

```
<body>
<h1>What to Bring:</h1>
<ul>
<li>A beverage of choice.</li>
<li>Munchies.</li>
<li>Music and movies.</li>
</ul>
</body>
</html>
```

No need for classes; there's only one image needed. This image will now replace the marker (see Figure 10-13).

FIGURE 10-13   Using images instead of text-based markers to customize your bullets.

Another list property you can use is the list-style-position property, with a value of either outside or inside. The outside value positions the marker outside the block, so when the line wraps, it indents—typical list behavior. Placing the marker inside results in no indent (see Figure 10-14).

FIGURE 10-14   The top option uses outside and the bottom inside for the list's position.

Shorthand CSS for List Styles

Another shorthand property is the `list-style` property. It takes properties from lists and enables you to author them in shorthand (see Example 10-9).

EXAMPLE 10-9   Using the `list-style` shorthand property

```
<!DOCTYPE html PUBLIC "-//W3C//DTD XHTML 1.0 Transitional//EN"
           "http://www.w3.org/TR/xhtml1/DTD/xhtml1-transitional.dtd">
<html xmlns="http://www.w3.org/1999/xhtml">
<head>
<title>working with style</title>
<style type="text/css">
body {font: 14px Georgia, Times, serif; color: black; background-image:
url(balloons.gif); background-position: right top; background-repeat: no-repeat;}
h1 {font: italic 20px Georgia, Times, serif; color: red; text-transform:
lowercase;}
ul {list-style: url(arrow.gif) inside;}
</style>
</head>
<body>
<h1>What to Bring:</h1>
<ul>
<li>A beverage <br />of choice.</li>
<li>Munchies.</li>
<li>Music <br />and movies.</li>
</ul>
</body>
</html>
```

In this case, I've styled the `ul` element using an image and a position. You could swap the image for a keyword if you don't want to use an image. You'll notice that I purposely broke the lines so you can see the influence of the `inside` value (see Figure 10-15).

FIGURE 10-15   Styling the list using the `list-style` shorthand property.

List-Based Vertical Navigation Using Color

Things begin to get really exciting when you combine links and lists for navigation. You'll begin here by first styling a simple list and getting rid of the bullets using the `list-style-type` property with a value of `none`. This removes the markers completely, leaving a list of links (see Example 10-10).

EXAMPLE 10-10 Styling a list of links

```
<!DOCTYPE html PUBLIC "-//W3C//DTD XHTML 1.0 Transitional//EN"
         "http://www.w3.org/TR/xhtml1/DTD/xhtml11-transitional.dtd">

<html xmlns="http://www.w3.org/1999/xhtml">
<head>
<title>working with style</title>
<style type="text/css">
body {font: 14px Georgia, Times, serif; color: black;}
ul {list-style-type: none;}
a {color: orange; text-decoration: none;}
a:link {color: orange;}
a:visited {color: yellow;}
a:hover {color: fuchsia; text-decoration: underline;}  /* font-style: italic;
font-weight: bold; background-color: aqua; */
a:active {color: red;}
</style>
</head>
<body>
<ul>
<li><a href="home.html">Home</a></li>
<li><a href="products.html">Products</a></li>
<li><a href="services.html">Services</a></li>
<li><a href="about.html">About Us</a></li>
<li><a href="contact.html">Contact</a></li>
</ul>
</body>
</html>
```

Figure 10-16 shows the list of styled links with no markers.

FIGURE 10-16 Simple list-based vertical navigation with styled links.

Okay, so that's not so fancy. Hang on! It gets better. By using a range of styles, including border effects and padding (see Chapter 11, "Margins, Borders, and Padding"), you can add a lot to this simple navigation bar. You can also add background colors and images to make the list more visually interesting (see Example 10-11).

EXAMPLE 10-11   Adding styles to the list

```
body {font: 14px Georgia, Times, serif; color: black;}
ul {list-style-type: none; padding: 0; width: 100px; background-image:
url(swirls.gif); border: 2px solid orange;}
li {padding-left: 5px; padding-bottom: 5px; border-bottom: 1px solid orange;}
a {color: orange; text-decoration: none;}
a:link {color: orange;}
a:visited {color: yellow;}
a:hover {color: fuchsia;}
a:active {color: red;}
```

Okay, that's definitely getting a little more interesting (see Figure 10-17).

FIGURE 10-17   Looks like a navigation bar now.

NOTE

As you try out different styles with your navigation, you will find differences in the way browsers manage styling lists. Mozilla and Mozilla Firefox, for example, interpret padding and widths carefully, while IE tends to be more forgiving.

Vertical List Navigation with Image Effects

By tapping into background graphics and the `:hover` selector, you can create a navigation list that will have an attractive background for each list item. Add a contrasting background graphic to the hover state for impressive results (see Example 10-12).

EXAMPLE 10-12 Using background images to create sophisticated navigation effects

```
body {font: bold 15px Georgia, Times, serif; color: black;}
a {color: white; text-decoration: none; display: block;}
a:link {color: white;}
a:visited {color: yellow;}
a:hover {color: white; background-image: url(linkhover.gif);}
a:active {color: red;}
#nav, #nav a, #nav li {width: 100px; margin: 0; padding: 0; list-style-type:
none;}
li {background-image: url(linkback.gif); border-bottom: 3px solid white;}
```

You'll notice that I've set a background graphic for the list item, as well as a background graphic for the hover state. This results in a richly designed navigation bar with visually advanced effects (see Figure 10-18).

FIGURE 10-18 Adding background graphics to the list item and hover state to create graphically rich mouseover effects previously unattainable without JavaScript.

NOTE

I've changed the display of the anchor element from `inline` (in-text) to `block` (followed by a break). This is necessary to match the width of the anchor element to the width of the list item element so that the hover state's background graphic displays properly across all browsers.

Horizontal List-Based Navigation with Color

In the last section, you used the `display: block;` property to turn the anchor element from an inline element to a block element. Using the `display: inline;` property, you can make lists operate inline, which means they'll display horizontally (see Example 10-13).

EXAMPLE 10-13 Markup and CSS for a horizontal list navigation using color effects

```
<!DOCTYPE html PUBLIC "-//W3C//DTD XHTML 1.0 Transitional//EN"
         "http://www.w3.org/TR/xhtml1/DTD/xhtml1-transitional.dtd">
<html xmlns="http://www.w3.org/1999/xhtml">
<head>
<title>working with style</title>
<style type="text/css">
body {font: 14px Georgia, Times, serif; color: black; }
ul#navlist {margin-left: 0; padding-left: 0; white-space: nowrap;}
#navlist li {display: inline; list-style-type: none;}
#navlist a { padding: 3px 10px; }
#navlist a:link, #navlist a:visited {color: white;  background-color: orange;
text-decoration: none;}
#navlist a:hover {color: orange; background-color: yellow; text-decoration: none;}
</style>
</head>
<body>
<div id="navcontainer">
<ul id="navlist">
<li><a href="home.html">Home</a></li>
<li><a href="products.html">Products</a></li>
<li><a href="services.html">Services</a></li>
<li><a href="about.html">About Us</a></li>
<li><a href="contact.html">Contact</a></li>
</ul>
</div>
</body>
</html>
```

This results in a very nice horizontal navigation bar (see Figure 10-19).

FIGURE 10-19 Using a list and color effects to achieve horizontal list-based navigation.

Horizontal List Navigation with Images

Just as you could swap images in the background with vertical lists, you can do the same thing with horizontal lists. I made a few modifications to the previous style sheet: I added the link and hover state background images. Then I bolded the font and set its color to white for both the link and hover states, to allow for good contrast as the image is swapped upon mouseover (see Example 10-14).

EXAMPLE 10-14   List navigation using background images

```
body {font: bold 14px Georgia, Times, serif; color: black; }
ul#navlist {margin-left: 0; padding-left: 0; white-space: nowrap;}
#navlist li {display: inline; list-style-type: none;}
#navlist a { padding: 3px 10px; }
#navlist a:link, #navlist a:visited {color: white;  background-image:
url(linkback.gif); text-decoration: none;}
#navlist a:hover {color: white; background-image: url(linkhover.gif); text-
decoration: none;}
```

Figure 10-20 shows the elegant navigation scheme.

FIGURE 10-20   List-based horizontal navigation using image swapping.

QUANTUM LEAP: HOVER AND INTERNET EXPLORER

As you work with lists for navigation, especially horizontal lists, you'll find that there are dramatic inconsistencies in the way that Internet Explorer deals with styles compared to Mozilla, Firefox, Opera, and Safari. Sadly, Internet Explorer hasn't been updated in years, and version 6.0 for Windows is missing significant support for CSS. As a result, you have to come up with savvy styles to ensure that your work looks good in the widest range of browsers possible (as those depicted here do).

One major issue with IE is the fact that it supports the `:hover` selector only for the anchor element, whereas all other browsers support it for *any* element. If this support were available in IE, there'd be less muss and fuss when dealing with list-based navigation—not to mention a wide range of additional options available for styling lists dynamically without using JavaScript. For other dynamic list navigation, such as drop-down or fly-out navigation that does not work in IE, see Eric Meyer's CSS Edge, at http://www.meyerweb.com/eric/css/edge/.

Rich Links, Lists, and Navigation

It's important to point out that the techniques in this chapter, particularly the way lists are being used in navigation, are a relatively new concept in web design. The mere fact that CSS lets you change the display of an element makes it very compelling to rely as little on imagery for effects as possible.

NOTE

Learn all about CSS lists by visiting Listamatic, a tutorial and gallery of great CSS-based navigation, http://css.maxdesign.com.au/listamatic/.

If you're interested in a tool that will make some of these lists for you right online, check out List-O-Matic, http://www.accessify.com/tools-and-wizards/list-o-matic/list-o-matic.asp.

Next up, you'll be getting a bit more involved in the actual control of margins and padding, which is important for gaining a firm hand over your visual page elements. This will help segue you into the more complex aspects of CSS: laying out pages.

 CHAPTER 11

Margins, Borders, and Padding

One of the coolest things about CSS is that you can style features such as margins, borders and padding. It's not even just being able to style such things that I find so exciting, but the flexibility we have with the styles available.

Consider that *all elements* have a margin, a border, and padding within the CSS visual model. The reason for this is that every element creates a box. Two types of boxes exist: block boxes (related to block-level elements) and line boxes (related to inline boxes). Figure 11-1 shows the difference.

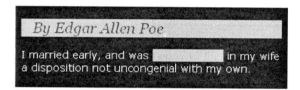

FIGURE 11-1 Examining boxes in the CSS visual model.

I've added a light gray background color to help with the visualization of block and line boxes. The h2 header is a block box. It runs the width of the available browser space (width can control this) and is followed by a line break after the block terminates at the right edge. The line box is demonstrated by a link and sits inline with the surrounding text. You can see how its edges run as close to the content as possible.

By tapping into the CSS visual model, which is referred to as the *Box Model*, you can add styles to various portions of the box. I'll show you the Box Model in the following section of this chapter so you can see exactly how the Box Model works, but the point now is that you can style not just all sides of a given box, but also specific sides of that box.

Margins give you the capability to control the box's margins in both positive and negative values. Borders enable you to style the box's border using a range of predefined border styles, and padding enables us to add padding to the box (much like adding cellpadding to a table). Being able to style these aspects of any element is one of the reasons CSS is far more powerful than any formerly available technology in terms of being able to style your pages with great control.

Exploring the Box Model

The Box Model is a standardized bit of browser technology. The W3C oversees standardization of browsers, so it has defined the Box Model (see Figure 11-2).

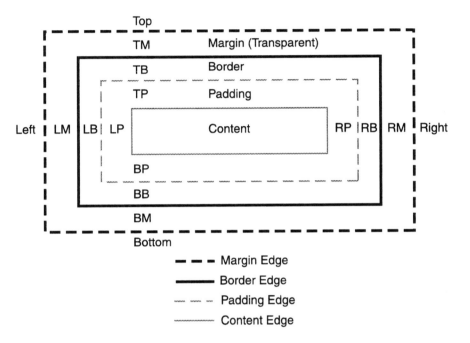

FIGURE 11-2   The Box Model as defined by the W3C.

Compare this figure with Figure 11-1, and imagine how the highlighted background of each box contains all these portions: margins, borders, padding, and the content area. Understanding this correlation will help you greatly as you proceed not only through this chapter, but also through chapters to come.

QUANTUM LEAP: THE BOX MODEL IN CSS DESIGN

You'll be spending all the remaining chapters working with aspects of the Box Model. Because CSS is used so much for visual styling, understanding the Box Model and the way it is both interpreted and misinterpreted in browsers becomes a key issue in how well you will learn and, in turn, apply CSS to your pages. As you'll find out in Chapter 12, "Positioning, Floats, and Z-index," the Box Model relates not only to how you style margins, borders, and padding, but also to how you use CSS as a positioning tool to achieve your layouts.

Using Margins

Margins are commonly styled to control the space between elements. You'll have noticed that there's always a certain amount of space, by default, around content displayed in web browsers (visible in Figure 11-1). This can be controlled by changing the margin values in the body element (see Example 11-1).

EXAMPLE 11-1 Setting margin values for the body element

```
body {font: 14px Verdana, Arial, Helvetica, sans-serif; color: white; background-
color: black; margin-top: 0; margin-left: 0; border: 2px solid white;}
h1 {font-size: 24px; color: orange;}
h2 {font: italic 20px Georgia, Times, serif; color: #999; text-indent: 15px;}
```

NOTE
You'll see that I have no length value such as px or em after my 0. That's because a 0 value requires no length; the meaning is implicit.

By setting the top and left margins to 0 in the body, the entire body element shifts, along with its children elements (see Figure 11-3).

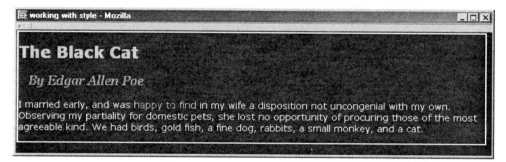

FIGURE 11-3 Zeroing the body margins to the top and left—notice the white border surrounding the body element and how it's flush to the top and left of the viewport.

Check out Figure 11-3 and notice how all the children elements are now flush left, with the exception of the h2, which has a `text-indent` property set to 15 pixels. But the h1 and paragraph elements, both children of the body with no other identified margins, are flush left and flush top. Or are they? What's the space between the h1 and the outline of the body element? Although the element is obviously flush top, the h1 is not. This is because Mozilla browsers expect a top margin value of 0 for the first element if you want it to be flush with the containing element's top margin. In Internet Explorer, this expectation is ignored and the same style results in the h1 also being flush left and top.

In Example 11-2, I created styles to even more dramatically demonstrate the use of margins with elements, including zeroing out the h1 element.

EXAMPLE 11-2   Setting a range of margins and values to demonstrate their use

```
body {font: 14px Verdana, Arial, Helvetica, sans-serif; color: white; background-
color: black; margin-top: 0; margin-right: 0; margin-bottom: 0; margin-left: 0;
border: 2px solid white;}
h1 {font-size: 24px; color: orange; margin-top: 0; margin-right: 100px; border:
2px solid green;}
h2 {font: italic 20px Georgia, Times, serif; color: #999; text-indent: 15px;}
p {margin-left: 100px; margin-top: 5px; margin-bottom: 0; border: 2px solid
yellow;}
```

Figure 11-4 shows how the margins are applied. I've slipped some borders in there to help visualize the margins. You'll learn more about borders later this chapter.

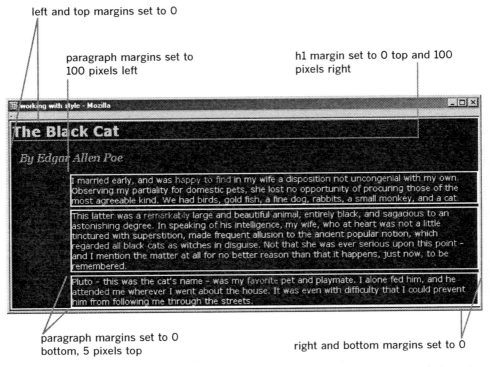

FIGURE 11-4   Applying margins to a range of elements including the body, h1, and paragraph elements.

Using Negative Margins

You can also use negative values with margins. This practice is helpful to achieve certain design needs, but it should be used with relative caution because browsers handle negative margins inconsistently.

Typically, negative margins are used to make visual adjustments, to manage workarounds for centering liquid designs in layout, or to offset specific elements outside the box in which they are contained (see Example 11-3).

EXAMPLE 11-3   Using negative margins to override a containing element

```
body {font: 14px Verdana, Arial, Helvetica, sans-serif; color: white; background-
color: black; margin-top: 30px; margin-right: 30px; margin-bottom: 30px; margin-
left: 130px; border: 2px solid white;}
p {margin-left: -65px; margin-top: 5px; margin-bottom: 0;}
```

Now the paragraph margins are offset to the body's left margin (see Figure 11-5).

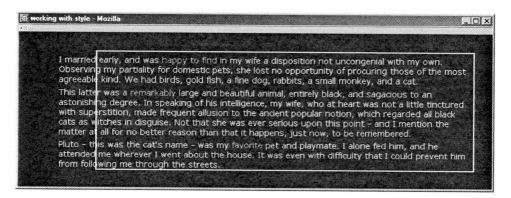

FIGURE 11-5   Using negative margins to override a containing block—in this case, the body element.

QUANTUM LEAP: NEGATIVE MARGIN SOLUTIONS FOR DESIGNERS

If you're interested in using negative margins to solve some known design issues, there are some terrific articles on the Web to help you out. "Creating Liquid Layouts with Negative Margins," by Ryan Brill, is terrific—read it now or hold off 'til you read the next two chapters (see http://www.alistapart.com/articles/negativemargins/). You can center elements using negative margins, too, as described by Rob Chandanais at http://www.bluerobot.com/web/css/center2.html. As with so many issues in CSS, the way browsers implement a property differs. Negative margins fall into this category because they are interpreted differently by different browsers. So use with care—and, as a good rule of thumb, if there's an easier way to accomplish the end result, use it.

Margin Shorthand

Margin properties have a shorthand counterpart using the `margin` property. You'll have noticed that CSS shorthand properties tend to have quirks of their own, such as the order of values. Margins are no exception to this.

Using the `margin` property, you set up the values for your margins in this *exact* order: top, right, bottom, left. The popular mnemonic for this in the industry is "TRouBLe." In Example 11-3, I'd set all the longhand properties for the body:

```
body {margin-top: 30px; margin-right: 30px; margin-bottom: 30px; margin-left: 130px;}
```

Although longhand doesn't require the specified margin order, I thought it would be helpful for you to see how this translates to shorthand:

```
body {margin: 30px 30px 30px 130px;}
```

You'll note that there are *no commas* separating each value, and the values will be applied in the exact TRBL order.

But wait, there's more. You can shorten your shorthand by relying on the fact that opposite side values automatically take their counterpart's value if they are not set:

```
Body {margin: 30px 20px}
```

That results in 30 pixels top and bottom, and 20 pixels right and left. So what happens when there are three values?

```
body {margin: 30px 20px 70px;}
```

The left value takes from the right, so this results in a margin of 30 pixels top, 20 pixels right, 70 pixels bottom, and 20 pixels left.

If all your margins are of equal size, simply use the value once:

```
body {margin: 100px;}
```

This results in a 100-pixel margin for all sides of the body element.

You also can use percentages as well as width values:

```
body {margin: 20%}
```

That results in a margin of 20% all the way around. Finally, remember that you do not need to define length or percentages if your value is 0:

```
body {margin: 0 30px 20px 0;}
```

Styling Borders

In the past chapters, you've seen me use borders to help you visualize CSS concepts. Here, I'll go into a bit more detail with you.

You can style borders based on their side, width, style, and color. Each of these uses a different border property: `border-width`, `border-style`, and `border-color`. You place the side of the border in between the two portions of the border property: `border-left-color`, `border-right-style`, and `border-top-width`. See the "Border Shorthand" section of this chapter for a more streamlined approach to border properties.

Border Width

Border widths can be specified using length values such as pixels or ems or keywords, which include `thin`, `medium`, and `thick`:

`border-bottom-width: 2px;`

`border-left-width: thick;`

Border Style

Here's where things get really fun. Currently eight style values will create a unique border, and two additional values are used for the `border-style` property (see Table 11-1).

TABLE 11-1 Border styles in CSS

Style	Effect
dotted	A series of dots
dashed	A series of dashes
solid	A solid line
double	Two solid lines
groove	A groove set into the canvas
ridge	A ridge coming out of the canvas
inset	An embedded appearance
outset	A raised appearance
hidden	Hidden border, which you can unhide using scripting
none	No border is ever visible

Here's a look at a border style property and value in action:

`border-right-style: dotted`

Border Color

Colors can be set using any of the available values: hex, hex shorthand, RGB values, RGB percentages, or supported color names:

```
border-top-color: #808080;
```

All Together Now!

Example 11-4 shows you how to use different combinations of border properties.

EXAMPLE 11-4 Combining border property styles

```
body {font: 14px Verdana, Arial, Helvetica, sans-serif; color: white; background-
color: black; margin-top: 0;}
h1 {font-size: 24px; color: orange; border-left-width: 3px; border-left-color:
red; border-left-style: dotted; border-bottom-width: thick;  border-bottom-color:
lime; border-bottom-style: inset;}
h2 {font: italic 20px Georgia, Times, serif; color: #999; text-indent: 15px;
border-bottom: thin; border-bottom-style: dotted; border-color: fuschia;}
p {border-left-width: medium; border-left-style: solid; border-left-color: blue;}
```

You can see all the border styles in use in Figure 11-6.

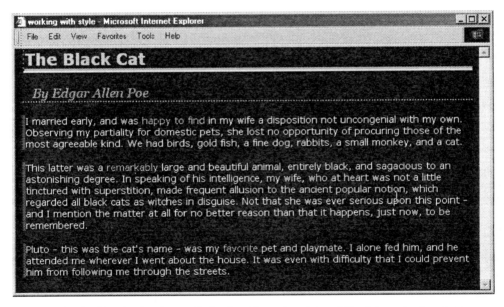

FIGURE 11-6 Applying borders to specific border sides and applying width, style, and color values.

Border Shorthand

Border shorthand is the most extended shorthand for a single property. You have several shorthand options.

Shorthand for Side, Width, Style, and Color

Each category of shorthand has corresponding shorthand, as follows:

```
border-right, border-left, border-top, border-bottom
```

```
border-width
```

```
border-style
```

```
border-color
```

So, you can write this:

```
border-right: 1px dotted red;
```

The property then causes the selected element to have a right border of 1 pixel, dotted, and of the color red.

The *border* Property

This shorthand property sets the width, style, and color for all four sides of the element in question:

```
border: thick ridge white;
```

In Figure 11-7, you can see the results for this.

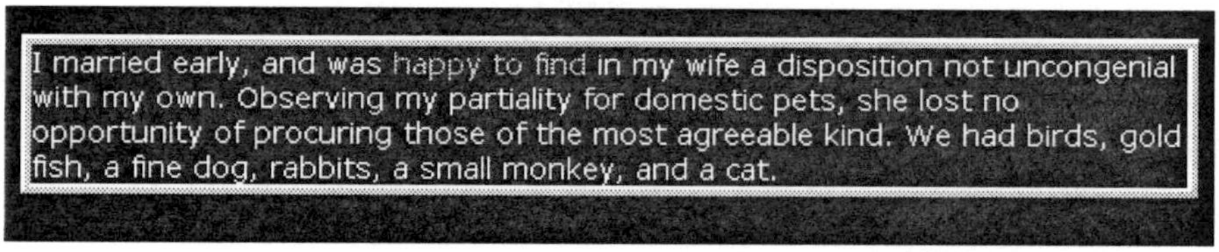

FIGURE 11-7   Using border shorthand.

NOTE

Unlike with margins (and padding), you cannot set differing widths in the `border` property itself. Also, if you want to style one border differently than the other three, just add another rule using that border's nonshorthand property, such as `border-right-width`.

Using Padding

Padding enables you to style the space that lies between the content and its border. In this chapter's previous examples, you'll notice elements that are flush against their borders and margins. Padding helps to solve this issue. You can add padding to an individual side using length values such as pixels or percentages. The individual padding properties are padding-top, padding-right, padding-bottom, and padding-left. You can see each of these in use in Example 11-5.

EXAMPLE 11-5 Using padding properties to add whitespace

```
body {font: 14px Verdana, Arial, Helvetica, sans-serif; color: white; background-
color: black; margin-top: 10px;}
h1 {font-size: 24px; color: orange; border-bottom: 2px dotted lime; padding-
bottom: 10px;}
h2 {font: italic 20px Georgia, Times, serif; color: #ccc; text-indent: 15px;}
p {border: thin solid orange; padding-top: 15px; padding-right: 30px; padding-
bottom: 0; padding-left: 30px;}
```

You'll notice the padding separating the h1 text from its border, and the padding to the top, right, bottom, and left of the paragraph (see Figure 11-8).

FIGURE 11-8 Adding padding to gain whitespace.

Padding Shorthand

You can use shorthand with padding, too, using the `padding` property. Shorthand for padding most closely resembles the way margin shorthand is managed.

This means that order is imperative, and you'll run into TRouBLe really quickly if you don't remember that! You must place your values in the top, right, bottom, left order for them to work:

```
p {padding: 15px 30px 25px 0;}
```

This rule results in a paragraph with 15 pixels of padding to the top, 30 pixels to the right, 25 pixels to the bottom, and 0 pixels to the left (see Figure 11-9).

FIGURE 11-9   Using the padding shorthand property to manage the padding of the paragraph.

You can also use combinations of two and three values, which work the same way as described for margin shorthand earlier this chapter. Finally, a single value applies to all four sides of the element's box.

Toward Gaining More Control...

Certainly, beginning to explore the Box Model and understand how elements work when CSS is added to the mix brings you even further along the road to gaining more control over your designs.

One area that I want to remind you of is having the correct document structure. Because of the DOCTYPE switching technology mentioned early on in this book, it becomes imperative to ensure that you are using a correct DOCTYPE, to make sure you don't have problems with the Box Model in IE 6.0.

If you've followed the methods in this book, you won't need to worry about it. See? There really is a method to my madness!

Next up, the holy grail of CSS: positioning. Are you ready? Let's go!

CHAPTER 12

Positioning, Floats, and Z-index

I
f you've been having a good time adding color, backgrounds, text styles, and margins to your pages, the fun has just begun. You'll be expanding your knowledge (which, at this point in the book should be quite sophisticated) to include the most significant aspects of CSS to be put to use in the past few years.

The combination of technologies you'll be working with in this chapter will provide you with the basis for what you need to know about creating great CSS-based layouts, instead of the table-based ones discussed so often in this book. Fortunately, contemporary browsers have enough CSS support—and we have enough knowledge of workarounds—to apply these techniques to create great-looking pages.

Positioning refers to the scheme in CSS that enables you to use elements to create boxes and move them around in relation to the document and browser. You'll learn what these schemes are and how to begin applying them.

Float refers to a CSS technique that places an element to the right or left. The text in the document can then flow around that element. This is likely to be most familiar to you in the context of images. You can float an image to the right, and the text will flow around the image. Add a little padding, and you've got a great look.

The use of floating has expanded to include floating div elements, allowing for the use of floated boxes for navigation or, even more adventuresome, the creation of multiple columns that can be used with or without positioning in the design of various layouts.

A z-index serves as a means to place element boxes along the z-axis. So far, I've discussed only the x- and y-axes, with x being horizontal and y being vertical. The z-axis provides the third dimension.

Think of it this way: Hold up a deck of cards in front of you. The order in which the cards appear from the closest one to you to the farthest one away is a good way to think of the z-index. Using it, you can literally stack items on top of one another and offset them. This is somewhat useful in layouts and to create effects, but the use of the z-index usually comes into play when combined with JavaScript. It's an interesting aspect of CSS, so you'll get to play with it a bit here, too. Okay, then—on with the show!

Getting into Position

By now, you know I'm just a wee bit interested in details. I feel it's very important that you learn the why as well as the how of things. So before I show you how to position elements, I want to go over some terminology and concepts important when working with positioning. Surely you're itching to start positioning elements and working with layouts, but bear with me. I assure you, there *is* method to my madness.

First off, it's important to remember that CSS positioning is a part of CSS, not something separate from it. Many people do refer to positioning as a separate concept, calling it CSS-P or other terms, but it's not a separate part of CSS.

In fact, positioning is really at the heart of CSS—it's the piece that gives you ultimate control over the visual results of a page. The separation is a false one, which grew mainly out of the fact that positioning wasn't well supported and, thus, was mostly unusable until the past few years.

We're past that now, fortunately, and can begin to look at positioning in earnest. Are there flaws still within browsers? You bet there are, and I'll be discussing some of them in this chapter and the next one.

To best prepare you to quickly grasp what some have spent years trying to clarify, I'll be using some terms to describe these positions and what they mean. The biggest part of the hurdle for many people who want to use CSS as a means of laying out pages is that the terminology is sometimes confusing, misleading, or downright unclear.

The CSS positioning scheme allows for four types of positioning, as follows:

- Absolute
- Relative
- Static
- Fixed

Positioning can make use of the offsets top, bottom, left, and right to position the box with specific values.

You'll learn the details of how each of these works as you go through the chapter. But first, here's a bit about *normal flow, containing blocks*, and *the browser viewport*. It's a little dry, I suppose, but it's necessary to discuss nonetheless.

Normal Flow

The term *normal flow* refers to the normal behavior of the browser. As you've surely noticed, everything defaults to the left of the browser unless otherwise modified by HTML or CSS. Consider Example 12-1.

EXAMPLE 12-1   Unstyled content to help visualize normal flow in a browser

```
<!DOCTYPE html PUBLIC "-//W3C//DTD XHTML 1.0 Transitional//EN"
          "http://www.w3.org/TR/xhtml1/DTD/xhtml1-transitional.dtd">

<html xmlns="http://www.w3.org/1999/xhtml">
<head>
<title>working with style</title>
</head>

<body>
<h1>The Black Cat</h1>
<h2>By Edgar Allen Poe</h2>
<p>I married early, and was <a href="http://www.poemuseum.org/">happy to find</a>
in my wife a disposition not uncongenial with my own. Observing my partiality for
domestic pets, she lost no opportunity of procuring those of the most agreeable
kind. We had birds, gold fish, a fine dog, rabbits, a small monkey, and a cat.</p>

<p>This latter was a <a href="http://www.poemuseum.org/">remarkably</a> large and
beautiful animal, entirely black, and sagacious to an astonishing degree. In
speaking of his intelligence, my wife, who at heart was not a little tinctured
with superstition, made frequent allusion to the ancient popular notion, which
regarded all black cats as witches in disguise. Not that she was ever serious
upon this point - and I mention the matter at all for no better reason than that
it happens, just now, to be remembered.</p>
</body>
</html>
```

Because you already have an understanding of the box model, you now can visualize how each block element (the headers and paragraphs) are stacked on top of one another and flow normally to the left.

The inline elements (the links) go with the flow. If you resized the browser, they would simply reflow to their new position without breaking the line.

Figure 12-1 shows how the document appears in a browser window, and Figure 12-2 shows that browser upon resizing. You'll see how the text adjusts to the available space, always flowing to the left.

After looking at these examples, try it out: Open a simple document with no tables or CSS positioning, and size and resize your browser. What you're observing is the normal flow of elements within that browser.

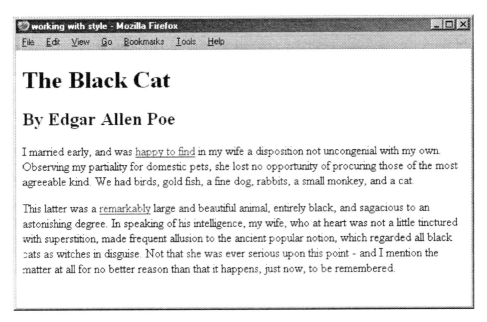

FIGURE 12-1   Unstyled document in the normal flow.

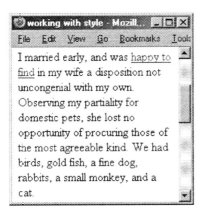

FIGURE 12-2   Resizing the browser reflows the text to the left.

Containing Blocks

Another important concept when working with CSS positioning is the *containing block*. A containing block is any parent block box to the element you're trying to position. Consider Example 12-2.

EXAMPLE 12-2   Understanding containing blocks

```
<div id="content">
<h1>The Black Cat</h1>
<h2>By Edgar Allen Poe</h2>

<p>I married early, and was <a href="http://www.poemuseum.org/">happy to find</a>
in my wife a disposition not uncongenial with my own. Observing my partiality for
domestic pets, she lost no opportunity of procuring those of the most agreeable
kind. We had birds, gold fish, a fine dog, rabbits, a small monkey, and a cat.</p>

<p>This latter was a <a href="http://www.poemuseum.org/">remarkably</a> large and
beautiful animal, entirely black, and sagacious to an astonishing degree. In
speaking of his intelligence, my wife, who at heart was not a little tinctured
with superstition, made frequent allusion to the ancient popular notion, which
regarded all black cats as witches in disguise. Not that she was ever serious
upon this point - and I mention the matter at all for no better reason than that
it happens, just now, to be remembered.</p>
</div>
```

As you see, I've placed all the content into a div element, which I've given an id of content (how's that for brilliant?) All the blocks within the content div are now *contained* by the div.

Suppose you went a step further and placed a container around the content:

```
<div id="main">
<div id="content">
...
</div>
</div>
```

The content div is now contained by the main div, which becomes the content div's containing box.

That's pretty simple so far, I think. But if you're having trouble visualizing this, think about those lacquered Chinese boxes that come nested one inside the other. The largest box contains the middle box, which contains the small box. So, the small box's containing block is the middle box, whose containing box is the large box.

It's important to understand this concept because when you begin to use positioning, the containing block of an element can have a lot to do with how the element or elements it contains are actually positioned.

Step back for a moment to Example 12-1. There's no obvious containing block, is there? Will you be surprised if I tell you that there's still a containing block? Here's how it works: If there is no specified containing block, the containing block is the *root element*. We know that the root element is html, so that's the containing block.

QUANTUM LEAP: BROWSER DEFAULTS

Why does it matter that html is the containing block when no other is specified? In the sense of positioning, it matters because there are browser default styles for many elements, including html. I discussed this a bit in Chapter 7, "Using CSS." Each browser has a default style sheet so that if you do not apply styles, some visual styling will still occur. This is why, without style, headers, paragraphs, links, and more still have a font, font size, and weight. When working with positioning, it's going to look as if certain positioned boxes are positioned in relation to the browser edges (also known as *chrome*). In reality, the positioning of certain uncontained blocks is due to the default styles given to the html element.

For Figure 12-3, I simply styled the html element to have a 2-pixel border. You can see how different browsers interpret the html element.

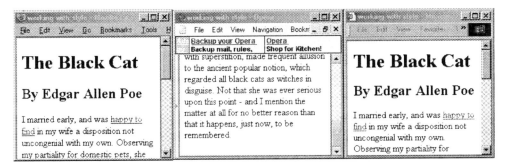

FIGURE 12-3   From left to right: Firefox, Opera, and Internet Explorer 6.0—note how Firefox and Opera interpret the html element and its styled borders within the document, whereas, in IE, the bottom and left portions of the element include portions of the browser such as the scrollbar.

IE's implementation is quirky, although not incorrect, because the specs are not very clear regarding how browsers should implement containing blocks. That's all the more reason to understand the why of positioning as well as the application of positioning.

The Browser Viewport

The *browser viewport* is the window in the browser through which the document content is viewed. This is a fairly simple concept, but, again, it's a distinct one from containing blocks.

In positioning, in some cases, element boxes are positioned in relation to the viewport and not normal flow or containing blocks. So understanding the viewport is important (see Figure 12-4).

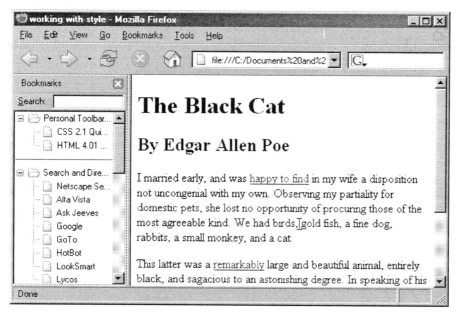

FIGURE 12-4   The Firefox browser with sidebar, menus, and status bar—the viewport is *only* the window through which you're seeing the document.

NOTE

It is considered conventional browser behavior to include a scrollbar in the viewport when the content is longer or wider than the available viewport space. Browsers behave differently in this regard, partly because the guidelines are not very specific when it comes to how browsers should ideally behave. As a result, there will be inconsistencies in the way users experience your designs, no matter what techniques you use.

Absolute Positioning: To the Root Element

Okay, enough terminology. It's time to have some fun and actually put positioning to work! Absolute positioning positions an element box *in relation to its containing block*. When you position something absolutely, you take it completely *out of the normal flow*. In easy terms, this means that any box you position will always be positioned to either its explicit container or to the html root element (not the viewport), no matter what other content might be on the page.

Oh, good! Now you get to see why I had to spend time up front to detail the terminology. In Example 12-3, I've placed a header and a paragraph into a containing block, and then positioned the block to an offset of 100 pixels from the left and 50 pixels from the top.

EXAMPLE 12-3   Absolutely positioning a block to the root element

```
<!DOCTYPE html PUBLIC "-//W3C//DTD XHTML 1.0 Transitional//EN"
          "http://www.w3.org/TR/xhtml1/DTD/xhtml1-transitional.dtd">
<html xmlns="http://www.w3.org/1999/xhtml">
<head>
<title>working with style</title>
<style type="text/css">
#content {
          position: absolute;
          left: 100px;
          top: 50px;
          border: 1px solid red;
          }
</style>
</head>
<body>
<div id="content">
<h1>The Black Cat</h1>
<p>I married early, and was <a href="http://www.poemuseum.org/">happy to find</a>
in my wife a disposition not uncongenial with my own. Observing my partiality for
comestic pets, she lost no opportunity of procuring those of the most agreeable
kind. We had birds, gold fish, a fine dog, rabbits, a small monkey, and a cat.</p>
</div>
</body>
</html>
```

Because there's no other containing block explicitly defined, the block will be positioned to the root element of html. I placed a screen shot that excluded any browser chrome in Photoshop so you can see how the box is now positioned *absolutely* to its containing block (see Figure 12-5). Figure 12-6 shows the same box in relation to other page elements.

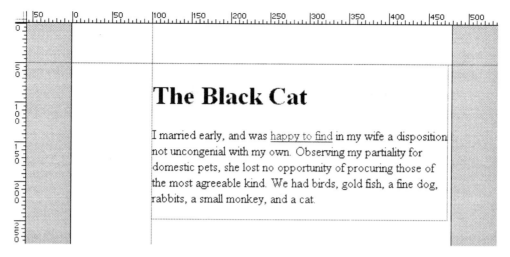

FIGURE 12-5 Absolutely positioning the `content` `div`.

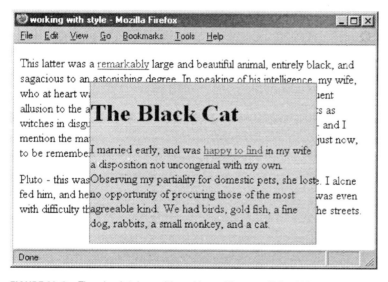

FIGURE 12-6 The absolutely positioned box with an explicit width—content flows within the box, which remains positioned despite other document elements, making it crystal clear what is meant by an absolute box being completely removed from the normal flow.

Absolute Positioning: To Another Block

Returning to the earlier example in which I described a containing block for the content block, you can move on to see how an absolutely positioned block is positioned only in relation to its containing block (see Example 12-4).

EXAMPLE 12-4   Absolutely positioning a block to its containing block

```
<!DOCTYPE html PUBLIC "-//W3C//DTD XHTML 1.0 Transitional//EN"
        "http://www.w3.org/TR/xhtml1/DTD/xhtml1-transitional.dtd">
<html xmlns="http://www.w3.org/1999/xhtml">
<head>
<title>working with style</title>
<style type="text/css">
#main {
        position: absolute;
        left: 50px;
        top: 20px;
        border: 1px solid green;
        }
#content {
        position: absolute;
        left: 100px;
        top: 50px;
        width: 300px;
        border: 1px solid red;
        background-color: #ccc;
        }
ul, li, a {
        list-style-type: none;
        display: inline;
        text-decoration: none;
        }
</style>
</head>
<body>
<div id="main">
<div id="nav">
<ul>
<li><a href="home.html">Home</a></li>
<li><a href="products.html">Products</a></li>
<li><a href="services.html">Services</a></li>
<li><a href="about.html">About Us</a></li>
<li><a href="contact.html">Contact</a></li>
</ul>
</div>
<div id="content">
<h1>The Black Cat</h1>
```

```
<p>I married early, and was <a href="http://www.poemuseum.org/">happy to find</a>
in my wife a disposition not uncongenial with my own. Observing my partiality for
domestic pets, she lost no opportunity of procuring those of the most agreeable
kind. We had birds, gold fish, a fine dog, rabbits, a small monkey, and a cat.</p>
  </div>
  </div>
  </body>
  </html>
```

Here, the containing block main is absolutely positioned 50 pixels from the left and 20
pixels from the top. The navigation block isn't positioned at all, but it is contained within
the main and, therefore, flows normally within its block. I've provided some minimal
style so you can see this coming together. Finally, the content div is absolutely positioned. Watch what happens (see Figure 12-7).

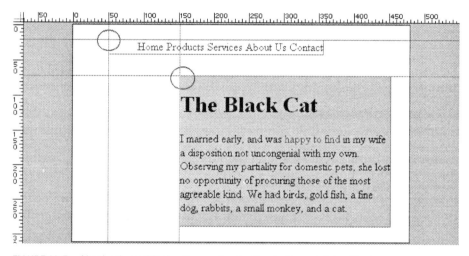

FIGURE 12-7 Absolutely positioning the content div to its containing block.

Note the two circles in the image. The first one highlights the starting point of the containing block, main. The second highlights the starting point of the content block. Notice
how the content block is positioned to the containing block: 100 pixels in from the left of
the containing block, 50 pixels from the top of the containing block.

The box now sits 150 pixels from the left and 70 pixels from the top. The reason is clearly
because it's being positioned in relation to the position of its containing block, not the
html element or the browser viewport.

NOTE

A containing block does not have to be positioned absolutely. The positioning
scheme as described remains in effect no matter what the position type is: An
absolutely positioned box *always* is positioned to its containing block, and it is
always removed from the normal flow, with no exceptions.

Relative Positioning

As mentioned, the terminology used in CSS positioning is a bit vague. Relative positioning is often confusing at first because it begs the question: Relative to what? Most people automatically—and quite logically—think that the position would be relative to another element.

But it's not (you knew that was coming). Relatively positioned boxes are positioned to the *normal flow*. This means that they are not removed from the normal flow the way an absolutely positioned box is. Here, I've removed all margins using the universal selector (*); this is to get rid of all default whitespace so you can see exactly how the relative positioning is being measured (see Example 12-5).

EXAMPLE 12-5   Relative positioning

```
<!DOCTYPE html PUBLIC "-//W3C//DTD XHTML 1.0 Transitional//EN"
        "http://www.w3.org/TR/xhtml1/DTD/xhtml1-transitional.dtd">
<html xmlns="http://www.w3.org/1999/xhtml">
<head>
<title>working with style</title>
<style type="text/css">
* {margin: 0;}
#content {
        position: relative;
        left: 45px;
        top: 10px;
        width: 400px;
        border: 1px solid red;
        }
</style>
</head>

<body>
<h1>The Black Cat</h1>
<p>I married early, and was <a href="http://www.poemuseum.org/">happy to find</a>
in my wife a disposition not uncongenial with my own. Observing my partiality for
domestic pets, she lost no opportunity of procuring those of the most agreeable
kind. We had birds, gold fish, a fine dog, rabbits, a small monkey, and a cat.</p>
<div id="content">
<p>This latter was a <a href="http://www.poemuseum.org/">remarkably</a> large and
beautiful animal, entirely black, and sagacious to an astonishing degree. In
speaking of his intelligence, my wife, who at heart was not a little tinctured
with superstition, made frequent allusion to the ancient popular notion, which
regarded all black cats as witches in disguise. Not that she was ever serious
upon this point - and I mention the matter at all for no better reason than that
it happens, just now, to be remembered.</p>
</div>
```

```
<p>Pluto - this was the cat's name - was my <a
href="http://www.poemuseum.org/">favorite</a> pet and playmate. I alone fed him,
and he attended me wherever I went about the house. It was even with difficulty
that I could prevent him from following me through the streets.</p>
</body>
</html>
```

Figure 12-8 shows how the `content` `div` is now positioned relative to the *normal flow* of
the document, not any other boxes.

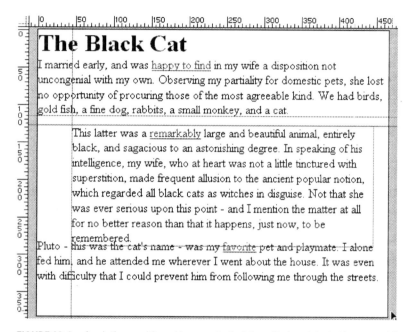

FIGURE 12-8 A relative positioned box—note that the offsets relate to the normal flow, not any other
element.

So, the box is offset 10 pixels from the earlier element box and 45 pixels to the left of the
flow—exactly the same place where the text begins because it's in the normal flow, too.
You see that the flow is uninterrupted by the positioning; the ensuing content flows as it
should both before and after the relatively positioned box.

NOTE

Relative positioning is used when the normal flow shouldn't be broken. Absolute
positioning is best used for items that have to be positioned very specifically. Often
the two are combined, such as having a relatively positioned `div` with an absolutely
positioned `div` contained within it, or vice versa. You'll see more of this in action in
Chapter 13, "CSS Layouts."

Fixed Positioning

Fixed positioning is a brilliant piece of CSS. Now you know that if I'm starting off a section like that, I'm giving you the good news first to soften the blow. Because as brilliant as fixed positioning is, it's not supported in Internet Explorer and, as such, can be used only for Mozilla, Opera, Safari, and other browsers that do support it. Phooey!

Fixed positioning enables you to fix a box anywhere on the page. Unlike absolute positioning, fixed elements are positioned in relation to the *viewport* (you *knew* that just had to be somewhere in this chapter). Look at Example 12-6.

EXAMPLE 12-6   Fixed positioning

```
<style type="text/css">
#nav {
          position: fixed;
          left: 0px;
          top: 0px;
          background: #ccc;
          width: 100%;
          }
ul, li, a {
          list-style-type: none;
          display: inline;
          text-decoration: none;
          padding-left: 3px;
          padding-right: 3px;
          }
</style>
```

So check out what I just did. By positioning the nav div to 0 left and 0 top, adding a gray background, and setting my width to 100%, I oh-so-cleverly made my navigation look pretty darned close to a standard menu, just as you'd find in the browser itself (see Figure 12-9).

NOTE

Although IE 6.0 doesn't support the fixed scheme, it doesn't entirely disallow you from using it. You'll get the positioned box, but it will scroll off along with the rest of the content instead of remaining fixed in place.

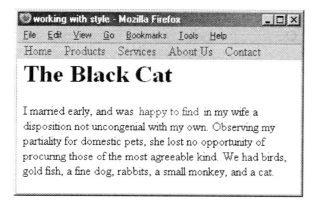

FIGURE 12-9   A fixed-position navigation bar.

In browsers that support fixed positioning, this menu will remain fixed no matter what else moves. So, if I scroll the content, it will disappear under the menu (see Figure 12-10).

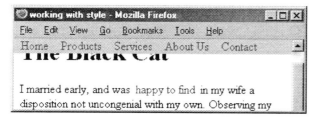

FIGURE 12-10   The content scrolls beneath the fixed-position nav.

You can see why I'm frustrated by IE's lack of support for fixed positioning—what a useful positioning scheme.

NOTE

Static positioning is the fourth positioning type. It simply positions a box in the normal flow and, because of that, is rarely used. You can think of using static positioning as similar to using the `text-align: left;` property and value. It's the default behavior, so it is used only to override an earlier rule. You'll rarely see static position in use as a result.

Floating Elements

As mentioned in the chapter's introduction, floating is *not* a positioning scheme. It gets confused with positioning sometimes because it can be used alone or with positioned boxes to create layouts.

The reason floating was introduced in CSS at all wasn't for layout, per se. The intent was to be able to float elements, particularly images, and have content flow around the image (see Example 12-7).

EXAMPLE 12-7   Floating an image

```
<style type="text/css">
img {
        float: right;
        padding: 15px;
        }
</style>
```

Figure 12-11 shows the results. I've added styles to spice up the look.

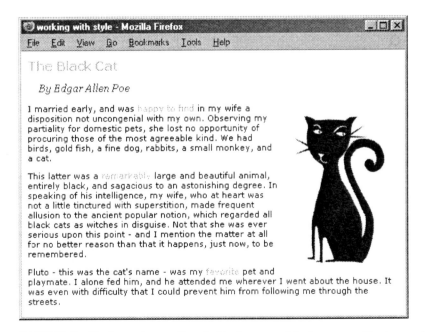

FIGURE 12-11   Floating an image allows text to flow around the image, resulting in a sophisticated look.

Just as you can float an `img` element, you can float any element. So, if your navigation is in a `div` and you want to float that element, you can do so (see Example 12-8).

EXAMPLE 12-8   Floating a `div`

```
#nav {
          float: right;
          border: 1px solid red;
          padding-right: 20px;
          padding-top: 10px;
          margin-left: 10px;
          }
```

Figure 12-12 shows how the nav `div` and the elements it contains are now floated to the right, just as the image would be. By doing this, you've actually created a floating navigation system that you can style to your heart's content.

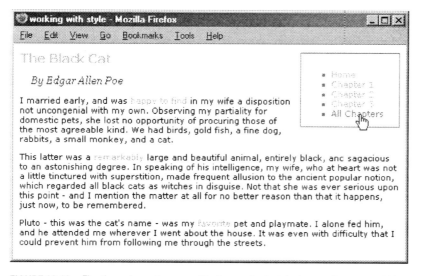

FIGURE 12-12   Floating a box—the nav `div` is now floated, just as an image would be.

You can now quite easily imagine how floats can be used for laying out portions of a document.

Clearing Floats

Clearing a float means clearing away all subsequent content so that the element is still floated but is not surrounded by the other elements. The `clear` property takes a value of `left`, `right`, or `both`. By adding the `clear: right;` property to the content division, the floating navigation remains in place, but the text is cleared (see Figure 12-13).

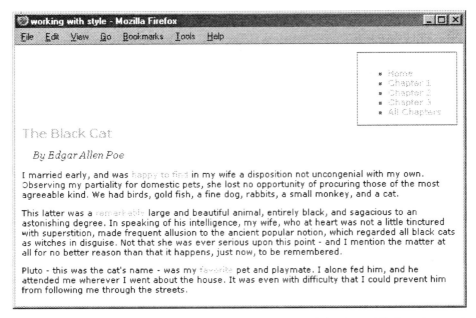

FIGURE 12-13   Clearing a float allows the floated element to remain in place, while the subsequent content is cleared from around it.

I created two floating boxes in Example 12-9.

EXAMPLE 12-9   Styling two floating boxes, one to the left and one to the right

```
#nav {float: right; border: 1px solid red; padding-right: 20px;   padding-top: 10px;
         margin-left: 10px;}

#nav2 {float: left; border: 1px solid red; padding-right: 20px;   padding-top:
10px;
         margin-right: 10px;}
```

Figure 12-14 shows what happens when I don't use a `clear` property for the content.

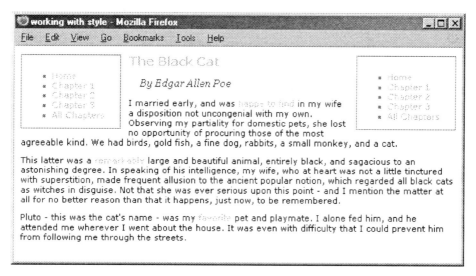

FIGURE 12-14 Without a clear, the content flows normally with the floated boxes.

I added a clear: both to the content style (see Figure 12-15).

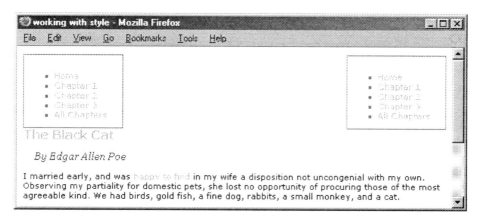

FIGURE 12-15 Clearing both the left and right floated boxes.

Interesting, eh? You can see the beginnings of columns. You'll be working with floated columns in Chapter 13.

Z-index

The z-index creates the dimensional axis upon which you can "stack" and overlap items. This comes in handy in positioning because you can use it to determine which boxes come to the foreground and which ones will flow behind upon browser resize. Other uses for the z-index relate mostly to DHTML, in which element boxes are scripted for dynamic purposes such as when creating animations or games.

Example 12-10 shows three boxes, each absolutely positioned to overlap one another and styled in such a way that you can visualize the stacking order.

EXAMPLE 12-10   Z-index with positioned boxes

```
#box1 {
         position: absolute;
         top: 10px;
         left: 10px;
         background: #000;
         width: 300px;
         height: 200px;
         z-index: 1;
         }

#box2 {
         position: absolute;
         top: 20px;
         left: 20px;
         background: #999;
         width: 300px;
         height: 200px;
         z-index: 2;
         }

#box3 {
         position: absolute;
         top: 30px;
         left: 30px;
         background: #ccc;
         width: 300px;
         height: 200px;
         z-index: 3;
         }
```

You'll note that the higher the number is, the "closer" the box appears in the stack. So, a box with a z-index of 3 appears to be the closest to you in the stack (see Figure 12-16).

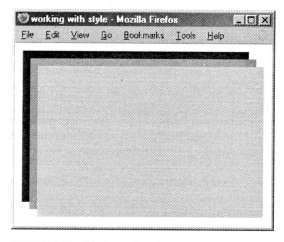

FIGURE 12-16 Z-index and stacking order—the higher the integer value is, the closer to you in the stack the element appears.

Just Like a Pro...

If it's taking a bit of time to get the concepts in this chapter down, please don't fret. These are some of the most complicated, confusing, and challenging aspects of CSS.

There's really no way to comfort you if you are having a bit of trouble, other than to say that you must give it time. No one learns this stuff overnight—and if you have, well, you're ready for prime time!

It takes constant practice and play to really get the hang of working with positioning; it's simply part of the nature of the CSS beast.

Of course, the rewards are richly worth it. As you'll find out in the next chapter, everything in this chapter will come together—at least, conceptually—when you begin to study layouts. After that, you'll want to practice, practice, practice to really get your skills as finely honed as a pro's.

CHAPTER 13

CSS Layouts

The past few years, people have sought a means to transcend all the problems related to table-based layouts and use CSS specifically for managing the visual layouts of their designs. In this chapter, you get a chance to work with the primary types of layouts in CSS that are typically used to achieve a range of design. Some of these layouts are based on positioning schemes, which you explored in Chapter 12, "Positioning, Floats, and Z-index." Some of the layouts use floats, which, you'll recall, are not a positioning scheme but do enable you to create columnar layouts. The combination of floating and positioning is common as well, and you'll get to see examples of that in action.

NOTE

For the purposes of clarity, I'm going to teach you how to create these designs in their most pure form. This means that I'm leaving out a number of popular hacks that might be necessary for you to implement, depending upon your browser base. Without the hacks, these designs will work very well in the browsers described in Table 13-1.

TABLE 13-1 Browser Support for CSS Layouts in This Chapter

Browser	OS	Version
Internet Explorer	Windows	6.0
Mozilla	All available	1.x+
Netscape	All available	6.x+
Firefox	All available	All
Opera	All available	6.x+
Safari	Macintosh	1.x+

All contemporary browsers in use will have no trouble with these layouts. The need for hacks or workarounds comes in when you have to support browsers outside this list, particularly Internet Explorer versions 5.0 and 5.5 for Windows, all IE versions for Macintosh, and Netscape earlier than 6.0; all have incorrect or partial implementation of the portions of CSS required.

Three Columns with Fixed Flanking Menus

One of the most desirable layouts for websites is a three-column layout with the flanking columns fixed to a specific width and the inside of the column fluid (see Figure 13-1).

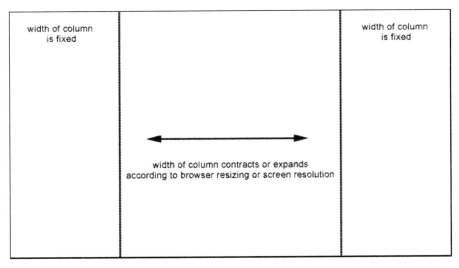

FIGURE 13-1   Three-column layout with fixed flanks and fluid center column.

Creating this layout involves using absolute positioning to position the left and right columns. You then give these explicit widths in pixels (that's how they become fixed). The trick here is to leave a width out of the center column so that it remains fluid and expands or contracts according to available space (see Example 13-1).

EXAMPLE 13-1   Three-column layout with fixed flanks and fluid center

```
<style type="text/css">
#nav {position: absolute; left: 10px; top: 50px; width: 200px;}
#content {margin-left: 200px; margin-right: 200px; margin-top: 10px;}
#sidebar {position: absolute; right: 10px; top: 10px; width: 200px;}
</style>
```

You'll notice that the #content div has left and right margins. The numeric value of these should be adjusted to accommodate any padding or borders you add to the columns themselves. The top margin is there just for visual balance, and you'll see that there's no width whatsoever. Figure 13-2 shows a page laid out using this technique with additional styles for the text, whitespace, and imagery. Figure 13-3 shows the same page resized, so you can see how the content will flow into the available space.

FIGURE 13-2 Fixed flanking columns with a fluid center column.

The Black Cat

By Edgar Allen Poe

I married early, and was happy to find in my wife a disposition not uncongenial with my own. Observing my partiality for domestic pets, she lost no opportunity of procuring those of the most agreeable kind. We had birds, gold fish, a fine dog, rabbits, a small monkey, and a cat.

FIGURE 13-3 Here you see how the text will reflow upon browser resizing.

NOTE

If you want to fix the center column, you can do so by adding an explicit width. However, on browser resize, columns will overlap.

NOTE

The templates are available at www.phptr.com/title/0131855867.

Three Columns with Masthead and Footer

Another very desirable layout is a three-column layout with a masthead and a footer (see Figure 13-4).

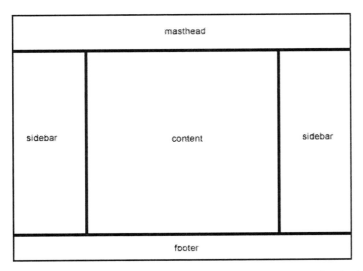

FIGURE 13-4 A sophisticated three-column layout with a masthead and a footer.

This layout uses floats, not positioning, to achieve the desired results (see Example 13-2).

EXAMPLE 13-2 Using floats for layout

```
<style type="text/css">
#masthead {width: 768px;}
#nav {float: left; width: 200px;}
#content {float: left; width: 368px;}
#sidebar {float: left; width: 200px;}
#footer {width: 768px; clear: both;}
</style>
```

This is a fixed-width layout, which means that none of the columns will dynamically change width-wise. Notice how the columns are simply all floated to the left, placing them one after another along the horizon. You'll also note that the #footer div uses the clear property with a value of both. This ensures that the footer completely clears the floated columns (see Figure 13-5).

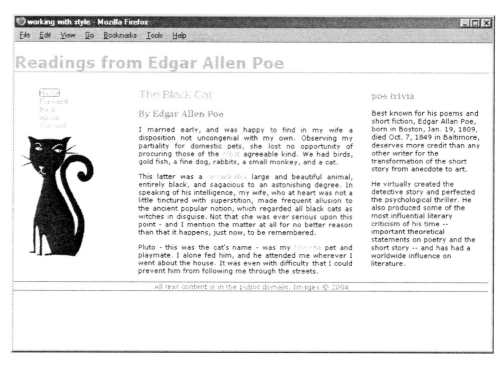

FIGURE 13-5   A three-column, fixed layout with a masthead and a footer.

You can make a fluid version of this layout simply by using percentages instead of fixed widths (see Example 13-3).

EXAMPLE 13-3   Using percentages to create a fluid version

```
<style type="text/css">
#masthead {width: 100%;}
#nav {float: left; width: 20%;}
#content {float: left; width: 60%;}
#sidebar {float: left; width: 20%;}
#footer {width: 100%; clear: both;}
</style>
```

NOTE

"Containing Floats" is an excellent article on working with floats from CSS expert Eric Meyer; see http://www.complexspiral.com/publications/containing-floats/.

Nested Float

A very simple but useful layout is the nested float. This layout floats a box within the main content area. You can then use this box for navigation, imagery, or whatever your preference (see Figure 13-6).

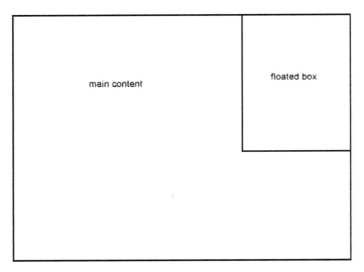

main content

floated box

FIGURE 13-6   Floated box within a content section.

Example 13-4 shows how this layout is achieved.

EXAMPLE 13-4   Nested float layout

```
<style type="text/css">
#content {margin: 10px; border: 1px solid orange;}
#content #nav {float: right; width: 150px; border: 1px solid orange; margin-left:
5px;}
</style>
```

I gave the content a margin and a border so you can visualize it better. To achieve the nested float, I used a descendant selector of #content #nav and then floated the nav within the #content to the right. The margin-left value adds a little whitespace between the border and the text. A very important issue is that when you write the HTML for this (which you can see in the template itself), the nav div *must be nested* inside the #content div:

```
div id="content">
<div id="nav">
<ul>
```

```
<li><a href="home.html">Home</a></li>
<li><a href="poe3.html">Forward</a></li>
<li><a href="poe1.html">Back</a></li>
<li><a href="about.html">About</a></li>
<li><a href="contact.html">Contact</a></li>
</ul>
</div>
<h1>The Black Cat</h1>
<h2>By Edgar Allen Poe</h2>
<p>I married early, and was happy to find in my wife a disposition not uncongenial
with my own. Observing my partiality for domestic pets, she lost no opportunity of
procuring those of the <a href="http://vig.prenhall.com/">most</a>
agreeable kind. We had birds, gold fish, a fine dog, rabbits, a small monkey,
and a cat.</p>   . . .
</div>
```

As you can see in Figure 13-7, I used additional styles (as I have been doing) to achieve
the decorative aspects of the design.

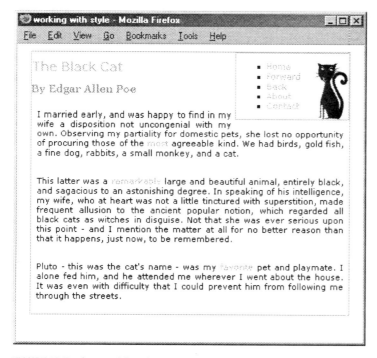

FIGURE 13-7 A nested float layout—simple, but very useful.

Centered Designs

An extremely popular layout technique is to center a fixed design along the horizon. This means that the design will always be centered, and whitespace will flow evenly to the right and the left (see Figure 13-8).

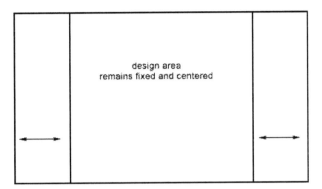

FIGURE 13-8   Fixed, centered layout.

Accomplishing this is somewhat challenging because of the way that elements are centered horizontally in CSS. A number of centering options exist. I'm going to use what's known as the negative-margin approach to horizontal centering. Although it's not the preferred method according to CSS best practices, it is the most supported across browsers (see Example 13-5).

EXAMPLE 13-5   A fixed, centered design

```
<style type="text/css">
#container {position: absolute; left: 50%; width: 400px; margin-left: -200px;
border: 1px solid orange;}
#content {margin-top: 75px;}
#nav {position: fixed; top: 0; width: 400px; border-top: 1px solid orange; border-
bottom: 1px solid orange;}
</style>
```

To accomplish the layout, you first create a container div, which will then be absolutely positioned. The content, navigation, and any other design components within the centered portion of the design are placed into the container. The negative margin moves the container right into the middle of positioning offset. Figure 13-9 shows the results. I also added a fixed navigation and some additional styles for fun.

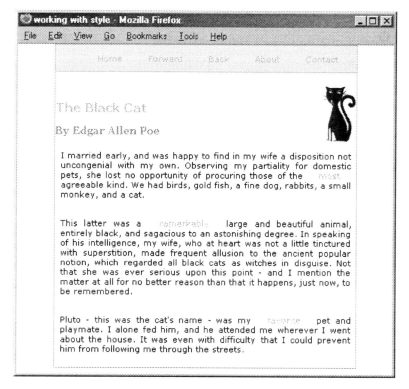

FIGURE 13-9　Fixed, centered design—an extremely popular layout.

If you'd like to create a design that is centered but has fluid flow within the content, you can do so by switching to percentage values (see Example 13-6).

EXAMPLE 13-6　A fluid, centered design

```
#container {position: absolute; left: 50%; margin-left: -200px; border: 1px solid
orange;}
#content {margin-top: 75px;}
#nav {position: fixed; top: 0; border-top: 1px solid orange; border-bottom: 1px
solid orange;}
```

Complex Layouts

Now the task before you is to begin combining techniques to come out with more advanced layouts. A good example is a fixed, centered design with three columns. If you're thinking you'd mix the positioning technique for centered, fixed designs with floats for the columns, go to the head of the class! Example 13-7 shows how.

EXAMPLE 13-7   Complex layout with centering, positioning, and floats

```
"http://www.w3.org/TR/xhtml1/DTD/xhtml1-transitional.dtd">
     <html xmlns="http://www.w3.org/1999/xhtml">
<head>
<title>working with style</title>
<style type="text/css">
#container {position: absolute; left: 50%; margin-left: -300px; width: 600px;
margin-top: 10px;}
#masthead {width: 600px;}
#nav {float: left; width: 150px;}
#content {float: left; width: 290px; margin-right: 5px; margin-left: 5px;}
#sidebar {float: right; width: 140px; margin-right: 10px;}
#footer {clear: both; width: 600px;}
</style>
<link rel="stylesheet" type="text/css" href="layout.css">
</head>
<body>
<div id="container">
<div id="masthead">
<h1>Readings from Edgar Allen Poe</h1>
</div>
<div id="nav">
<ul>
<li><a href="home.html">Home</a></li>
<li><a href="poe3.html">Forward</a></li>
<li><a href="poe1.html">Back</a></li>
<li><a href="about.html">About</a></li>
<li><a href="contact.html">Contact</a></li>
</ul>
</div>
<div id="content">
<h1>The Black Cat</h1>
<h2>By Edgar Allen Poe</h2>
<p>I married early, and was happy to find in my wife a disposition not uncongenial
with my own. Observing my partiality for domestic pets, she lost no opportunity
of procuring those of the <a href="http://vig.prenhall.com/">most</a> agreeable
kind. We had birds, gold fish, a fine dog, rabbits, a small monkey, and a cat.</p>
<p>This latter was a <a href="http://vig.prenhall.com/">remarkably</a> large and
beautiful animal, entirely black, and sagacious to an astonishing degree. In
speaking of his intelligence, my wife, who at heart was not a little tinctured
with superstition, made frequent allusion to the ancient popular notion, which
```

```
regarded all black cats as witches in disguise. Not that she was ever serious
upon this point - and I mention the matter at all for no better reason than that
it happens, just now, to be remembered.</p>
<p>Pluto - this was the cat's name - was my <a
href="http://vig.prenhall.com/">favorite</a> pet and playmate. I alone fed him,
and he attended me wherever I went about the house. It was even with difficulty
that I could prevent him from following me through the streets.</p>
</div>
<div id="sidebar">
<h2>poe trivia</h2>
<p> Best known for his poems and short fiction, Edgar Allan Poe, born in Boston,
Jan. 19, 1809, died  Oct. 7, 1849 in Baltimore, deserves more credit than any
other writer for the transformation of the short story from anecdote to art.</p>
<p>He virtually created the detective story and perfected the psychological
thriller. He also produced some of the most influential literary criticism of his
time -- important theoretical statements on poetry and the short story -- and has
had a worldwide influence on literature.</p>
</div>
<div id="footer">
<p class="footertext">All text content is in the public domain. Images &copy;
2004</p>
</div>
</div>
</body>
</html>
```

I've got a couple of things to point out: First, you'll see how I've used embedded style to
demonstrate the fundamental layout technique, and linked a style sheet to handle my
other styles. Next, I've included all the divs within the main container div. This enables
me to center the float-based design (see Figure 13-10).

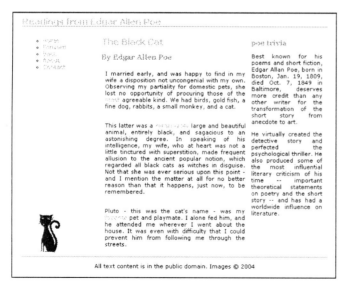

FIGURE 13-10 Complex CSS layout.

Repeat After Me...

Remember, I said it might take a little time to grasp all the layout concepts shared here. That's because there's a lot of technical information to grasp hold of, and the only way it's going to take firm grasp is for you to get your hands very dirty with the code.

At this point, I recommend downloading all the samples on the site and playing with them. Make mistakes—go ahead! It's an important part of discovery. What's more, there's nothing like that moment when you solve a problem that's been nagging at you for days.

No matter what your interest is in HTML and CSS, I hope this book has helped you grasp how today's web designers and developers are approaching the increasingly complex field. There's so much that a book like this can't cover (good information architecture, usability). I've worked to point out helpful tips and tricks along the way, but I heartily encourage you to visit the many sites I've mentioned and dig in deeper.

If you find yourself solving CSS problems in your sleep, you'll know that you're really starting to think like a web designer.

XHTML 1.0 Annotated Reference

The following appendix covers all elements in the XHTML 1.0 Transitional DTD. Note that many of these elements are presentational in nature and have been removed from the Strict DTD. Notes on support and best practices are included for each element.

Key to Element Types: Display

Block: A block-level element is one that creates a block box by default. All subsequent elements will appear on the next line.

Inline: An inline element is one that creates a line box and doesn't break the line.

Structural: This is an element that is used for document structure or that structures other elements within a specific portion of a document, such as Table, Head, and so on.

NOTE

Note that an element's display type can be altered using the display property in CSS. The terminology used here is meant to describe the primary default behavior of the element. Some elements can have multiple display types, such as structural and block. Here the primary display type is noted.

Key to Element Types: Empty and Non-Empty

Empty: An element that contains no data but, rather, is an instruction to the browser to perform some action, such as force a line break or display an image. Empty elements in XHTML are terminated with a trailing slash, as in <br />.

Non-empty: An element that contains data. All nonempty elements in XHTML must be closed, as in this example:

```
<p>This is a paragraph, it contains data and is therefore non-empty.</p>
```

Element: a

Description: Used for linking to external documents or intrapage references

Element Type: Inline, nonempty

Example:

```
<a href="http://www.pearson.com/">Go to the Pearson Web Site</a>

<a name="reference1">Go to Reference One</a>
```

Tips: There are no known tips for this element. You cannot have an anchor element within another anchor element.

Element: abbr

Description: Denotes abbreviations and is especially useful for accessibility purposes

Element Type: Inline, nonempty

Example:

```
<abbr title="department">dept.</abbr>
```

Tips: This element is well supported in contemporary browsers and often is used in place of acronym because of poor support for that element.

Element: acronym

Description: Denotes acronyms and is especially useful for accessibility purposes

Element Type: Inline, nonempty

Example:

```
<acronym title="Hypertext Markup Language">HTML</a>
```

Tips: Support for acronym is spotty, at best. At this time, it is being dropped from the XHTML 2.0 specification. As a result, it's best to use abbr in all cases of abbreviations and acronyms.

Element: `address`

Description: Denotes an address

Element Type: Inline, nonempty

Example:

```
<address>1600 Pennsylvania Avenue</address>
```

Tips: This element is very widely supported. Browsers will typically display text marked with the `address` element in italics.

Element: `applet`

Description: Denotes an applet

Element Type: Block, nonempty

Example:

```
<applet code="nervoustext.class"
width="300" height="60">
<param name="text" value="Java Comes Alive" />
</applet>
```

Tips: The element is deprecated in favor of the `object` element but can be used in XHTML 1.0.

Element: `area`

Description: Denotes an input area within an image map

Element Type: Structural (map), empty

Example:

```
<area shape="circle" href="http://molly.com/" coords="0,10,8" />
```

Tips: This element is well supported in contemporary browsers.

Element: b

Description: Presentational element used to denote bold text

Element Type: Inline, nonempty

Example:

```
<b>This sentence will appear in bold text.</b>
```

Tips: This element is widely supported but considered presentational; the `strong` element should be used in its place.

Element: base

Description: Defines the base URI information for relative paths within a document. Also used to define the base target for linked frames within the document. Placed within the head element.

Element Type: Structural (head), empty

Examples:

```
<base href="http://molly.com/" />
```

```
<base target="_top" />
```

Tips: Very broad support exists for this element.

Element: basefont

Element Type: Structural (head), empty

Description: Denotes a base font.

Example:

```
<basefont color="#ff0000" size="4" face="Arial" />
```

Tips: This is a deprecated element and, therefore, should not be used in XHTML 1.0 strict, but it may be used in XHTML 1.0.

Element: bdo

Description: Denotes bidirectional text. Its primary usage is in internationalization, to denote text that is running in a different direction.

Element Type: Inline, nonempty

Example:

```
<bdo lang="he" dir="rtl">I would enter Hebrew characters here and they would appear right to left.</bdo>
```

Tips: This element is well supported in contemporary browsers. CSS allows for bidirectional styling also.

Element: big

Description: Presentational element used to format a large text style

Element Type: Inline, nonempty

Example:

```
<big>This text will appear bigger than default body text</big>
```

Tips: Very wide support exists, but use of this element should be restricted because it is a presentational element and CSS provides an alternative.

Element: blockquote

Description: Used for quotations

Element Type: Block, nonempty

Example:

```
<blockquote>"To be or not to be, that is the question."</blockquote>
```

Tips: Very wide support exists. This element is often used for presentation because browsers will format block quotes with margins, but this usage should be avoided. Instead, use CSS to achieve margins and padding for any element.

Element: body

Description: Denotes the portion of any nonframeset XHTML document that contains the content to be displayed

Element Type: Structural (document), nonempty

Example:

```
<body>All content for the page goes here </body>
```

Tips: No tips are known.

Element: br

Description: Forces a line break

Element Type: Block, empty

Example:

```
To break my line<br />

A break is fine.
```

Tips: In some older browsers, a trailing slash appearing immediately after the last character in empty elements can cause rendering problems. Placing a space between the last character of the element and the trailing slash solves this problem.

Element: button

Description: Allows for the inclusion of an image-based button in forms

Element Type: Inline, nonempty

Example:

```
<button type="submit" id="button" value="clicked">
<img src="images/submit.gif" width="50" height="30" alt="submit" />
</button>
```

Tips: Wide support exists for this element, with the exception of Netscape 4.x browsers.

Element: caption

Description: Declares a caption in tables. It is especially helpful for accessibility purposes.

Element Type: Structural (table), nonempty

Example:

`<caption>This is the Table's purpose</caption>`

Tips: This element is widely supported but will render differently across browser version and types.

Element: center

Description: A presentational element used to center text or other content on a page

Element Type: Block, nonempty

Example:

`<center>This text will now be centered on the page</center>`

Tips: This is a presentational element and should be avoided in favor of CSS.

Element: cite

Description: Denotes a citation or reference to another source

Element Type: Inline, nonempty

Example:

`He said <cite>"Don't cry honey, it's only spilt milk!"</cite> but she kept crying anyway.`

Tips: Widely supported, this element should be used for inline quotations, citations, and references. Most browsers will style this element with italics, but using CSS, you can modify that to your liking.

Element: code

Description: Denotes code samples

Element Type: Inline, nonempty

Example:

```
The <code>code</code> element is used to denote code items that appear inline.
```

Tips: Very widely supported, this element is typically displayed in most browsers using a monospaced font.

Element: col

Description: Defines and controls the appearance of a column within a column group; useful for making tables more accessible.

Element Type: Inline, empty

Example:

```
<col span="2" align="right" />
```

Tips: This element is unreliable in many browsers, and because it is most often used for presentation, contemporary practices suggest using a well-structured table and CSS for more consistent results.

Element: colgroup

Description: Denotes a column group within a table

Element Type: Inline, nonempty

Example:

```
<table>
<colgroup align="center" span="2"></colgroup>
<colgroup valign="bottom"></colgroup>;
<tr>
<td>column one, spans two columns, is centered.</td>
<td>column two, part of the two column span, is centered</td>
<td>column three, aligned to the bottom</td>
</tr>
</table>
```

Tips: This element is unreliable in many browsers and is most often used for grouping columns for presentational reasons. The presentation is best handled by CSS for consistent results.

Element: dd

Description: Creates a definition list description

Element Type: Block, nonempty

Example:

```
<dl>
    <dt>XHTML</dt>
    <dd>Extensible Hypertext Markup Language</dd>
</dl>
```

Tips: This element is very widely supported and, sadly, underused.

Element: del

Description: Denotes deleted text, usually from a previous version of the same document or in a document that's being edited

Element Type: Inline, nonempty

Example:

```
<del>This text is to be deleted</del>
```

Tips: Unsupported in Netscape 4.x, this element typically appears with a strikethrough in supporting browsers.

Element: dfn

Description: Describes a term the first time it's used in a document

Element Type: Inline, nonempty

Example:

```
<dfn>XHTML</dfn> is the Extensible Hypertext Markup Language.
```

Tips: Unsupported in Netscape 4.x, this element is otherwise well supported. It is typically interpreted by the browser as italics.

Element: `dir`

Description: Defines a directory list

Element Type: Block, nonempty

Example:

```
<dir>
<li>Item one</li>
<li>Item two</li>
<li>Item three</li>
</dir>
```

Tips: Widely supported, this a deprecated element in favor of the `ul` element and so should be avoided.

Element: `div`

Description: Denotes divisions within a document. It is used primarily as a means to identify sections of a document that can then be positioned and styled with CSS.

Element Type: Block, nonempty

Example:

```
<div id="content">

This section will contain the document's primary content.

</div>
```

Tips: Very good support exists. This is one of the primary elements used to manage effective styling of page divisions.

Element: `dl`

Description: Denotes a list of definition terms

Element Type: Block, nonempty

Example:

```
<dl>
   <dt>XHTML</dt>
   <dd>Extensible Hypertext Markup Language</dd>
</dl>
```

Tips: This element is very well supported.

Element: dt

Description: Denotes the term to be defined

Element Type: Block, nonempty

Example: See dl.

Tips: This element is very well supported.

Element: em

Description: A structural, nonempty, inline element used to denote text that is emphasized

Element Type: Inline, nonempty

Example:

```
<em>This text is marked up as emphasized text.</em>
```

Tips: This element is very broadly supported. Although browsers will typically display emphasized text as italic, this is a convention. The em element is not considered presentational.

Element: fieldset

Description: Provides a means to group form labels and controls that are related. Used for accessibility.

Element Type: Block, nonempty

Example:

```
<form>
<fieldset>
<input type="text" id="firstname" value="firstname" />
<input type="text" id="lastname" value="lastname" />
</fieldset>
</form>
```

Tips: No Netscape 4.x support exists, but otherwise, this element is well supported in contemporary browsers. Most browsers will style the content of a fieldset with a border.

Element: font

Description: Enables a document author to add fonts to the document

Element Type: Inline, nonempty

Example:

```
<font face="Arial" color="blue" size="2">This will appear as Arial blue text one
size smaller than the default text</font>
```

Tips: This is a deprecated element, and although it is allowed in XHTML 1.0 Transitional, it should be avoided.

Element: form

Description: Denotes a form

Element Type: Block, nonempty

Example:

```
<form>
<input type="text" id="firstname" value="firstname" />
<input type="text" id="lastname" value="lastname" />
</form>
```

Tips: Typically, you will need to point to a script for forms processing. These scripts vary greatly; check with your service provider should you require more information as to scripts that are specific to your environment.

Element: frame

Description: Defines a frame within a frameset document. It can be used only with the frameset DTD, and it replaces the body element in that document type.

Element Type: Structural (frames), empty

Example:

```
<frame src="frame1.html" id="frame1" scrolling="no" />
```

Tips: Support exists in all modern browsers. This element must be used within a frameset, with a frameset DOCTYPE.

Element: frameset

Description: Defines a frameset, the control of a frame-based site

Element Type: Structural (frames), nonempty

Example:

```
<frameset cols="30%,100%" scrolling="auto">
    <frame src="nav.html">
    <frame src="content.html" />
    <frame src="frame3.html" />
</frameset>
```

Tips: Support exists in all contemporary browsers. This element is available only in the frameset DTD.

Element: h1–h6

Description: Used for headers, level 1–6

Element Type: Block, nonempty

Example:

```
<h1>Welcome to the site that does it all!</h1>
```

Tips: This element is extremely well supported. Headers should be used semantically for well-structured documents, not to control header sizing. h1 is considered the most important header on a page, akin to a chapter title. Many professional authors advocate using only one incidence of h1 in any document, but this isn't a hard and fast rule.

Element: head

Description: Denotes the head portion of a document. This is a required element within all XHTML documents and must contain a title element within it. The head portion of the document is used to define the page title and can be used for the meta, link, style, and script elements.

Element Type: Structural (document), nonempty

Example:

```
<head>
```

```
<title>The title element must always appear within a head element</title>
</head>
```

Tips: Some much older browsers will display style or script information if it's not contained within comments, but this occurs rarely anymore.

Element: `hr`

Description: Displays a horizontal rule

Element Type: Block, empty

Example:

```
I want to separate my text with a rule, so I'll place a horizontal rule element
after.
```

```
<hr />
```

Tips: This element is very well supported. Many markup experts suggest avoiding the use of horizontal rules and relying on CSS to style a bottom border for the element in question; this gives more flexibility and control over the appearance of the rule.

Element: `html`

Description: Considered the root element of all HTML and XHTML documents. It is the "ancestor" element—all elements in an HTML or XHTML document are descendants of the root.

Element Type: Structural (document), nonempty

Example:

```
<html xmlns="http://www.w3.org/1999/xhtml">
<head>
<title></title>
</head>
<body>
</body>
</html>
```

Tips: This element is very well supported. In XHTML, the opening tag must always contain the `xmlns` (XML namespace) attribute. Some HTML editors do not include this, and not having it will cause an otherwise valid document to not validate.

Element: i

Description: A presentational element that is used to create italicized text

Element Type: Inline, nonempty

Example:

```
<i>This text will appear as italicized.</i>
```

Tips: This element is available in XHTML transitional and strict DTDs, but purists recommend avoiding it in favor of the em element, which is considered structural rather than presentational.

Element: iframe

Description: Creates an inline frame

Element Type: Block, nonempty

Example:

```
<iframe src="about.html" width="100"
height="100" id="message">
</iframe>
```

Tips: The iframe element is supported by all contemporary browsers but is not supported by Netscape versions prior to 7.0.

Element: img

Description: Calls an image

Element Type: Inline, empty

Example:

```
<img src="images/molly.gif" width="150" height="200" alt="picture of Molly" />
```

Tips: This element is very widely supported but is expected to be deprecated in XHTML 2.0 in favor of the object element, which becomes ubiquitous for all objects in that language.

Element: `input`

Description: Used within forms to denote a form control such as text box

Element Type: Inline, empty

Example:

`<input type="text" id="firstname" value="firstname" />`

Tips: Very broad support exists for this element.

Element: `ins`

Description: Denotes inserted text within the document

Element Type: Inline, nonempty

Example:

`<ins>Inserted text here.</ins>`

Tips: No support exists in Netscape 4.x, but this element is well supported in all contemporary browsers. It typically displays as underlined text.

Element: `isindex`

Description: Used by web authors to provide a line of input to search an index. Also, marks a document as part of the searchable index.

Element Type: Block, empty

Example:

`<isindex />`

Tips: Very widespread support exists for this element. It is deprecated in XHTML, so it can't be used in strict documents. The preference now is to use a form with search engine software. Typically it displays the text "This is a searchable index. Enter search keywords:", followed by a searchable text box.

Element: kbd

Description: Defines text that the reader should input via the keyboard

Element Type: Inline, nonempty

Example:

```
Please type the following into your practice document: <kbd>Hello, World!</kbd>
```

Tips: This element is very widely supported and typically displays the text in a monospaced font.

Element: label

Description: Enables authors to label form controls. This is especially useful for accessibility purposes.

Element Type: Inline, nonempty

Example:

```
<label for="fullname"><input type="text" id="fullname" /></label>
```

Tips: This element is supported in all contemporary browsers, and is also supported in Netscape 4.*x.*

Element: legend

Description: Provides a caption for fieldsets within forms

Element Type: Block, nonempty

Example:

```
<form>
<fieldset>
<legend>Personal Info</legend>
<input type="text" id="firstname" value="firstname" />
<input type="text" id="lastname" value="lastname" />
</fieldset>
</form>
```

Tips: This element is not available in Netscape 4.*x* but is supported in most contemporary browsers.

Element: li

Description: Denotes individual list items within ordered and unordered lists

Element Type: Block, nonempty

Example:

```
<ul>
<li>By default, unordered list items display with a bullet.</li>
</ul>
```

Tips: No known support issues for this element.

Element: link

Description: Links to related files, such as an external style sheet from the head portion of a document

Element Type: Structural (head), nonempty

Example:

```
<link href="my.css" rel="stylesheet" type="text/css" />
```

Tips: This element is well supported in all browsers with at least some CSS support.

Element: map

Description: Denotes an image map

Element Type: Block, nonempty

Example:

```
<map name="map2">
<area shape="rect" href="http://www.molly.com/" coords="0,0,10,20" />
<area shape="circle" href="http://www.pearson.com/" coords="0,10,8" />
<area shape="poly" href="http://www.google.com/" coords="10,0,20,10,0,10" />
</map>
<img src="images/map.gif" usemap="#map2" />
```

Tips: Wide support exists in all contemporary browsers.

Element: menu

Description: Creates a single-column menu list

Element Type: Block, nonempty

Example:

```
<menu>
<li>option one</li>
<li>option two</li>
<li>option three</li>
</menu>
```

Tips: This element is widely supported but deprecated in favor of the ul element.

Element: meta

Description: Manages a wide range of metadata in HTML and XHTML documents

Element Type: Structural (head), empty

Example:

```
<meta name="description" content="Enter your description here" />
```

Tips: This element always appears in the head element of a document.

Element: noframes

Description: Used in frameset documents only. Its purpose is to allow document authors to add a section within the frameset that will be viewable in browsers without frames support or for folks using assistive technology devices to access frame-based sites.

Element Type: Block, nonempty

Example:

```
<frameset cols="30%,100%" scrolling="auto">
<frame src="nav.html">
<frame src="content.html" />
<frame src="frame3.html" />
<noframes>
It appears your browser does not support frames. Please use this <a
href="noframes.html">version</a> for access to the content.
</noframes>
</frameset>
```

Tips: This element is very widely supported and should be used in all frameset documents to assist individuals without access to frames.

Element: `noscript`

Description: Provides alternate content to browsers that don't support JavaScript

Element Type: Block, nonempty

Example:

```
<script src="scripts/myscript.js" type="text/javascript"></script>
<noscript>
Your browser either does not support JavaScript, or you have it disabled, thank
you.
</noscript>
```

Tips: This element is widely supported and should be used to provide information regarding script support to those who do not have an enabled browser or who have their JavaScript disabled for some reason.

Element: `object`

Description: Defines any external object. It is currently used primarily for Flash, video, audio, and Java applets, but it will become ubiquitous in XHTML 2.0 for all external objects, including images.

Element Type: Special (can be block or inline, depending upon context), nonempty

Example:

```
<object codebase="http://www.molly.com/java/classes" classid="FunApplet.class"
width="50" height="100">Applet</object>
```

Tips: This element should be used wherever possible in place of the `applet` element, which is deprecated in favor of `object`. The `embed` element, which is a wholly proprietary element and does not appear in any specification, should be replaced by `object` or, when backward compatibility is necessary, used along with `embed`.

Element: `ol`

Description: Denotes an ordered list. Without styling, the default behavior in browsers is to begin with the numeral 1. This can be modified using CSS properties (See Appendix B, "CSS 2.1 Annotated Reference").

Element Type: Block, nonempty

Example:

```
<ol>
<li>This is the first item in the list</li>
<li>This is the second item in the list</li>
</ol>
```

Tips: This element is widely supported and should be used in all logical circumstances in which a sequential list is required.

Element: `optgroup`

Description: Enables you to group options within form select menus

Element Type: Block, nonempty

Example:

```
<form>
<select id="browsers">
<option>Name your favorite web browser</option>
<optgroup label="standards-compliant">
<option>Mozilla</option>
<option>Firefox</option>
<option>Safari</option>
<option>Opera</option>
</optgroup>
<optgroup label="needs-updating">
<option>Internet Explorer</option>
<option>AOL</option>
</optgroup>
</select>
</form>
```

Tips: This element is supported only in contemporary browsers such as IE 6.0, Mozilla, and Mozilla Firefox. It is very helpful for accessibility and general comprehension, so it is recommended for use. If a browser doesn't support the element, the option list will still display and function properly.

Element: `option`

Description: Describes the individual options within a form menu

Element Type: Block, nonempty

Example: Please see optgroup element.

Tips: This element is widely supported.

Element: p

Description: Denotes a paragraph of text

Element Type: Block, nonempty

Example:

```
<p>This is a paragraph of text.</p>
```

Tips: This element is supported in all known browsers.

Element: param

Description: Specifies values for applets and objects

Element Type: Structural (object), empty

Example:

```
<object codebase="http://www.molly.com/java/classes" classid="FunApplet.class"
width="50" height="100">
<param name="FunStuff" value="lgh" />
Fun Stuff Java Applet</object>
```

Tips: This element is widely supported and often required by the object in question to perform properly.

Element: pre

Description: An extremely useful element that denotes a section where all text, carriage returns, and whitespace will be interpreted by the browser

Element Type: Block, nonempty

Example:

```
<pre>

This text will
```

```
appear    with     all the spaces

and carriage returns intact.

</pre>
```

Tips: This element is very widely supported. It is most often used to display longer chunks of code. It displays in a monospaced font in almost all browsers.

Element: q

Description: Defines short quotations inline

Element Type: Inline, nonempty

Example:

```
<q>Don't put all your eggs in one basket.</q>
```

Tips: All contemporary browsers support the q element, although how they display the tagged text differs. In some browsers, quotation marks are added; in others, no change occurs. You can use CSS to modify the look.

Element: s

Description: Displays the text with a line through it (strikethrough)

Element Type: Inline, nonempty

Example:

```
<q>Don't put all your <s>eggs</s> hopes in one basket.</q>
```

Tips: This element is widely supported but deprecated in favor of style sheets, which can accomplish the same results with more control.

Element: samp

Description: Shows sample output from scripts or other programs

Element Type: Inline, nonempty

Example:

```
<p>Enter the following text into your code: <samp>Hello, World!</samp></p>
```

Tips: This element is widely supported and useful for displaying sample code inline because most browsers will display the contained text in a monospaced font.

Element: `script`

Description: Embeds or links to scripts, typically JavaScript

Element Type: Structural (head), nonempty

Example:

```
<script type="text/javascript">(javascript code here)</script>
```

```
<script href="myscript.js"></script>
```

Tips: This element is very widely supported.

Element: `select`

Description: Creates an option menu within forms

Element Type: Block, nonempty

Example:

```
<form>
<select name="browsers">
<option>Your favorite browser:</option>
<option>IE</option>
<option>Mozilla / Firefox</option>
<option>Opera</option>
<option>Safari</option>
</select>
</form>
```

Tips: This element is widely supported.

Element: `small`

Description: Presentational element for rendering text smaller than the default browser text size

Element Type: Inline, nonempty

Example:

```
What do you know - <small>this text will appear smaller</small> than the
surrounding text.
```

Tips: Use CSS in place of the small element for greater type size control.

Element: span

Description: Inline generic container for text

Element Type: Inline, nonempty

Example:

```
In this paragraph <span style="color: blue; font-weight: bold;">I've styled this
text</span> differently than the surrounding text.
```

Tips: Widely supported, this element is used primarily to apply style inline. The span element is under scrutiny by markup purists, who feel that other elements such as q or cite or code are better for marking up text that has a specific significance.

Element: strike

Description: Creates strikethrough text (just like the s element)

Element Type: Inline, nonempty

Example:

```
Don't put all your <strike>eggs</strike> dreams in one basket.
```

Tips: This element is widely supported, but CSS is favored over it for applying strikethrough text styles.

Element: strong

Description: Structural element to denote a strongly emphasized portion of text

Element Type: Inline, nonempty

Example:

```
I want to <strong>shout out the good news</strong> for everyone to hear!
```

Tips: Widespread support exists. `strong` is favored over the `b` element. Both typically display the text as bold, by default.

Element: `style`

Description: Denotes a section of embedded style

Element Type: Structural (head), nonempty

Example:

```
<style type="text/css">
h1 {font-family: Arial, font-size: 1.5em; color: #000;}
</style>
```

Tips: This element is supported in all browsers with any measure of CSS support. Although embedded style can be very useful in certain situations, external style is recommended for better document management.

Element: `sub`

Description: Describes subscript text

Element Type: Inline, nonempty

Example:

```
What do you know - <sub>this text will appear as subscript</sub> that is, lower
than the surrounding text.
```

Tips: This element is very widely supported.

Element: `sup`

Description: Describes superscript text

Element Type: Inline, nonempty

Example:

```
On the 24<sup>th</sup> of June, my niece got married to the nicest guy!
```

Tips: This element is very widely supported.

Element: `table`

Description:

Element Type: Block, nonempty

Example:

```
<table>
<tr>
<th>Table header</th>
<td>Table cell</td>
<td>Another table cell</td>
</tr>
</table>
```

Tips: Very widely supported, the table element is ideally used structurally—that is, to describe tabular data—rather than as a tool for layout. You can use CSS to manage all aspects of a table's presentation.

Element: `tbody`

Description: Groups rows within tables. It is useful when making tables more accessible.

Element Type: Structural (table), nonempty

Example:

```
<table>
<tr>
<th>Table header</th>
<td>Table cell</td>
<td>Another table cell</td>
</tr>
<tbody id="row2">
<tr>
<th>Table header</th>
<td>Table cell</td>
<td>Another table cell</td>
</tr>
<tbody>
</table>
```

Tips: This element is available in contemporary browsers only. It is useful when breaking up sections of a table to make them more comprehensible.

Element: td

Description: Contains the content for a table column

Element Type: Structural (table), nonempty

Example: See table and tbody.

Tips: This element is very widely supported.

Element: textarea

Description: Creates multiple-line text areas within forms

Element Type: Block, nonempty

Example:

```
<form>
<textarea name="feedback" rows="2" cols="25">This text will appear within the text
area</textarea>
</form>
```

Tips: Very broad support exists for this element.

Element: tfoot

Description: Defines a footer row section within a table

Element Type: Structural (table), nonempty

Example:

```
<tfoot>
<t^>
<th>Table header</th>
<td>Table cell</td>
<td>Another table cell</td>
</:r>
</:foot>
```

Tips: This element is available in contemporary browsers and is used for enhanced accessibility.

Element: th

Description: Table header for table data columns

Element Type: Structural (table), nonempty

Example: See table and tbody.

Tips: Very broadly supported, this element is essential when creating structural data tables. Default display is typically bold and centered, although this can easily be modified with CSS.

Element: thead

Description: Defines the table head portion within a multirow table

Element Type: Structural (table), nonempty

Example:

```
<thead>
<tr>
<th>Table header</th>
<td>Table cell</td>
<td>Another table cell</td>
</tr>
</thead>
```

Tips: Support is limited to contemporary browsers only, used to enhance accessibility and comprehension within multirow tables.

Element: title

Description: Denotes a page title within the browser's title bar

Element Type: Structural (head), nonempty

Example:

```
<title>Welcome to Molly.Com!</title>
```

Tips: This element is very widely supported. It must be present within the head portion of the document for the document to validate.

Element: tr

Description: Creates a table row

Element Type: Structural (table), nonempty

Example: See table and tbody.

Tips: This element is very widely supported.

Element: tt

Description: Creates teletype text

Element Type: Inline, nonempty

Example:

`In this sentence <tt>these words represent teletype text</tt>.`

Tips: This element is broadly supported. It typically displays in a monospaced font and is considered presentational because CSS can easily reproduce this visual style.

Element: u

Description: Presentational element used to underline text

Element Type: Inline, nonempty

Example:

`In this sentence, <u>these words are underlined</u>.`

Tips: This element is very widely supported, although use of CSS is preferred. Many experts advise against using underlines because people tend to confuse underlined text onscreen as being linked text.

Element: ul

Description: Creates an unordered list

Element Type: Block, nonempty

Example:

```
<ul>
<li>List item one</li>
<li>List item two</li>
</ul>
```

Tips: Very wide support exists. Unordered lists are displayed with a bullet by default, although this can be modified using CSS.

Element: var

Description: Indicates a variable

Element Type: Inline, nonempty

Example:

```
Locate for the <var>book.php</var> file before continuing.
```

Tips: This element is rarely used, but has wide browser support.

CSS 2.1 Annotated Reference

In this reference, you'll find information about the selectors and properties available for use in CSS 2.1. Selectors are defined and described, an example is provided, and usage tips are offered. For properties, each property is first defined and described, with its media classification given. This is followed by an example and helpful usage tips.

Selectors, Pseudo Classes, and Pseudo Elements

The following selector types, pseudo classes, and pseudo elements are available for use in CSS 2.1.

Selector: Adjacent sibling selector

Description: Selects an adjacent sibling (one that is directly adjacent to the first defined selector and that shares the same parents)

Example:

```
h1 + p {
        text-indent: 0;
        }
```

Tips: This selector is unavailable for use in Internet Explorer and, therefore, is used primarily for enhancing styles in browsers that do support it, or for hacks.

Selector: Attribute selector

Description: Selects an element based on its attributes

Example:

```
acronym [title] {
          color: red;
          }
```

Tips: This selector is unavailable for use in Internet Explorer and, therefore, is used primarily for enhancing styles in browsers that do support it, or for hacks.

Selector: Child selector

Description: Selects the children of a given element

Example:

```
#content > p {
          padding: 10px;
          }
```

Tips: This selector is unavailable for use in Internet Explorer and, therefore, is used primarily for enhancing styles in browsers that do support it, or for hacks.

Selector: Class selector

Description: Allows the creation of a custom class. Called in the HTML or XHTML using the class attribute within the element to be selected.

Example:

```
.notation {
          font-size: xx-small;
          }
```

Tips: This selector is widely supported and, therefore, overused. Avoid overuse by stream-lining CSS with descendant selectors instead.

Selector: Descendant selector

Description: Selects all the descendant elements of a parent element

Example:

```
#content p {
          font-family: Arial, Helvetica, sans-serif;
          }
```

Tips: This selector is widely supported and should be used as often as possible, to reduce reliance on class selectors.

Selector: ID selector

Description: Allows the creation of a uniquely identified selector. Called in the HTML or XHTML using the id attribute within the element to be selected. Can be used only once per document.

Example:

```
#content {
          margin-left: 25px;
          margin-right: 25px;
          }
```

Tips: This selector is widely supported and typically used to describe sections of a document used for layout. It is also used to bind elements to scripts in DHTML.

Selector: Universal selector

Description: Selects all elements

Example:

```
* {
        border: 1px dashed blue;
        }
```

Tips: This selector is very helpful when working with diagnostics, but it should be avoided for general use. Some problems with universal selector behavior exist in Internet Explorer versions.

Selector: Element (type) selector

Description: A selector matching the element type

Example:

```
h1 {
        font-size: 22px;
        }
```

Tips: Very widely supported, this is the most commonly used selector.

Selector: :active dynamic pseudo class

Description: Selects an element while that element is being activated by the user

Example:

```
a:active {
        color: red;
        }
```

Tips: This selector is widely supported. When styling links, you must follow the LoVe/HAte order of link, visited, hover, active, or results might be inconsistent.

Selector: :after pseudo element

Description: Used to insert generated text after the selected element

Example:

```
a:after {
        content: link;
        }
```

Tips: This selector is unavailable for use in Internet Explorer and, therefore, is used primarily for enhancing styles in browsers that do support it.

Selector: :before pseudo element

Description: Used to insert generated text before the selected element

Example:

```
a:before {
        content: link;
        }
```

Tips: This selector is unavailable for use in Internet Explorer and, therefore, is used primarily for enhancing styles in browsers that do support it.

Selector: :firstchild pseudo class

Description: Used to select the first child of an element only

Example:

```
p:firstchild em {
        font-weight: bold;
        }
```

Tips: This selector is unavailable for use in Internet Explorer and, therefore, is used primarily for enhancing styles in browsers that do support it.

Selector: :firstletter pseudo element

Description: Used to select the first letter of an element only

Example:

```
#content p:firstletter {
        font-size: larger;
        }
```

Tips: Good support exists in all contemporary browsers. This selector is helpful in creating non–image-based drop caps.

Selector: :firstline pseudo element

Description: Used to select the first line of an element only

Example:

```
#content p:firstline {
         color: red;
         }
```

Tips: Good support exists in all contemporary browsers. This selector applies the style to the first line. If the line length changes because of browser resize, the style is still applied to whatever the first line is.

Selector: :focus dynamic pseudo class

Description: Applies the style when an element has focus (is accepting keyboard input, such as in a form)

Example:

```
input:focus {
         border: 1px solid red;
         }
```

Tips: This selector is unavailable for use in Internet Explorer and, therefore, is used primarily for enhancing styles in browsers that do support it.

Selector: :hover dynamic pseudo class

Description: Applies the style when an element is hovered over with the mouse or pointing device

Example:

```
#tcggle:hover {
         border: 1px solid green;
         }
```

Tips: This selector is unavailable for use in Internet Explorer except as applied to the a element. Therefore, it is used primarily for enhancing styles in browsers that do support it.

Selector: :lang pseudo class

Description: Selects an element based on its language

Example:

```
p:lang(de) {
            quotes: '»' '«' '\2039' '\203A'
            }
```

Tips: Inconsistent support exists. This selector is used for multilingual documents and internationalization.

Selector: :link link pseudo class

Description: Selects a link in the normal state

Example:

```
a:link {
            color: #ccc;
}
```

Tips: This selector is very widely supported. Remember the LoVe/HAte order rule, to avoid inconsistent behavior.

Selector: :visited link pseudo class

Description: Selects a link in the visited state

Example:

```
a:visited {
            color: #333;
}
```

Tips: This selector is very widely supported. Remember the LoVe/HAte order rule, to avoid inconsistent behavior.

CSS 2.1 Properties

Property: background

Media Type(s): Visual

Description: Shorthand property for all individual background properties

Example:

```
body: {
            background: url(images/body-back.gif) #ccc 50% no-repeat fixed;
            }
```

Tips: Shorthand properties are often unique. In this case, you need to watch order: image, color, position, repeat, and attachment. If you aren't using all the options, just be sure to keep the integrity of the order.

Property: background-attachment

Description: Used to manage scrolling of backgrounds

Media Type(s): Visual

Example:

```
body {
            background-attachment: scroll;
            }
```

Tips: A scroll value means the background scrolls with the content; if fixed is used, the background remains fixed while the content scrolls over it.

Property: background-color

Description: Defines a color for an element background

Media Type(s): Visual

Example:

```
div#content {
            background-color: #fff;
            }
```

Tips: Use a background color along with a background image, and choose a color that is close to the end effect of the image. This will help you avoid problems that can arise when a background image doesn't load for some reason.

Property: `background-image`

Description: Specifies an image path for an element background

Media Type(s): Visual

Example:

```
div#nav {
        background-image: url(images/nav.gif);
        }
```

Tips: You will sometimes see quotations around the image's path and filename. This is not necessary; leaving out the quotes might actually save you a few bytes of data.

Property: `background-position`

Description: Enables you to position a background image in relation to its element

Media Type(s): Visual

Example:

```
div#nav {
        background-position: top left;
        }
```

Tips: You can position backgrounds using percentages or length value keywords (`top`, `right`, `center`, `bottom`, `left`). If only one value is given, it sets the horizontal position only. If both values are provided, the horizontal value is first in the order. You can use negative position percentage values.

Property: `background-repeat`

Description: Describes the way a background image repeats or does not repeat

Media Type(s): Visual

Example:

```
div#content {
          background-repeat: repeat-x;
          }
```

Tips: Once upon a time, all backgrounds simply tiled into the main body. Now you can control tiling within an element, tile the image completely, tile only along the x- or y-axis, or not tile at all.

Property: border

Description: Shorthand property that enables you to apply width, style, and color to all four sides of an element box

Media Type(s): Visual

Example:

```
blockquote {
          border: 1px dotted red;
          }
```

Tips: Using the border property to help outline elements can be very helpful for diagnostics, as well as provide a nice design option for the element's presentation. You cannot set four different sides using this shorthand property; you need to specify the longhand, individual sides to do so.

Property: border-collapse

Description: Defines the border model for table borders. A value of separate enables you to display cell borders separately; a value of collapse sets the collapsing border model.

Media Type(s): Visual

Example:

```
#table01 {
          border-collapse: separate;
          }
```

Tips: The model you choose to display table borders is wholly an aesthetic choice.

Property: `border-color`

Description: Sets a border color for any element. Can be used in place of `border-top-color`, `border-right-color`, `border-bottom-color`, and `border-left-color`.

Media Type(s): Visual

Example:

```
#sidebar {
        border-color: red blue green yellow;
        }
```

Tips: If you're setting more than one color, you must follow the TRouBLe order rule: top, right, bottom, left. If there is only one value, it applies to all sides. If there are two values, the top and bottom borders are set to the first value, and the right and left are set to the second. If there are three values, the top is set to the first value, the left and right are set to the second, and the bottom is set to the third. If there are four values, they apply to the top, right, bottom, and left.

Property: `border-spacing`

Description: Defines the space between adjoining cells within tables

Media Type(s): Visual

Example:

```
table {
        border-spacing: 1.0em;
        }
```

Tips: If one length is specified, it gives both the horizontal and vertical spacing. If two are specified, the first gives the horizontal spacing and the second the vertical spacing. Lengths may not be negative.

Property: `border-style`

Description: Sets the style of an element's borders. Can be used in place of `border-top-style`, `border-bottom-style`, `border-left-style`, and `border-right-style`.

Media Type(s): Visual

Example:

```
#sidebar {
          border-style: solid dotted dashed none;
          }
```

Tips: If you're setting more than one style, you must follow the TRouBLe order rule: top, right, bottom, left. If there is only one value, it applies to all sides. If there are two values, the top and bottom borders are set to the first value, and the right and left are set to the second. If there are three values, the top is set to the first value, the left and right are set to the second, and the bottom is set to the third. If there are four values, they apply to the top, right, bottom, and left.

Property: border-top

Description: Shorthand property to style an element's top border with a width, style, and color

Media Type(s): Visual

Example:

```
#sidebar {
          border-top: 2px dashed green;
          }
```

Tips: You don't have to use all three values. If you want to set only the width, for example, you can do so and use the border-style and border-color properties to set those values.

Property: border-right

Description: Shorthand property to style an element's right border with a width, style, and color

Media Type(s): Visual

Example:

```
#sidebar {
          border-right: 2px solid green;
          }
```

Tips: You don't have to use all three values. If you want to set only the width, for example, you can do so and use the border-style and border-color properties to set those values.

Property: `border-bottom`

Description: Shorthand property to style an element's bottom border with a width, style, and color

Media Type(s): Visual

Example:

```
#sidebar {
        border-bottom: 2px dashed green;
        }
```

Tips: You don't have to use all three values. If you want to set only the width, for example, you can do so and use the `border-style` and `border-color` properties to set those values.

Property: `border-left`

Description: Shorthand property to style an element's left border with a width, style, and color

Media Type(s): Visual

Example:

```
#sidebar {
        border-bottom: 2px solid green;
        }
```

Tips: You don't have to use all three values. If you want to set only the width, for example, you can do so and use the `border-style` and `border-color` properties to set those values.

Property: `border-top-color`

Description: Sets the color for the top border of an element

Media Type(s): Visual

Example:

```
#nav {
        border-top-color: #c30;
        }
```

Tips: Using shorthand options can result in more streamlined CSS. Use longhand border properties only when really necessary.

Property: `border-right-color`

Description: Sets the color for the right border of an element

Media Type(s): Visual

Example:

```
#nav {
          border-right-color: red;
          }
```

Tips: Using shorthand options can result in more streamlined CSS. Use longhand border properties only when really necessary.

Property: `border-bottom-color`

Description: Sets the color for the bottom border of an element

Media Type(s): Visual

Example:

```
#nav {
          border-bottom-color: #808080;
          }
```

Tips: Using shorthand options can result in more streamlined CSS. Use longhand border properties only when really necessary.

Property: `border-left-color`

Description: Sets the color for the left border of an element

Media Type(s): Visual

Example:

```
#nav {
          border-left-color: red;
          }
```

Tips: Using shorthand options can result in more streamlined CSS. Use longhand border properties only when really necessary.

Property: `border-top-style`

Description: Sets the style for the top border of an element

Media Type(s): Visual

Example:

```
blockquote {
          border-top-style: dashed;
          }
```

Tips: Using shorthand options can result in more streamlined CSS. Use longhand border properties only when really necessary. Styles include `dotted`, `dashed`, `solid`, `double`, `groove`, `ridge`, `inset`, and `outset`. There are also values for `none` (displays none) and `hidden`.

Property: `border-right-style`

Description: Defines the style for the right border of an element

Media Type(s): Visual

Example:

```
blockquote {
          border-right-style: groove;
          }
```

Tips: Using shorthand options can result in more streamlined CSS. Use longhand border properties only when really necessary. Styles include `dotted`, `dashed`, `solid`, `double`, `groove`, `ridge`, `inset`, and `outset`. There are also values for `none` (displays none) and `hidden`.

Property: `border-bottom-style`

Description: Sets the style for the bottom border of an element

Media Type(s): Visual

Example:

```
blockquote {
          border-bottom-style: ridge;
          }
```

Tips: Using shorthand options can result in more streamlined CSS. Use longhand border properties only when really necessary. Styles include dotted, dashed, solid, double, groove, ridge, inset, and outset. There are also values for none (displays none) and hidden.

Property: border-left-style

Description: Sets the style for the left border of an element

Media Type(s): Visual

Example:

```
blockquote {
          border-left-style: none;
          }
```

Tips: Using shorthand options can result in more streamlined CSS. Use longhand border properties only when really necessary. Styles include dotted, dashed, solid, double, groove, ridge, inset, and outset. There are also values for none (displays none) and hidden.

Property: border-top-width

Description: Sets a width for the top border of an element

Media Type(s): Visual

Example:

```
#content {
          border-top-width: 2px;
          }
```

Tips: Using shorthand options can result in more streamlined CSS. Use longhand border properties only when really necessary.

Property: `border-right-width`

Description: Defines the width for the right border of an element

Media Type(s): Visual

Example:

```
#content {
          border-right-width: 4px;
          }
```

Tips: Using shorthand options can result in more streamlined CSS. Use longhand border properties only when really necessary.

Property: `border-bottom-width`

Description: Defines the width for the bottom border of an element

Media Type(s): Visual

Example:

```
#content {
          border-bottom-width: 2px;
          }
```

Tips: Using shorthand options can result in more streamlined CSS. Use longhand border properties only when really necessary.

Property: `border-left-width`

Description: Sets the width for the left border of an element

Media Type(s): Visual

Example:

```
#content {
          border-left-width: 4px;
          }
```

Tips: Using shorthand options can result in more streamlined CSS. Use longhand border properties only when really necessary.

Property: `border-width`

Description: Shorthand property used to define the width of an element's borders

Media Type(s): Visual

Example:

```
#content {
         border-width: 2px 4px 8px 10px;
         }
```

Tips: If you're setting more than one side's width, you must follow the TRouBLe order rule: top, right, bottom, left. If there is only one value, it applies to all sides. If there are two values, the top and bottom borders are set to the first value, and the right and left are set to the second. If there are three values, the top is set to the first value, the left and right are set to the second, and the bottom is set to the third. If there are four values, they apply to the top, right, bottom, and left.

Property: `bottom`

Description: Specifies the offset of a positioned box's bottom

Media Type(s): Value

Example:

```
#content {
         position: absolute;
         bottom: 45px;
         }
```

Tips: The positioning scheme used affects which aspect of the element box will be offset. Absolutely positioned boxes compute the value according to the containing block. With relatively positioned boxes, the offset is in relation to the element's box.

Property: `caption-side`

Description: Used to position the caption box in tables with a caption element

Media Type(s): Visual

Example:

```
caption {
caption-side: bottom;
}
```

Tips: Poor support in current browsers limits the use of this property.

Property: clear

Description: Used to clear elements away from floated elements.

Media Type(s): Visual

Example:

```
#tipscolumn {
            clear: both;
            }
```

Tips: Values include left, right, and both. This property is used in the same manner the HTML clear attribute was used in presentational markup.

Property: clip

Description: Defines which portion of a box is visible

Media Type(s): Visual

Example:

```
#dynamicbox {
            clip: rect(15px, 20px, 15px, 25px);
            }
```

Tips: This property is often used along with scripting and the Document Object Model (DOM) to add a dynamic behavior to the element in question.

Property: color

Description: Defines the foreground color of an element's text content

Media Type(s): Visual

Example:

```
p           {
            color: blue;
            }
```

Tips: No known issues exist. This property has been in widespread use since the earliest days of CSS.

Property: content

Description: Used for generated content along with the pseudo elements :before and :after

Media Type(s): All

Example:

```
a:after     {
            content: "link"
            }
```

Tips: Generated content is not supported by IE 6.0. As a result, use of this property is, unfortunately, quite limited at this time.

Property: cursor

Description: Defines the kind of cursor to be displayed

Media Type(s): Visual, interactive

Example:

```
a           {
            cursor: pointer;
            }
```

Tips: This property is very helpful in providing additional cues about an item that has focus. It is useful for accessibility and improved usability.

Property: direction

Description: Specifies writing direction within blocks

Media Type(s): Visual

Example:

```
p          {
           direction: rtl;
           }
```

Tips: Values are rtl (right to left) and ltr (left to right). This is incredibly important in internationalization and multilingual document development.

Property: display

Description: Sets the visual display type of an element

Media Type(s): All

Example:

```
ul, li     {
           display: inline;
           }
```

Tips: This property is extremely useful for layout and navigation design in contemporary practices.

Property: empty-cells

Description: Determines whether to show or hide empty cells within a table

Media Type(s): Visual

Example:

```
table      {
           Empty-cells: show;
           }
```

Tips: This property is used with the separated borders model (see border-collapse).

Property: float

Description: Allows an element to be floated to the right or left

Media Type(s): Visual

Example:

```
#contentcolumn    {
            float: right;
            }
```

Tips: Floats were originally developed to manage such floating elements as images.

Property: font

Description: Shorthand property to manage font display

Media Type(s): Visual

Example:

```
p          {
            font: italic small-caps bold 100%/100% Arial, sans-serif;
            }
```

Tips: You must always follow the required order with the font shorthand property: font-style, font-variant, font-weight, font-size/line-height, font-family. You do not need to include all properties, but the order is significant. You must also have at least the font size and family identified.

Property: font-family

Description: Sets the font family for the element's text

Media Type(s): Visual

Example:

```
p          {
            font-family: Georgia, "Times New Roman", serif;
            }
```

Tips: It's always wise to include the generic font family (serif, sans-serif, fantasy, monospace) for the fonts you're using. Also, note that each font name is comma delimited, and the only time quotes are used is for multiword font names.

Property: font-size

Description: Determines the size of the font

Media Type(s): Visual

Example:

```
.notation     {
        font-size: small;
        }
```

Tips: You can use absolute sizing via keywords (xx-small to xx-large), relative sizing keywords (larger, smaller), and the common length and percentage values.

Property: font-style

Description: Sets the font's style, typically italic and oblique

Media Type(s): Visual

Example:

```
.notation   {
        font-style: italic;
        }
```

Tips: Use font styles for auxiliary text such as notes and captions. Italic and oblique styles are not ideal for larger sections of text.

Property: font-variant

Description: Sets a variant of small caps

Media Type(s): Visual

Example:

```
h1        {
        font-variant: small-caps;
        }
```

Tips: This property can be very useful for creating attractive headings and accent text. It is not meant for body text. If a browser doesn't support the property, normal display of the font occurs.

Property: `font-weight`

Description: Sets the weight of the font

Media Type(s): Visual

Example:

```
.highlight {
        font-weight: bold;
        }
```

Tips: Numeric values 100 to 900 are inconsistently supported and, therefore, should not be relied upon.

Property: `height`

Description: Sets the content height of an element

Media Type(s): Visual

Example:

```
#content {
        height: 400px;
        }
```

Tips: This property is inconsistently supported and should not be relied upon. Note that `height` does not apply to nonreplaced inline elements.

Property: `letter-spacing`

Description: Specifies spacing between text characters

Media Type(s): Visual

Example:

```
#content p {
        letter-spacing: 0.1em;
        }
```

Tips: Designers with a taste for control over type appreciate this property, but support is somewhat inconsistent. If a browser can't render the property, the default spacing is used.

Property: line-height

Description: Describes the height of a given line of text

Media Type(s): Visual

Example:

```
#content p {
          line-height: 120%;
          }
```

Tips: Typically, line-height should be close to the size of the font. The shorter the line height is in relation to the font, the closer the lines will be, and vice versa. Too much or too little space in either direction can cause problems with readability.

Property: list-style

Description: Shorthand property to manage the list's type, position, and image

Media Type(s): Visual

Example:

```
#content ul {
          list-style: disc outside url(images/bullet.gif);
          }
```

Tips: If the image is unavailable, the style disc will be displayed in its place.

Property: list-style-image

Description: Adds an image to list items

Media Type(s): Visual

Example:

```
#nav ul   {
          list-style-image: url(images/nav-bullet.gif);
          }
```

Tips: If you'd like to add a list style in case the image doesn't load, you can gain a little more control over display. If you don't add a list style value and the image doesn't display, the default list style for that list type will be displayed.

Property: list-style-position

Description: Describes the positioning of the marker box for the list

Media Type(s): Visual

Example:

```
#content ul {
            list-style-position: inside;
            }
```

Tips: A value of inside starts the second line of text within a list item directly below the marker. A value of outside starts the second line of text within a list item outside the box, resulting in the conventional and familiar indents seen in most lists.

Property: list-style-type

Description: Sets the style of the list marker

Media Type(s): Visual

Example:

```
#content ol {
            list-style-type: decimal-leading-zero;
            }
```

Tips: Markers include disc, circle, square, decimal, decimal-leading-zero, lower-roman, upper-roman, lower-greek, lower-latin, upper-latin, armenian, georgian, none, and inherit. Note that a value of none removes all markers, which is useful in list-based navigation design.

Property: margin

Description: Shorthand property for an element's margin values.

Media Type(s): Visual

Example:

```
#content {
            margin: 10px 20px 30px;
            }
```

Tips: You must follow the TRouBLe order rule: top, right, bottom, left. If there is only one value, it applies to all sides. If there are two values, the top and bottom borders are set to the first value, and the right and left are set to the second. If there are three values, the top is set to the first value, the left and right are set to the second, and the bottom is set to the third. If there are four values, they apply to the top, right, bottom, and left. Margin values are *not* inherited.

Property: `margin-right`

Description: Sets the margin for an element's right margin

Media Type(s): Visual

Example:

```
#nav {
          margin-right: 20px;
          }
```

Tips: Margin values are not inherited.

Property: `margin-left`

Description: Sets the margin for an element's left margin

Media Type(s): Visual

Example:

```
#nav {
          margin-left: 2.0em;
          }
```

Tips: Margin values are not inherited.

Property: `margin-top`

Description: Sets the margin for an element's top margin

Media Type(s): Visual

Example:

```
#nav {
          margin-top: 10%;
          }
```

Tips: Margin values are not inherited.

Property: `margin-bottom`

Description: Defines the margin for an element's bottom margin

Media Type(s): Visual

Example:

```
#nav {
          margin-bottom: 20px;
          }
```

Tips: Margin values are not inherited.

Property: `max-height`

Description: Sets a maximum height for an element box

Media Type(s): Visual

Example:

```
h2 {
          max-height: 35px;
          }
```

Tips: No negative values are allowed. This doesn't apply to nonreplaced inline elements or tables.

Property: `max-width`

Description: Sets a maximum width

Media Type(s): Visual

Example:

```
p {
        max-width: 80%
        }
```

Tips: This property is helpful in limiting lines of text so they don't become overly long. Unfortunately, this property is unsupported in Internet Explorer 6.0, causing frustration for visual designers who appreciate being able to have this intended level of typographic control.

Property: min-height

Description: Sets a minimum height for an element box

Media Type(s): Visual

Example:

```
h2 {
        min-height: 100px;
        }
```

Tips: This doesn't apply to nonreplaced inline elements or tables.

Property: min-width

Description: Sets a minimum width for an element box

Media Type(s): Visual

Example:

```
p {
        min-width: 80%
        }
```

Tips: This property is helpful in ensuring that lines of text are at least a minimum width. Unfortunately, this property is unsupported in Internet Explorer 6.0, causing frustration for visual designers who appreciate being able to have this intended level of typographic control.

Property: `outline`

Description: Shorthand that creates a dynamic outline for form controls and objects

Media Type(s): Visual, interactive

Example:

```
img {
          outline: red solid thick;
}
```

Tips: All dynamic outline properties are unlike borders, in that they do not take up space (are not calculated as part of the box model width or height) and they may be nonrectangular. Support for these properties is very limited (Safari 1.2 has support for outline properties), so they are rarely used at this time.

Property: `outline-color`

Description: Defines an outline color for form controls and objects

Media Type(s): Visual, interactive

Example:

```
img {
          outline-color: blue;
          }
```

Tips: All dynamic outline properties are unlike borders, in that they do not take up space (are not calculated as part of the box model width or height) and they may be nonrectangular. All colors are available for this property, with the addition of a value of `invert`. This inverts the color, which can be helpful to ensure that the outline is visible when the control or object is in focus. Support for these properties is very limited (Safari 1.2 has support for outline properties), so they are rarely used at this time.

Property: `outline-style`

Description: Sets an outline style for form controls and objects

Media Type(s): Visual, interactive

Example:

```
img {
        outline-style: groove;
        }
```

Tips: All dynamic outline properties are unlike borders, in that they do not take up space (are not calculated as part of the box model width or height) and they may be nonrectangular. This property accepts the same styles as for `border-style`, with the exception of the `hidden` value. Support for these properties is very limited (Safari 1.2 has support for outline properties), so they are rarely used at this time.

Property: `outline-width`

Description: Sets the outline width for form controls and objects

Media Type(s): Visual, interactive

Example:

```
input {
        outline-width: 2px;
        }
```

Tips: All dynamic outline properties are unlike borders, in that they do not take up space (are not calculated as part of the box model width or height) and they may be nonrectangular. This property accepts the same styles as for `border-width`. Support for these properties is very limited (Safari 1.2 has support for outline properties), so they are rarely used at this time.

Property: `overflow`

Description: Used to manage content that overflows an element box

Media Type(s): Visual

Example:

```
#tipscolumn {
        overflow: scroll;
        }
```

Tips: Values include `visible`, which makes the content visible outside the box; `hidden`, which hides all overflow; `scroll`, which forces a scrollbar into the element box that contains the content; and `auto`, which automatically provides a scroll if it's required.

Property: `padding`

Description: Shorthand property to define the padding of an element box

Media Type(s): Visual

Example:

```
#content {
          padding: 10px 20px 15px 0;
          }
```

Tips: You must follow the TRouBLe order rule: top, right, bottom, left. If there is only one value, it applies to all sides. If there are two values, the top and bottom borders are set to the first value, and the right and left are set to the second. If there are three values, the top is set to the first value, the left and right are set to the second, and the bottom is set to the third. If there are four values, they apply to the top, right, bottom, and left.

Property: `padding-top`

Description: Sets the padding for the top of an element box

Media Type(s): Visual

Example:

```
#content>p {
          padding-top: 10px;
          }
```

Tips: Padding is considered a part of the box model, and values must be included when calculating widths and heights.

Property: `padding-right`

Description: Sets the padding for the right side of an element box

Media Type(s): Visual

Example:

```
#content p {
          padding-right: 10%;
          }
```

Tips: Padding is considered a part of the box model, and values must be included when calculating widths and heights.

Property: `padding-bottom`

Description: Sets the padding for the bottom of an element box

Media Type(s): Visual

Example:

```
#content+p {
          padding-bottom: 2.0em;
          }
```

Tips: Padding is considered a part of the box model, and values must be included when calculating widths and heights.

Property: `padding-left`

Description: Sets the padding for the left side of an element box

Media Type(s): Visual

Example:

```
#content {
          padding-left: 16px;
          }
```

Tips: Padding is considered a part of the box model, and values must be included when calculating widths and heights.

Property: `page-break-after`

Description: Forces a page to break according to the values included

Media Type(s): Visual, paged

Example:

```
#content {
          page-break-after: always;
          }
```

Tips: The values for page-break properties include auto (no forced break), always (always force the break), avoid (avoid breaking a page at the element in question), left (break the page and resume content on the left page), and right (break the page and resume content on the right page).

Property: page-break-before

Description: Forces a page to break according to the values included

Media Type(s): Visual, paged

Example:

```
h2 {
        page-break-before: right;
        }
```

Tips: The values for page-break properties include auto (no forced break), always (always force the break), avoid (avoid breaking a page at the element in question), left (break the page and resume content on the left page), and right (break the page and resume content on the right page).

Property: page-break-inside

Description: Forces a page to break according to the values included

Media Type(s): Visual, paged

Example:

```
h2 {
        page-break-inside: avoid;
        }
```

Tips: The values for page-break properties include auto (no forced break), always (always force the break), avoid (avoid breaking a page at the element in question), left (break the page and resume content on the left page), and right (break the page and resume content on the right page).

Property: position

Description: Defines a positioning scheme of static, relative, absolute, or fixed

Media Type(s): Visual

Example:

```
#topnav {
          position: absolute;
          top: 0;
          left: 0;
}
```

Tips: Fixed positioning is not supported by Internet Explorer. Static positioning refers to the default normal flow of the browser.

Property: quotes

Description: Specifies quotation marks for embedded quotations

Media Type(s): Visual

Example:

```
blockquote:before {
          content: open-quote
}
blockquote:after   {
          content: close-quote
}
```

Tips: This property is typically used with generated content, as the example demonstrates. Because generated content is unavailable in older browsers and Internet Explorer 6.0, its use is limited to supported environments only, or workarounds are employed to manage other browsers.

Property: right

Description: Specifies a right margin offset in positioning

Media Type(s): Visual

Example:

```
#topnav {
          position: absolute;
          right: 20px;
          }
```

Tips: The positioning scheme used affects which aspect of the element box will be offset. Absolutely positioned boxes compute the value according to the containing block. With relatively positioned boxes, the offset is in relation to the element's box.

Property: `table-layout`

Description: Controls the way browsers manage tables

Media Type(s): Visual

Example:

```
table {
        table-layout: fixed;
        }
```

Tips: Two algorithms are used for managing tables. One is fixed, which is considered a faster rendering method because it doesn't depend upon the content of cells to determine width. The other is auto, which does depend on width and is the typical default behavior of most browsers. Although `table-layout` has fairly good support, the results vary enough among browsers that most people avoid using it and rely on the native agent's algorithm instead.

Property: `text-align`

Description: Specifies an alignment of `left`, `right`, `center`, or `justify` for text

Media Type(s): Visual

Example:

```
p {
        text-align: justify;
        }
```

Tips: Broad browser support exists. Many designers recommend avoiding the `justify` value because they feel that it's not appropriate for onscreen; others feel that judicious use is fine.

Property: `text-decoration`

Description: Sets a decoration for selected text

Media Type(s): Visual

Example:

```
a {
        text-decoration: none;
        }
```

Tips: Values include none, underline, overline, line-through, and blink. The use of none with anchors as described in the example removes underlines from links. Most web designers avoid using underline because it's felt that underlining is too easily confused with the default behavior for links. The values of overline and line-through are typically used for editing or for whimsical design features. The blink value should be used with extreme caution; the fact that it even exists is probably more of an inside joke than a realistic desire to provide this less-than-accessible or attractive style to text.

Property: text-indent

Description: Sets an indentation

Media Type(s): Visual

Example:

```
p {
        text-indent: 5px;
        }
```

Tips: Using this property, you can create a very professional look for long sections of text. You may also use negative values to create an outdent effect.

Property: text-transform

Description: Transforms selected text into capital case, upper case, or lower case, no matter how the text is input in the document

Media Type(s): Visual

Example:

```
h3 {
        text-transform: uppercase;
        }
```

Tips: Widespread support exists. This property is helpful in keeping headers and other important text items consistent.

Property: top

Description: Specifies the offset of a positioned box's bottom

Media Type(s): Visual

Example:

```
#nav {
            position: relative; top: 20px;
            }
```

Tips: The positioning scheme used affects which aspect of the element box will be offset. Absolutely positioned boxes compute the value according to the containing block. With relatively positioned boxes, the offset is in relation to the element's box.

Property: unicode-bidi

Description: Helps to manage the bidirectional algorithm used to determine the direction of letters within a given language

Media Type(s): Visual

Example:

```
p.hebrew {
            direction: rtl;
            unicode-bidi: embed;
}
```

Tips: The use of unicode-bidi is limited to document authors concerned with maintaining control over the bidirectional algorithms within browsers.

Property: vertical-align

Description: Sets a vertical alignment using the keywords baseline, sub, super, top, text-top, middle, bottom, text-bottom, or a percentage or length value.

Media Type(s): Visual

Example:

```
img {
            vertical-align: baseline;
            }
```

Tips: This property works only with images in Netscape 4.x browsers.

Property: visibility

Description: Determines whether the box generated by an element will be rendered as visible, hidden, or collapsed.

Media Type(s): Visual

Example:

```
#container {
          visibility: hidden;
          }
```

Tips: Invisible boxes affect layout. If you want to completely suppress box generation, use the display property with a value of none instead. The collapse value is used with tables.

Property: white-space

Description: Determines how whitespace within an element is managed

Media Type(s): Visual

Example:

```
td {
          white-space: nowrap;
          }
```

Tips: Values are pre, which acts just like preformatted text; nowrap, which suppresses line breaks; pre-wrap, which breaks lines at new lines within the source; and pre-line, which collapses sequences of whitespace.

Property: width

Description: Sets the content width of an element

Media Type(s): Visual

Example:

```
#content p {
          width: 225px;
          }
```

Tips: This does not apply to nonreplaced inline elements.

Property: `word-spacing`

Description: Sets the spacing between words

Media Type(s): Visual

Example:

```
#content p {
            word-spacing: 1.0em;
            }
```

Tips: You can use negative values to decrease the space between words.

Property: `z-index`

Description: Used with position boxes to determine stacking order

Media Type(s): Visual

Example:

```
.boxtwo {
            position: absolute;
            top: 10px;
            left: 10px;
            z-index: 2;
            }
```

Tips: The higher the integer is, the closer to the viewer the box in the stack appears.

Index

Q-R

q element, 249
quotes property, 293

radio buttons in forms
   adding, 74
   preselecting, 75
ragged right text, 149
rel attribute, 113
relative keywords for font sizing, 144
relative length values for font sizing, 144-145
relative linking, 22
relative positioning (CSS), 204-205
removing
   frame borders, 99-100
   image border, 37
   underlined text from links, 165
reset buttons in forms, adding, 80
resizing
   browsers, 195-196
   frames, 96
RGB percentages in CSS, 121
RGB values in CSS, 121
rich, defined, 31
right property, 293
right-aligned text, 149
root element, 4
   absolute positioning to, 200-201
   as containing block, 198
rows
   in framesets
      adding, 94
      combining with columns, 95
   in tables
      adding, 52
      grouping, 66
      spanning, 58-59, 62
rows attribute, 78, 94
rowspan attribute, 58-59, 62
rules (CSS)
   defined, 108
   formatting, 117
   order of precedence, 109

S

s element, 249
Safari, small caps text in, 154
samp element, 249
sans-serif fonts, 140
saving HTML page template, 11
script element, 5, 43-44, 250
scripts
   defined, 31, 43
   embedding, 43-44
   hiding from browsers, 45
   linking to, 44
   noscript element, 45-46
   websites for, 46
scrollbars in browsers, 199
scrolling
   and accessibility, 133
   background images, 132-133
   in frames, 96
scrolling attribute, 96
search engines and keywords in meta
   element, 8
select element, 76, 250
selected attribute, 76-77
selecting fonts, 140-141
selectors (CSS)
   class selectors, 124
      multiple link styles, 166
      versus ID selectors, 167
   defined, 108
   descendant selectors, 167-168
   grouping, 127
   ID selectors, 167
   pseudo element selectors
      for links, 162
      for text, 157
   types of, 260-265
   universal selector, 204
serif fonts, 140
SGML (Standardized General Markup
   Language), 2
shadows, creating drop shadows, 158
shorthand (CSS), 137
   backgrounds, 136-137
   borders, 189
   fonts, 158
   hexadecimal color, 120

text. *See also* fonts
    adding to template, 28-29
    aligning, 149
    alternative text for images, 35
    coloring, 148
    decorating, 150
    definition lists, 21
    drop shadows, 158
    font families, applying, 142-143
    headers, 14
    hiding, 10
    indenting, 151-152
    line breaks, 16
    line height, 155
    nesting lists, 19-20
    ordered lists, 17
    paragraphs, 15
    spacing, 156
    styling first letter/line, 157
    transforming case, 153-154
    underlined text, removing from links, 165
    unordered lists, 18
    unsupported properties, 158
    varying, 153-154
text-align property, 149, 294
text-decoration property, 150, 165, 294
text-indent property, 151-152, 295
text-shadow property, 158
text-transform property, 153-154, 295
textarea element, 78-79, 254
textareas in forms, adding, 78-79
textboxes in forms. *See* input textboxes in forms
tfoot element, 66, 254
th element, 54, 255
thead element, 66, 255
three columns with fixed flanking menus
    (CSS layout), 216-217
three columns with masthead and footer
    (CSS layout), 218-219
tiling background images, 128-129
title attribute, 23, 25, 39
title element, 5-6, 255
top property, 295
tr element, 52, 256
tracking (of text), setting, 156
transforming text case, 153-154
transitional design, 49

transparent backgrounds, 134-135
tt element, 256
type attribute, 71, 73, 81, 111, 113
typography. *See* fonts; text

U

u element, 256
ul element, 18, 256
underlined text, 150
    removing from links, 165
Unicode character sets, 7
unicode-bidi property, 296
universal selectors (CSS), 204, 262
unordered lists, 18, 171-172
uppercasing text, 153
usability and link styles, 164. *See also*
    accessibility
user style sheets, 108
UTF-8 character set, 7

V

validation, 1, 12
validators, 3
valign attribute, 64
value attribute, 74, 80
var element, 257
varying text, 153-154
vertical axis, tiling background images,
    128-129
vertical navigation
    with color, 174-175
    with images, 176
vertical-align property, 296
video files, links to, 38-39. *See also* multimedia
viewport
    defined, 9, 199
    fixed positioning to, 206-207
visibility property, 297
:visited link pseudo class, 162, 265
visited link state, 162

W

Web, origin of, 13
web browsers. *See* browsers
web graphics. *See* images
websites
    Crazy Netscape Navigator Frame Tricks
        Page, 94
    CSS Zen Garden, 138
    Eric Meyer's CSS Edge, 178
    floats information, 219
    font sizing information, 145
    forms processing information, 86
    FOUC (flash of unstyled content)
        information, 115
    hacking CSS, 115
    List-O-Matic, 179
    Listamatic, 179
    Macromedia Flash, 41
    negative margins information, 185
    for scripts, 46
    table accessibility information, 57
    for validating HTML pages, 12
    Wells Fargo (online banking), 87
weight of fonts, 146
Wells Fargo website, 87
white-space property, 297
whitespace. *See* padding (CSS)
width attribute, 50-51, 63
width of borders (CSS), 187
width property, 297
width values of images, 34
word-spacing property, 156, 298
words, spacing, 156

X-Z

x-axis, tiling background images, 128
XHTML, XML namespace for, 4
XHTML 1.0 Transitional DTD, 2-3
XHTML annotated reference, 227
XML namespace for XHTML, 4
xml:lang attribute, 4
xmlns attribute, 4

y-axis, tiling background images, 128-129

z-index (CSS), 193, 212-213
z-index property, 298

Register
Your Book

at www.awprofessional.com/register

You may be eligible to receive:

- Advance notice of forthcoming editions of the book
- Related book recommendations
- Chapter excerpts and supplements of forthcoming titles
- Information about special contests and promotions throughout the year
- Notices and reminders about author appearances, tradeshows, and online chats with special guests

Contact us

If you are interested in writing a book or reviewing manuscripts prior to publication, please write to us at:

Editorial Department
Addison-Wesley Professional
75 Arlington Street, Suite 300
Boston, MA 02116 USA
Email: AWPro@aw.com

Visit us on the Web: http://www.awprofessional.com